Creativity, Incentive and Reward

For Amy, Ricardo and Isaac

Creativity, Incentive and Reward

An Economic Analysis of Copyright and
Culture in the Information Age

Ruth Towse

*Department for the Study of the Arts and Culture (KCW),
Erasmus University Rotterdam, The Netherlands*

Edward Elgar

Cheltenham, UK • Northampton, MA, USA

Published by
Edward Elgar Publishing Limited
Glensanda House
Montpellier Parade
Cheltenham
Glos GL50 1UA
UK

Edward Elgar Publishing, Inc.
136 West Street
Suite 202
Northampton
Massachusetts 01060
USA

A catalogue record for this book
is available from the British Library

Library of Congress Cataloguing in Publication Data

Towse, Ruth, 1943–
    Creativity, incentive, and reward : an economic analysis of copyright and culture in the information age / Ruth Towse.
        p. cm.
    Includes bibliographical references and index.
    1. Copyright—Economic aspects—Europe. 2. Arts—Economic aspects—Europe.
I. Title.

Z581.T69 2001
306.3'094—dc21

2001033074

ISBN 1 84064 254 8

Printed and bound in Great Britain by Biddles Ltd, *www.biddles.co.uk*

Contents

Figures

Tables

Preface

This book collects together 10 years' research on one aspect of cultural economics, artists' labour markets. I started in 1988 with a Leverhulme Trust grant at the London School of Economics with research for my book *Singers in the Marketplace: Economics of the Singing Profession* (Towse, 1993). I was enabled to do this study by the fact that I had spent the previous 10 years studying singing and gaining a little experience of opera and recitals. I had a wonderful time doing that and living in a fantasy world that I was just not quite cut out for. For much of the time while I was studying singing, I worked as an economist one way or another, as a Senior Lecturer at Middlesex University, where I had started my academic career, then as a researcher at the Institute of Education, University of London. Alan Peacock gave me my first research work in cultural economics on the project he did for the Arts Council of Great Britain on inflation and the performed arts, which tested Baumol's Cost Disease hypothesis in the arts in Britain over the decade of the 1970s. I also did freelance work for the Policy Studies Institute, basically data-mining for *The Economic Importance of the Arts in Britain* edited by John Myerscough (Myerscough, 1988). My first publication in the field of cultural economics was my contribution as the Rapporteur to a Council of Europe conference in Munich in 1984, published as *Funding the Arts in Europe* and edited by John Myerscough (Myerscough, 1984). Thus began my career as a cultural economist. Shortly after, I taught arts administration at City University, while being active in that role myself (I promoted an opera, Offenbach's *The Brigands*, on the Edinburgh Fringe and did a recital series myself there too).

In 1990, I moved to Department of Economics at the University of Exeter, where I taught Economics of Social Policy and introductory economics. Few cultural economists are able to earn their living from that alone and that is not such a bad thing; it is important for any area of applied economics that ideas circulate. After writing a series of papers on artists' labour markets, some of them commissioned by the Arts Council of Great Britain (later of England) and the Arts Council of Wales, I began to work on the economics of copyright as it relates to artists. I obtained a grant from the Economic and Social Research Council under the Media Economics and Media Culture programme headed by Simon Frith for the research project 'Copyright, Performers' Rights and Incentives in Cultural Markets'. Millie Taylor worked with me on this project.

In 1994, I became joint editor (with Mark Crain) of the reconstituted *Journal of Cultural Economics*, which I now edit jointly with Mark Schuster. I also served for six years on the Executive Board of the Association for Cultural Economics International (ACEI) and was a founding member of the International Centre for Research in the Economics of the Arts (ICARE) in Venice, founded by Gianfranco Mossetto. The regular ACEI conferences and the ICARE workshops have provided a stimulating forum for meeting and discussing with cultural economists from all over the world. I am much indebted intellectually to Bruno Frey and to David Throsby. Alan Peacock and Will Baumol have also, it goes without saying, been major influences. I have had the particular privilege of editing a book of Baumol's work and to Alan I owe a very special debt of thanks for his continuing support and inspiration. I am also grateful to Arjo Klamer for his support and for encouraging me to join him at the Department for the Study of the Arts and Culture at Erasmus University Rotterdam, to which I moved in 1999. He and Roger van den Bergh of the Faculty of Law kindly supervised my promotion there. Thanks also go to William Baumol, Barbara Krug, Rudi Holzhauer and Jules Theeuwes for their questions and comments. Most of all, my greatest friend, critic, supporter and devil's advocate is my husband, Mark Blaug.

I have had the good fortune to have had very special secretarial assistance from Diana Moyse. We have worked together for over 10 years with great mutual respect and enjoyment. Miro de Ruiter added finishing touches.

This book consists of a combination of specially written material (Chapters 1, 2 and 9) and reprinted previously published work. An Individual Award from The Leverhulme Trust enabled me to prepare it. Chapter 3 was commissioned and published as a Research Report by the Arts Council of England, to whom I am grateful for permission to reprint it, and to Andy Feist for all the hard work he put into editing it and insisting I write clearly for non-economists! Chapter 4 was originally published in the first book I edited (with Abdul Khakee), *Cultural Economics*, published in 1992 by Springer Verlag and now out of print. Chapter 5 was written jointly with Millie Taylor and I am grateful to her for her contribution and for her permission to reprint the paper and also to Sage Publications, the publishers; the paper was published as 'The Value of Performers' Rights: An Economic Analysis', in *Media, Culture and Society*, Volume 20, number 4, October, 1998, pp. 631–52. Chapter 6 was published as 'Copyright and Economic Incentives: An Application to Performers' Rights in the Music Industry', in *Kyklos*, Vol. 52, 1999, Fasc. 3, pp. 369–90 and I acknowledge permission from Helbing and Lichtenhahn Verlag to reprint the paper. Chapter 7 appears in *Cultural Policy*, 6 (1), 91–107, 'Copyright, Risk and the Artist'. Chapter 8 was commissioned and published by the Intellectual Property Institute in the UK. I retain the copyright of both these – I have learned something useful from my studies!

PART I

Cultural economics, copyright and cultural industries

1. Creativity, incentives and rewards: cultural economics and copyright law

INTRODUCTION

This book is about incentives, rewards and creativity in the cultural sector and the institutions that co-ordinate them, the market for artistic labour and the law of copyright. The specific arena in which these institutions are examined is that of the creative industries. There we find the 'traditional' creative and performing arts (visual arts, literature, music, dance, opera, drama) and the cultural industries (film, radio, television, sound recording, multimedia). In most countries the arts are supported by some form of government intervention, whether state provision, government subsidy or indirect support via tax breaks and the like, in accordance with cultural policy. The cultural industries may be publicly or privately owned, subsidised, assisted through the tax system and, in the case of industries such as broadcasting, regulated. Other industries that are entirely private, such as fashion, advertising and computer software, depend on creativity and they are coming to be regarded as part of the 'creative' industries as well (Chapter 2). This is a development of the so-called 'information age' and at its core is the increasing significance in post-industrial economies of intangible production relying upon copyright law to establish property rights and protect revenues. The information age has also altered the perspective of earlier debates about high and popular culture; the focus is now on the creation of information and its delivery in various media, one of which is electronic. As digitalisation revolutionises the whole economy, including the cultural sector, fundamental questions are being asked about how markets will work and whether copyright law can be adapted.

Creativity is central to the cultural or creative industries. It plays the equivalent role in these industries to that of innovation in other sectors of the economy. Just as firms in manufacturing have outlays on research and development (R&D), so firms in the cultural industries search for new ideas and talented workers – artists – to create and supply them. And, as with technical innovation, we may distinguish product and process innovation. New products are very important in the cultural industries, with a stream of novelty being demanded and supplied. Ironically, this

1

is more a characteristic nowadays in the commercial rather than in the subsidised sector. Cultural policy for the subsidised arts in some countries (among them the USA and the UK) has tended to play safe, with subsidy being mainly devoted to well-established arts rather than to new ones. This would seem to be counter-intuitive, as one might suppose one of the main arguments for arts subsidy is to support new work that could not succeed on the market (Towse, 1994). The problem is, though, that the incumbent arts organisations with high production costs (especially opera and ballet) have come to expect regular funding and it becomes difficult for funding bodies to refuse support to vested interests. In the Netherlands, for example, the policy of the state distancing itself from the administration of subsidy and leaving decisions about arts supply to professional artists has inevitably reinforced the tendency towards path dependency and over-supply of subsidised output (Ministry of Education, Culture and Science, 1998). In former times, arts audiences expected novelty; for example, in Italy where opera was a popular art form, there were riots in the eighteenth and nineteenth centuries if not enough new operas were offered.[1] However, the unsubsidised commercial industries, being reliant on the market, have to please the public taste for novelty. Some economists even argue that the market is therefore a superior institution for fostering creativity and cultural innovation (Cowen, 1998).

It is misleading, however, to focus too much on product innovation because there has been enormous process innovation in the cultural industries as well. Indeed, the cultural industries are the product of technical developments of sound recording, film, video, television and computers. We live in an era of unprecedented speed of change in the provision of and access to information, including cultural goods, via the Internet. As with all technological revolutions, these changes have altered the pattern of demand for workers, reducing the employment in the cultural sector of some types of artists and increasing it for others; they also have been the cause of the superstar phenomenon in the cultural sector.

The contribution of this book is to offer the particular perspective of cultural economics to the reward of creativity in the cultural sector and to draw implications for cultural policy. Cultural economics deals, among other things, with analysis of cultural production and the supply of creativity in artists' labour markets. The economic analysis of copyright law offers a framework for considering the effects of technological change on the creative industries, in much the same way as the economic analysis of patents has considered R&D, innovation and economic growth. What unites the topics in this book is my empirical research on artists' earnings from fees and royalties. That began with my work on the singing profession (Towse, 1993); Chapter 4 of the present volume contains an economic analysis of the labour market for singers based on that research. Later, I extended this work to cover all artists' labour markets; Chapter 3 is a survey of my own research and that of others in the UK and of the field worldwide. Part III moves on to my empirical work on performers' earnings from copyright; Chapter 5 investigates the role of copyright law as a vehicle for strengthening artists' earning power; Chapter 6 analyses the economic role of royalties as an incentive and presents international data on payments to performers from one particular property right, public performance of music. Part IV is concerned with the policy implications of these research findings; Chapter 7 develops the theme of the riskiness of artists' careers and contrasts it with the risk faced by entrepreneurs in the cultural industries. Chapter 8 considers the implications of digitalisation for copyright and for markets in information goods with some preliminary empirical estimates on potential changes in fair dealing. The concluding chapter makes the case for a new focus in cultural policy in the information age, for greater cohesion between policy for the traditional arts, the cultural industries and copyright. This book is addressed to economists in general and to cultural economists in particular and with it I hope to persuade readers of the case for cultural economics to embrace more enthusiastically analysis of the creative industries and of the role copyright law plays in framing markets in the cultural sector.

CULTURAL ECONOMICS AND ARTISTS' LABOUR MARKETS

The field of cultural economics, previously known as the economics of the arts, was essentially founded by William Baumol and William Bowen, whose book *Performing Arts: The Economic Dilemma* was published in 1966. That book provided the seminal idea which has bound together much subsequent work in the field, and it also made economists aware that the cultural sector was a virtual *tabula rasa* for economic analysis. Thirty-five years later, we are still only beginning to understand the complexity of markets in the arts, heritage and cultural industries and how they interact with government policy, subsidy and regulation.

Baumol and Bowen's economic dilemma was this: the technology of artistic performance is fixed and cannot be subjected to productivity improvements. A Beethoven quartet must be performed by four string players and they take as long to perform it now as did the first players. Payments to labour in general, however, improve due to productivity increases and economic growth in the 'dynamic' sector of the economy. The arts are bound to become relatively more expensive – hence the terms 'Baumol's cost disease', 'Baumol's Law' or the earnings gap in the arts – and, so that the increase in the prices of artistic work are not pushed by cost inflation above the general rate of inflation, the arts will require subsidy in order to survive. This fundamental idea has become one of the focal points of work in the field and continues to generate empirical research. It may truly be said to have provided a unifying strand in the economic analysis of the arts.

One central theme of cultural economics, therefore, has been the question of artists' earnings and the extent to which they drive up costs of producing cultural output. Baumol and Bowen devoted a chapter of their book to an analysis of the US labour market for artists and hypothesised that the upward trend in artists' earnings, in real terms, would persist. Subsequent empirical work on the cost disease by Peacock et al. (1982) in the UK for the 1970s (a period of relatively high inflation – it reached 27 per cent at its zenith) called into question the role of artists' earnings in cost inflation in the arts, showing that the cost of materials and non–artistic labour had risen faster than aggregate artists' earnings. Having contributed to this study, I realised that disaggregated data could be assembled that would permit an analysis of earnings of classically trained singers, a group in which I had a particular interest. While doing this research, I became aware of two aspects of artists' earnings that have shaped my subsequent work: first, the importance of a thriving market for singers working by the 'session' in TV, radio and recording studios, recording backing music for pop groups, film music, advertising jingles and so on as a vital source of fees and royalties for singers preparing for careers in opera and concerts, testifying to the overlap between 'high art' and the cultural industries, and second, the role of copyright as an influence on artists' earnings.

Indeed, a cursory glance at the curriculum vitae of any performer, author, composer or visual artist, confirms the importance of the cultural industries in offering work to trained artists of every type. Almost no artist in the UK or the USA can survive without commercial work and many who have trained in the leading academies do nothing but commercial work. For some reason, the public chooses to remain blissfully unaware of the facts of life about artists' labour markets; for example, audiences for performances of Bach cantatas apparently do not care to know that the angelic-looking soprano singing such heavenly music was earlier that day making an advertising jingle that pays her rent, while her fee from the concert is hardly enough to pay for a meal after the performance and the taxi home! This scenario is not repeated to the same extent in all countries, however, because subsidies to the arts are so generous in some (the Nordic countries, the Netherlands, Germany) that artists are well-supported by government grants and are paid well by the subsidised organisations that hire them.[2] Nevertheless, almost all artists do some work in the cultural industries and it is there that protection from copyright law comes into play.

My appreciation of the role of copyright law came from reading the standard contracts (negotiated by artists' trade unions) that apply to casual work in the cultural industries. Later on, involvement in a UNESCO conference on the Status of the Artist alerted me to the lobbying by artists' representatives to promote recognition of artists as a professional group, using any means to that end, one being copyright law.[3] Governments have not been slow to see that they could easily placate artists by altering copyright law, which they could do without committing any funds, since a change in the law mostly redistributes rewards between participants (different rightsholders and consumers – see Chapter 5). The creative industries also lobby for increased global copyright protection at the national government level and internationally, through the World Intellectual Property Organisation (WIPO) and the World Trade Organisation (WTO). One result of this is that copyright policy has become increasingly important for cultural policy in general and for artists' labour markets in particular.

Curiously, cultural economists have been somewhat slow in analysis of the economic aspects of the cultural industries. For instance, it is only recently that there has been anything but a smattering of contributions to the *Journal of Cultural Economics* on film, broadcasting and publishing. This is in contrast to sociologists of culture, who have long analysed the social impact, organisation and role in social change of the cultural or media industries. There is also a body of research on the cultural industries by sociologists and political economists offering a radical analysis of economic power and its effect on communication; the collection of articles in Golding and Murdock (1997) demonstrates the range of this literature. On the other hand, a review of the first 10 years of the specialist *Journal of Media Economics,* which tends to concentrate more on the communication aspect of the media industries, concluded that there has been a 'lack of integration between the disciplines of economics and media research' (Chambers, 1998).

Cultural economics has had cultural policy issues at its centre for the last 35 years and cultural policy has had at its core subsidy of the 'traditional' arts and heritage. The cultural industries have perhaps seemed less worthy of attention and may even not be considered a fit subject for cultural policy. I discuss the increasing integration of the high arts and cultural industries in the next chapter. In many countries, cultural policy and policy on media and copyright law are kept separate and handled by different ministries. Yet all areas of cultural production, subsidised and commercial, have to respond to the challenge of new information age technologies and their effect on markets, as well as the use of copyright law to regulate these changes. This calls for greater integration of these policies, a theme developed in Chapter 9.

CREATIVITY AND TALENT, INCENTIVES AND REWARDS

A feature common to all artistic enterprise, subsidised or commercial, high art or pop culture is that it seeks out outstandingly talented 'personalities', the high income superstars.[4] Very talented and creative artists are, by definition and in contrast to the majority of artists trying to make a career, rare and in short supply. Consequently, great rewards fall to the chosen few. They do so also to those who successfully talent-spot and this provides the incentive for a host of 'middlemen', people and organisations whose function it is to search out and promote talented newcomers. Among those who perform this search and information service are artists' agents, literary agents, art dealers, gallery owners, artist and repertoire (A&R) departments of record companies and disc jockeys. Training institutions also perform this role, linked to their function of imparting skills and knowledge to prepare entrants for the different artistic professions; these institutions include higher education for artists, post-school vocational training and arts education in schools.

A large question mark that hangs over the notion of talent relates to the nature–nurture debate. This has an economic dimension because if we believe creativity can be learned, then the greater the expenditure on it, the greater its supply would be. On the other hand, if we believe that talent is inborn and will 'out' under any circumstances – the romantic view of the driven genius – then there is no need to spend resources training potential artists, only in supporting them once they emerge. A third way is to hedge one's bets as a society and do both: put in place training facilities to teach skills and to spot talent. That is the model that exists in many European countries, where training for artists is subsidised. This creates over-supply but it improves the chance of the cream rising to the top, thus maximising the social benefit of creativity (Towse, 1996).

One of the complicating factors in trying to understand the role of training and education in improving artistic talent and creativity is that because most courses for training artists in higher education, universities, art and music colleges and so on attract far more applicants than there are places for them, colleges are able to be highly selective in their admission, preferring the more obviously talented and able entrants. Thus the value-added of training is difficult to assess. The economic aspects of this, apart from the amount of resources that are devoted to training artists, are that labour markets for artists do not value paper qualifications as they do for other professions; employers prefer their own screening devices to seek out talent, such as auditions, membership of professional associations and personal recommendations. I have described these processes in detail in my study of classically trained singers (Towse, 1993) and they apply to many other artists' labour markets (see Chapter 3). Sometimes, the role of what is often called 'the Academy' is so strong that the affirmation of talent is politicised. In the absence of any objective measure of talent or creativity, we must regard it anyway as being socially determined. The rewards for being perceived as talented are very high for the superstars. Because markets for products with superstar input (records, films and so on) are global, there is a multiplicative effect on incomes as shown by Rosen (1981) in his economic analysis of superstars. I have put forward the theory (Chapter 4) that potential high prizes are a lure to would-be artists who risk forgoing considerable incomes to try their luck. The downside is that the risk of failure is very high. In Chapter 6, I argue that this analysis must also be applied to artists' royalty earnings and that the market alone, even with the protection and incentive of copyright law, does not sufficiently reward artists. Indeed, copyright favours the firms rather than the artists in the cultural industries.

Despite a now considerable body of work by sociologists and economists on artists' labour markets, we still do not understand the incentives to which artists respond.[5] Artists typically are multiple job-holders and spend long hours on artistic work; when their total earnings rise, they spend more hours on their artistic work and less on other work. That is not in itself a very surprising result. What is significant about this, however, is how elastic the supply of artistic work is, implying that even small rewards in the form of, say, commissions, grants or prizes have a considerable impact on creative supply. The policy implications are that small increments in income from any source – better rates of pay, higher royalties or subsidies to individual artists – could have significant results because artists have a strong preference for art work while being averse to other work. This observation calls for a theory of labour supply that is based on liking for work rather than dislike of it. Frey (1997) put forward an important behavioural theory which he later applied to artist supply (Frey, 1999). He distinguishes intrinsic and extrinsic motivation, the former being, in this context, the artistic drive to create, a non-pecuniary motive which has elsewhere been called psychic rewards, and the latter being a response to pecuniary rewards, as in money wages and income. The significance of Frey's theory is that monetary payment is not only not appropriate for intrinsic motivation, it also could cause crowding-out, that is it could act as a disincentive to effort. Frey (1999) makes the distinction between personal and institutional creativity and argues that cultural policy should find measures that are appropriate to both.

Frey does not reject the role of monetary payments but argues instead for a balance of intrinsic and extrinsic rewards to maximise creative supply. His approach rationalises the findings of surveys of artists' labour markets showing that artists value the professional recognition accorded by grants in addition to the financial benefit (Chapter 3). I suggest, in addition, that copyright law confers status for artists that makes it attractive even though pecuniary rewards are often low (*droite de suite* for visual artists is an example of this, see below). Data presented in Chapter 6 suggest that the average performer earns relatively little from copyright, though, as with artists' earnings from other sources, the superstars earn a great deal.

Understanding artists' labour market behaviour is important if as a society we wish to encourage creativity. For no amount of subsidies to arts organisations will lead to the production of high quality and novel output without a creative and talented workforce of artists. Some countries recognising this have had long-term policies of financial support in the form of grants for individual artists; other countries, including the UK and the USA have been unwilling to have such a policy.[6] As Frey's theory of intrinsic motivation suggests, payments in the form of a state grant provide more than just a monetary income to artists; they also symbolise recognition and status, especially as such grants are mostly awarded by peer groups. However, there is also a moral hazard element to this policy which is often ignored: it is difficult to measure output or, to be exact, measure the extra output from a grant, though that should be assessed somehow in order to evaluate the success of artistic policy in raising the quality and quantity of creative work. The result may also be affected by the choice of assessors: there is a danger of mutual back-scratching by a self-serving professional elite – the Academy – who block outside criticism from outsider artists or the public. The Arts Councils in the UK, which are 'arm's length' bodies of voluntary members of the public served by professional administrators, have been criticised for elitism but this organisational structure is less likely to be self-serving than that in the Netherlands or Finland, for example, where considerable grants are made to artists by their fellow professionals. Part II of this volume summarises my theoretical and empirical work on artists' labour markets, which has attempted to shed light on the economic aspects of talent and its reward.

ECONOMICS OF COPYRIGHT

In the remainder of this chapter, I review the literature on the economics of copyright that has particular relevance for artists' labour markets and for the work presented in Parts III and IV of this book.

Copyright has evolved into a dominant feature of the creative industries in the information age with considerable implications for incentives to artists. Copyright law was first enacted in England in 1709 with the Statute of Anne. It gives the right to authors (those who create works of art) to exclude others from copying their work without permission, thus creating intellectual property rights for literary and artistic works which overcome some of the public good aspects of information goods by preventing free-riding. It therefore provides an incentive to creative work. As techniques for reproducing and copying creative work have developed and the hardware for applying them has become cheaper, making it possible for the average household to own several copying devices (aural and video tape recorders, photocopiers, computers), the scope and degree of protection of copyright law has been increased. In addition, changes in social attitudes to creativity and to the status of artists have led to different forms of protection under copyright law, such as performers' rights. These developments have had an impact on artists' labour markets.

The acknowledged economic role of copyright law is to provide incentives to create and disseminate the expression of ideas. Unlike patents, which have the same economic purpose, copyright law does not protect ideas, only the expression of the work in fixed form (the fixation); copyright belongs initially to the author, the creator of the first fixation and is automatic in some countries. Copyright applies to a wide range of literary, dramatic, musical and artistic works in various media, such as broadcasts, films, recordings, computer software and the like. Whereas patent law requires proof of novelty, copyright law does not require any proven artistic merit, and accepts authorship on the basis of creative effort, not on creative achievement by any artistic standard; thus arrangements, compilations, listings, databases and so on are protected by copyright separately from the original material embodied in them.

The basic right conferred on the author, a term used throughout for the first owner of rights in a work (and note that rights apply work by work, so that the author of several works is a 'multiple-monopolist') is that of controlling or restricting the acts of copying, that is reproducing the work, issuing copies to the public, performing the work in public, broadcasting it by wire or satellite and including the work in a cable programme, playing and showing the work in public and renting or lending it to the public. The author may license, assign or sell these rights outright or in part or transfer them to an agent. All such transactions are made through contracts. Only the author's moral right in the work may not be sold or transferred. Typically, copyright for sales and other kinds of what may be called primary use is administered by the publisher; secondary use, such as photocopying and public performance of recorded works, is licensed by co-operative collecting societies.

The economic literature on copyright may be summarised briefly as follows: early writers, Plant (1934), Hurt and Schuchman (1966) and Breyer (1970) questioned the case for having copyright at all; the focus of their argument was the dynamic incentive that copyright provides in stimulating *author's* supply. Later writers, Novos and Waldman (1984), Johnson (1985) and Landes and Posner (1989) adopted a general welfare approach, using a comparative static model to consider the theoretical effect on *markets* of changes to copyright law. The merit of this approach is that it throws the emphasis on to the relation between the fixed costs of expression (writing the book, making the master tape) and the marginal cost of making copies, whether legal or pirated ones. The drawback is that these models simply assume that incentives to author and publisher work harmoniously and somehow produce the socially desired outcome. Indeed Landes and Posner, whose analysis of the law and economics of all aspects of intellectual property law has come to be regarded as definitive, not only do not question the case for copyright, they regard the basis of all legal doctrines as being a sort of modern invisible hand that overcomes market failure and promotes private economic efficiency and social welfare.

The third approach of economists writing on copyright is to consider the implementation of copyright. There has been some theoretical work, for example, by Smith (1986) and by Besen et al. (1992) on the economics of copyright collectives; another aspect of the literature is empirical work by Peacock and Weir (1975), Peacock (1979), MacQueen and Peacock (1995) and Taylor and Towse (1998, see Chapter 5) that investigates the complex institutional arrangements for the administration of copyright mainly in the music industry, where collection societies have been established longest. Finally, we come, as it were, full circle with a recent literature on the economic effects of digitalization, which provides a new spin on the old question of how markets for information goods will fare under changing technology. This last point is the subject of Chapter 8. In the remainder of this chapter, I consider these points, as a background to the applied work in Parts III and IV of this book.

Several features of the economics of copyright have particular relevance for the themes in this book – creativity, incentives and rewards in artists' labour markets.

Copyright law as an incentive to creative activity
The doctrine of fair use in the consumption and production of information goods
Work-for-hire doctrine
Droit de suite or artists' resale rights
The moral right.

Copyright as an Economic Incentive

The economic justification for statutorily giving authors copyright is an efficiency one: that it provides an incentive to create by enabling authors and publishers to recoup their outlays on the time and effort of creating the work on the part of the author and the cost to the publisher of making the master copy; together these constitute the fixed costs of the expression or its first fixation. Avoiding the fixed cost is not the only benefit that a copier could free-ride on if she were not prevented from doing so by having to obtain authorisation; the copier can also avoid the risk of testing the market for this original work because she will obviously only copy works that are successful and profitable. Plant (1934) saw this very clearly and concluded from it that copyright itself created inefficiency as it encouraged the production of sub-marginally risky works (he, like so many other economists, considered only books as examples of copyright material); in modern terminology, he thought copyright created moral hazard problems. He doubted that it created any real incentive to produce great works of art because great artists are not responsive to marginal pecuniary gain (and they could anyway be offered grants or subsidies to encourage them to do so) and saw copyright as merely drawing in poorer work that would not otherwise make it on the free market. He gave as evidence the publication in America of English works of fiction at a time when American authors had copyright but did not recognise foreign copyrights and therefore the claim to royalties of English authors, citing the particular example of Dickens.[7] He obviously agreed with Macaulay, whom he quoted with relish, that 'copyright is a tax on readers for the purpose of giving a bounty to authors'.

Plant rejected the case for copyright on economic grounds, seeing it as the cause of market failure rather than a solution; he believed the publisher of a new work had sufficient lead time (first mover advantage) to establish his product on the market. What Plant could not foresee was that lead time in copying, which in his day (1934) no doubt lasted months for books, would, 30 years later, be reduced to hours and 50 years later to minutes, even seconds. The acceleration of developments of copying technology of all kinds, from wax records and silent films to digital downloading of music and images, has completely wiped out the possibility of relying on lead time as a barrier to entry and an advantage in the market. With it has withered what Merges (1995) aptly called 'The Grand Question' – do we need copyright? In this respect Plant was really the last writer on the nineteenth-century patent controversies (he published a companion paper on the economics of patents in 1934).

Plant did recognise, however, that without some non-market system of rewards, authors would lack a sufficient incentive to create. He therefore proposed that private or public patronage in the form of grants and prizes be instituted to replace copyright. Hurt and Schuchman (1966) and Breyer (1970) also reached the same conclusion. Breyer's main concern was not the effect that the absence of copyright would have on the vast bulk of book production but rather what it would do to the creation of 'great works' of fiction. All these writers considered that a system of patronage and prizes could provide the same incentive as copyright (unlike Macaulay, who had considered the same options but concluded copyright was the lesser of the two evils). Breyer believed this solution to be preferable since it did not have any effect on 'access' because with a subsidy to authors, book prices would not be raised by the copyright monopoly. Thus the long-standing debate, originating with the mid-seventeenth-century claims of the Stationers' Company for restoration of their monopoly 'to encourage the advancement of learning' only really ceased with these economists' reluctant acceptance of copyright. Plant could not subscribe to copyright, which he found to be a blunt instrument; unlike patents, it did not discriminate quality, being accorded to all authors' works, whatever their literary merits, and it lasted too long since the majority of books went out of print long before the copyright expired. Plant's proposal was to have copyright made renewable like patents (as they originally were in both UK and US law).

Landes and Posner (1989) contribute a further insight into copyright's positive and negative incentives to creativity: the author's exclusive right removes works from the public domain for the duration of the copyright, thereby increasing the cost to subsequent authors of creating new works. For this reason ideas cannot be copyrighted; if, say, someone were able to copyright musical notation, she could effectively monopolise musical composition until a new notation were developed and disseminated or the copyright expired. Therefore, in order to maximise creative output, the law must strike a balance between too much protection of the author and the search costs for novel means of expression, of obtaining permission to use the copyrighted works of others, and suchlike. The following illustrates this tension between positive and negative incentives to create: imagine authors fishing for ways of expressing their ideas in a tank of water that is public; the more works they produce and copyright at any one time, the fewer the fish in the tank and the harder it gets for authors to catch them. How many fish there are in the tank depends on how often supplies are renewed by fish being released into the tank, the public domain, by the expiry of earlier copyrights and on how many authors are fishing. The longer copyright lasts, the less often stocks of fish are renewed. Equilibrium at any one time is when the marginal cost of fishing equals the marginal return to it, that is when the cost of extra protection by copyright, which inhibits creativity by restricting access to the public domain, equals the incentive it provides to authors.

Landes and Posner's model yields specific policy implications:

1. a greater (optimal) copyright protection is required for works that have greater social value; this implies that copyright should be discriminatory

and not applied across the board (Plant's conclusion). However, this is too difficult to administer. Since the (private) value of works increases with demand and demand shifts with income and markets expand with technical change, copyright protection should expand over time. This raises difficult problems for having a 'world standard' of copyright in countries with diverse incomes and levels of economic development (see, for example, Reichman, 1996/7).

2. the optimal level of copyright protection must take account of the higher transaction costs that it causes; the costs of tracing copyright owners increase with the duration of copyright, providing a brake on the number of years *post mortem autoris* that are desirable. The reason why there should not be perpetual copyrights as in property rights for land is that land is overused if not privately owned, whereas intellectual property is non-rival and cannot be overused.

3. the lower the costs of administering copyright *cet. par.* and the more authors respond to it, the greater will be the optimal extent of protection.

The analysis by Landes and Posner shows that the question of incentives is an intertemporal one and their static welfare model nearly bursts at the seams in places. Moreover, lumping together the bundle of rights and primary and secondary usage, inevitable in a general model, obscures the very different ways that markets work in different parts of the cultural industries and the different incentives to author and publisher. Above all, these models show how much answers to policy questions in economics rely on quantitative evidence; we may model the direction of changes but all too often the answer depends on the relative size of the costs and benefits.

Fair Use Doctrine

Fair use[8] may be characterised as a legal equivalent to Pigovian welfare analysis with its balance of social costs and benefits. The public interest in maximising creative output justifies both the incentive to create that copyright provides and its modification to ensure users' access to the works that are created. The exclusive right of authorisation is therefore limited in copyright statutes and exceptions made for certain types of 'fair use' – the use of copyrighted material without the author's consent and without payment. With the advent of cheap office- or home-based copying machinery, such as photocopiers and home video recorders and the facility for copying music via the Internet, unauthorised use, some of which is fair use but much of which is illegal, has increased considerably.

The underlying economic issue of fair use is market failure due to transaction costs exceeding the value of copies to individual users (Gordon, 1982). Gordon developed a 'three part test' for determining fair use: fair use is a defence against copyright infringement when there is market failure, when transferring control to the 'infringer' is in the public interest and when the incentives to the copyright owner are not substantially altered. Here market failure is used in the literal sense that a market fails to develop. The role of copyright law is then a Posnerian one of 'creating a market' by legal intervention. Such a creation might be by private collective agreement using blanket licensing as in the case of copyright collecting societies (see Chapter 5 on the music industry) or by government administration, such as the US Copyright Clearance Center, which could be strengthened if necessary by compulsory licensing (see Chapter 8 for the UK practice).

The problems that these copyright collecting arrangements overcome are the cost and bother to individual authors, publishers and users of clearing and paying for the use of copyright material and that of enforcing copyright in private homes and offices where infringement, often on a large scale, takes place. Digitalisation may or may not exacerbate these problems. The second point of Gordon's three part test is that the public interest may be served in some cases by allowing free use of new technology since the adoption of new technology promotes wealth maximisation. Fragile markets in new technology must be encouraged, not nipped in the bud, and fair use would achieve this by encouraging widespread use, even if some of it is free to the user. The Internet and the present economic and legal uncertainties surrounding some aspects of it come readily to mind in this context. Menell (2000) has led the field in applying the concept of network economies to new technologies and used what might be termed an infant industry argument for copyright – that copyright stimulates the development of new information goods industries.[9] Gordon's third test is loss of incentive fair use has for the copyright owner; for example, free use of out-of-print works could be a disincentive to a publisher to reprint them.

Fair use, therefore, is an important issue for incentives and rewards in the creative industries. A too strong copyright regime that tolerated little fair use would raise transaction costs and copyright-based earnings, transferring rents to artists from users; it would, however, raise the costs of creation to artists, as argued by Landes and Posner. A too weak regime, on the other hand, would not provide sufficient incentives to look for means of charging and therefore would reduce transaction costs and earnings but would make easier what Landes and Posner called 'productive' (as compared to 'reproductive') fair use of copyright material for creating new works and so benefit consumers.[10] Thus legal intervention has both efficiency and distributive effects, which must be separated. This distinction, one of the most fundamental in economics, is often fuzzy in policy-making.

Digitalisation and fair use

The impact of digitalisation on fair use and piracy will no doubt continue to dominate discussions of copyright as technical developments gather pace. It makes outdated some of the earlier economic analysis of copying, which was based on the idea that a copy is inferior, as digital copies are identical to the original (that is, they are perfect substitutes). In fact, there are two opposing versions of this discussion about the future of the cultural industries in the information age: one is that cheap downloading from the Internet of music, words and images in private homes will wipe out authors' and publishers' ability to collect royalties; the other is that it will so facilitate their collection that fair use is threatened.

Bell (1998) specifically deals with the question of the impact of the new technologies on fair use doctrine. He argues the scope of fair use will be reduced because courts will not accept fair use as a defence in situations where payment can be made (as was the case when the US Copyright Clearance Center made payment of 'small' copyright charges possible at low transaction costs). Instead, there will be vastly increased opportunity for what he cleverly calls 'fared use', that is charging for the use of digitally delivered material. As every item of material can potentially be traced and its use monitored, fair use gives way to fared use. Thus, not only will each and every piece of material have to be paid for, other expressive freedoms, quotation, citation, parody and the rest are under threat. Bell supports Gordon's view that fair use is a 'default' defence where markets do not exist and foresees that digitalisation can create functioning markets in the vacuum. He does not, however, conclude that fared use will necessarily reduce access to copyrighted material, as providers may well authorise free use of material under certain conditions (like fair use); moreover, increased opportunities to earn money from the creation of information goods offers an incentive to authors and publishers, so that we may expect supply to increase. Competition for users' time and budgets will also drive down prices. Thus the overall effect may be socially beneficial.

The question remains whether Internet trade can be achieved through contractual means. Bell argues that markets will evolve automated rights management conventions independently of statutory copyright protection if they are free (of government intervention) to do so. He envisages the development of reciprocal quasi-compulsory licensing which could be enforced through contract law. His view is that ' third parties', those not party to the contract, will be bound by a widely recognised 'default' implicit contract or general understanding that fared use is the norm, that is, people should expect to pay for material from the Internet.

Meurer (1997) explores price discrimination and fair use with respect to digital works; he argues that digitalisation may encourage the demand for excerpts, for example, for creating multimedia products, and that revenues could accordingly rise. This would make the formation of digital collecting societies worthwhile and hence cut down the amount of fair use 'excused' (my word) because no mechanism exists for charging. Online charging and shrinkwrap licensing (when software is purchased and the packaging broken for use, the terms of the contract are assumed to be accepted by the user) are forms of what Meurer aptly calls 'arm's length' transactions – with implicit contracts. Even with such possibilities for contracting, though, he argues that copyright owners will seek greater statutory protection because it offers greater benefits, such as damages and costs of litigation, to plaintiffs. With digital technology, price discrimination is aided by the producer's ability to alter content so as to inhibit 'arbitrage' and separate markets; it also facilitates the tracking of use, the development of encryption devices to prevent unauthorised use such as those built into DVD, and, indeed, of doing market research on users. Thus, price discrimination is likely to grow in the digital world and with it profits. But because price discrimination allows consumers to enter the market who would be otherwise deterred by a higher (monopoly) price, consumers are better off, and, one might add, this also deters piracy. Therefore, Meurer concludes, price discrimination obviates the need for vastly expanded statutory protection by copyright law.

This discussion throws up many questions which are particularly appropriate for investigation by cultural economists to whom pricing policy and access to cultural goods are a familiar theme. Many of the issues are essentially empirical ones, which require estimates of the relative size of costs and benefits, including the social impact on cultural production and consumption. What also requires more attention is the equity or redistributive effects of changes in technology and the law and in how the market responds to them.

Work-for-hire Doctrine

Copyright law has for a long time vested in the employer the copyright of works created by employees in the course of their employment; that is the basic work-for-hire doctrine and it is of particular interest for the type of labour market found in the cultural sector. Artists' labour markets are well known to be characterised by a range of non-permanent employment contracts, self-employment and freelance contracts for services. Labour markets in some areas, such as TV programme making, have been casualised by deregulation and changes in ownership (often the withdrawal of state ownership); these trends therefore make the question of who owns copyrights the more important. Hardy (1988) argues the work-for-hire doctrine has a sound economic basis. His analysis starts with the observation that there is tension between what he calls 'creators and copyright exploiters'. This characterisation leaves little doubt as to his view that there is not the harmonious relationship between the parties assumed by most economists writing on copyright, notably Landes and Posner.[11]

The simple question Hardy poses is: would abolition of the work-for-hire doctrine increase freelance creators' ability to make money? Evidence provided by artists' professional bodies to the US Congress suggests not. Nor would the supply of copyrightable works decrease without it, asserts Hardy. However, the real bone of contention is benefits from unbargained for, unforeseen uses which accrue as windfall rents to the copyright owner; where these exist (and every artists' representative I have ever spoken to believes they are widespread throughout the cultural sector), an ex ante 'fair' bargain can turn into an ex post rip-off. Thus, it is rights to unanticipated uses that are at the centre of work-for-hire disputes and these disputes have high transaction costs (making the Coase theorem irrelevant, as Hardy points out). He therefore investigates the possibility that copyright law could improve bargaining. Hardy argues that because there is asymmetric information and ability to bear risk as between freelance author and publisher the party best able to bear risk and exploit the market should have the copyright; however, the author should be the one to retain the rights to unanticipated uses and should therefore hold any rights not expressly granted to the publisher; the burden is then on the publisher, who is better placed to do so, to contract for a different result. (In practice, however, publishers frequently deal with the problem by requiring the author to sign away *all* rights for uses known and unknown.)

Hardy adopted an empirical approach to this matter. He analysed legal disputes over works for hire by looking for evidence of the courts' preference for the 'better exploiter' and their treatment of ambiguous contracts, using the cases cited by the authority on US copyright, Nimmer, concluding that the work-for-hire doctrine of copyright law reflected the tension in that law itself between maximising public access to a work and incentives to creators. A similar approach has been taken by Caves (2000), who explains the economic organisation of the creative industries in terms of contract theory.

Droit de Suite

Though not part of the copyright proper, *droit de suite* (known in the USA as the artists' resale right) is linked closely to it. It is an *ad valorem* tax on the resale of paintings over a certain price in public sales which exists in most European countries[12] and in the state of California; more often than not, it is not exercised by artists, as predicted when it was introduced (Rottenberg, 1975). It is an unalienable (unwaivable) right designed, with the best will in the world, to assist artists in bargaining with buyers but is generally believed by economists to reduce prices for the work of young artists and thus have unintended adverse incentive effects. As with other incomes of artists, it seems that *droit de suite* royalties, where they are collected, for example in France, are a significant source of income for the top artists but pay little to, or even harm, young artists by depressing prices (Perloff, 1998). Moreover, *droit de suite* is likely to act as a disincentive to dealers and others in promoting artists' work (Perloff, 1998). The effect of *droit de suite* on the art market should be testable empirically. But although there is now a considerable literature of econometric work in cultural economics on art as an investment, almost no one has tested the impact of *droit de suite* on art prices.

Solow (1998) introduces a new approach that challenges the negative view of *droit de suite*. He analyses its dynamic external effect on an artist's work over her lifetime. By having a claim on resale prices of past works, the artist has an interest in the future value of her early work, creating an incentive to maintain her reputation. Thus resale prices are 'endogenised'. The question of complementarity and substitutability between early and late works of a still-producing artist is an interesting one in other areas too, such as in sound recordings and literature, where the value of back catalogue can be enhanced by present activities, such as going on tour, being interviewed by the media and so on. Cheung (1986) is relevant to this question; he argues that unless both parties, licensor and licensee (author and publisher) share revenues, the licensee will obtain information on the value of the invention, which is otherwise not signalled directly to the licensor. Put simply, authors have the incentive to overstate the value of their work and publishers to understate it without full information.

An alternative to *droit de suite* is to give artists an exhibition payment right, a share of the entrance charge to public exhibitions of their work (Santagata, 1995). An interesting question that could be analysed in this context is the different values of the bundle of rights that are sold with a painting or other work of art; though the buyer acquires the painting, the copyright remains with the artist, who then has reproduction and other secondary use rights. An objection to a scheme for exhibition payments, however, is that it would have high tracing costs; any royalty scheme necessitates keeping in touch with copyright owners and that is also the case to a lesser extent for *droit de suite*. A similar proposal for a display right is discussed in a paper by Hansmann and Santilli (1997) in the context of artists' moral rights.

Moral Rights

The economic analysis of copyright, being largely by American authors, is almost exclusively concerned with what are called 'economic' rights, as contrasted to the 'moral' right. I dislike this terminology because it implies that economists are only interested in money, not welfare or the public interest nor, indeed, in the allocation of resources, which can perfectly easily be discussed without any reference to money prices. As suggested above, this is an area in which Frey's (1997) distinction between extrinsic and intrinsic motivation applies.

The European tradition of *droit d'auteur* stresses what have come to be called in English moral rights, the rights of attribution, integrity, disclosure and withdrawal. With the globalisation of the cultural industries and increasing standardisation of copyright worldwide, the distinction between the civil law countries' emphasis on moral rights and copyright in the common law tradition is eroding. Hansmann and Santilli (1997) consider both equity and efficiency arguments for artists' moral rights, which are beginning to be incorporated in US law, while Rushton (1998) argues that there is anyway pecuniary benefit from the moral right, so *droit moral* must be regarded as having efficiency effects; the moral right has an incentive effect for artistic production because it encourages artistic recognition of status and professionalism. Like the *droit de suite* (and some new performers' rights) in the EU, the moral right is unwaivable; in so far as moral rights have efficiency effects, this is a feature of interest to economists (see, in particular, Chapter 5).

One intriguing sideshoot of statutory moral rights for artists is that the question of what is art, and hence who are artists, becomes a legal matter. Hansmann and Santilli offer an economic perspective on this through the right of integrity; knowing who the artist is, and therefore the stock of works on which her reputation is based, is important market information. Though this explanation would seem to beg more questions about who says what art is than it answers, it is nevertheless interesting to see the connection being made in this way. While it is a relatively simple matter to identify the creator of a work of visual art, such as a painting or sculpture, however, it may be more difficult or even impossible to do so in other areas of the cultural industries, such as multimedia and sound recording. This is also an issue with performers' rights where costly arrangements have to be made to identify their contribution to works (Chapter 5).

COPYRIGHT AND GLOBALISATION

International co-operation for mutual enforcement of copyright for authors started in the mid-nineteenth century and was formalised in the Berne Convention of 1886. National collecting societies collaborate to collect and distribute royalties to foreign affiliates and courts enforce legal rights of authors and publishers who are nationals of signatory countries. Coverage of the Berne Convention has expanded along with national copyright law and the Rome Convention gives international protection to the neighbouring rights of performers, film makers, phonogram producers and the like, whose works were not included in copyright law as such in many countries and therefore required a separate agreement. The USA was not a signatory of either Convention until 1989 when it signed the Berne Convention; it is still not a signatory to the Rome Convention as it does not have rights in sound recordings nor the requisite performers' rights. The World Intellectual Property Organisation (WIPO), created as a UN policy forum, is another international organisation. None of these bodies has the power effectively to enforce compliance except by exhortation and international disapproval. The formation of the European Union and NAFTA (North American Free Trade Area) necessitated further harmonisation of inter-country IP law so as to promote effective competition; these trade areas can ultimately apply trade sanctions and fines on offending national governments when they do not observe the law. The international agreement that carries the greatest clout is the TRIPS (Trade-related Intellectual Properties) agreement of the GATT (General Agreement on Tariffs and Trade) which in the Uruguay Round, started in 1986, for the first time included 'intangible' goods and services alongside primary and manufactured goods. Thus copyright and other IP law became part of the business of international trade. International trade is now overseen by the WTO (World Trade Organisation, which replaced GATT) in which the USA is a dominant member; this organisation can evoke considerably greater worldwide trade sanctions for the international enforcement of IPs.

It is widely accepted that the USA made virtually no concessions in the recently concluded Uruguay negotiations of GATT and imposed upon the world not only the economic interests of its IP-based industries – the cultural industries, computers, pharmaceuticals and so on – but a degree of protectionism that is economically and culturally destructive to developing countries. David (1993) has argued that all countries throughout history, starting with Germany and England acquiring the technologies of the Venetian Republic in the fifteenth century, have copied the ideas and technologies of more developed countries and that was certainly true of the USA during its own period of industrialisation. Bettig (1996) connects the copyrighting of culture, as he calls it, to the political economy of capitalist development in general in a splendid and persuasive book which argues that copyright law is another weapon in the battery of property laws that are (mis)used to promote economic power and wealth. Moreover, he argues that the wealthy individuals who dominate the communications and entertainment industries are now globally supported by copyright law and its international enforcement through TRIPS. Reichman (1996/7) discusses the demands that greater international protection due to TRIPS makes on the administration and law enforcement of copyright and other IPs in developing countries, which they may be unable to meet. And though Reichman freely uses the term 'protectionism' pejoratively with respect to the strengthening of IP law for the benefit of developed countries, he does not appear to see the irony in an international organisation (GATT) that was founded to promote free trade and the dismantling of tariffs and other barriers to trade advocating an IP policy which introduces unfair trading advantage. Reichman admits that most developing countries have no need of enhanced IPs and should demand other trade concessions in exchange, but one has to write this off as exceptional naivety about economic power. The radical political economists have the advantage here; indeed, overexposure to intellectual property law and lawyers runs the risk of turning many of us into Marxists!

FINAL COMMENTS

It can be seen from this review of literature on the economics of copyright that, like copyright itself, its scope and volume have increased exponentially. In this partial survey I have concentrated on the literature of the economics of copyright that is most relevant to the creative industries. There is an extensive literature on the economics of intellectual property in general and on the economics of patents which contains much that is relevant to cultural economics – inventiveness in science and technology is after all not so different from creativity in the arts – but that has not been included for reasons of space. I have not referred to the growing number of publications on the economics of copyright in relation to computer software and databases. Nor have I referred to other rights that work alongside copyright in the cultural industries – design rights and trade marks, which are important for craft works, the manufacture of a host of design products, ranging from clothes to street lamps and also in the film, TV, music industries and publishing, where designs are utilised in the production process of the 'primary product', as well as in the production of all manner of ancillary merchandise that is now part and parcel of the marketing of films, CDs and the rest.

For all the sophisticated analysis by economists, economic historians, law-and-economists and lawyers, however, we still cannot say with any conviction that intellectual property law in general, and copyright law in particular, stimulates creativity. That is no argument for not having it but it should sound loud notes of caution about increasing it. And we still know very little about its empirical effects. These are issues of particular interest to cultural economists because they relate to the questions of how as a society we can stimulate artistic creativity and the role that reward plays in that process:

copyright, like subsidy, is an instrument of policy that is mostly assumed to work through pecuniary incentives.

The theme of this book is incentives and rewards to creativity in the arts and cultural industries. These industries are of increasing economic importance in both post-industrial and developing countries, whose culture is more and more globalised. But the arts and culture are important for their contribution to the cultural life of society, not only for their economic contribution. That recognition is the basis of cultural economics, which is concerned with the economic aspects of cultural policy by which governments seek to encourage cultural supply and its distribution. A vital part of this policy is the stimulation of creative innovation by artists. Thus the motivation of artists and their response to incentives is as much part of cultural economics as is the cost of artistic labour in public expenditures on cultural policy. Artists do not only work in the subsidised arts sector, however; employment in the cultural industries and earnings from that work are a necessary part of their economic viability. Nevertheless, most artists' pecuniary rewards are relatively low, as the surveys reported in Chapter 3 demonstrate and only a few superstars receive higher than average earnings from artistic work. Subsidy to the arts is not the only incentive to creativity; copyright law also seeks to provide incentives to cultural production and it is increasingly important in the cultural industries. But though much is made of the role of copyright in ensuring royalty earnings for artists, the majority of them again earn little from these sources (see Part III).

A central argument of this book is that copyright, like subsidy, is an instrument of cultural policy and the role of copyright in providing incentives and rewards to creativity must be considered side by side with subsidy. Copyright policy should therefore be integrated into cultural policy for the sake of the health of the creative industries. These themes are taken up in the following chapters.

NOTES

1. See Bianconi and Pestelli (1998).
2. But see IJdens (1999) for the situation of jazz musicians and entertainers in the Netherlands.
3. See Irjala (1992).
4. There is a strong similarity here with other 'entertainment' industries, particularly sport. Television has had an undoubted role in globalising information about sportspeople. In some sports the commercialisation of talent has gone further than in the arts; the market for sportspeople with transfer fees and the like has no direct parallel in the arts, though in the past, there were transfer fees for opera singers in Italy (see Bianconi and Pestelli, 1998).
5. Artists' labour markets have been studied by sociologists of culture as well as by cultural economists. There is an interesting overlap and consensus between their work (Menger, 1999). Sociologists have focused somewhat more on the status and professional organisation of artists while economists have focused more on the functioning of the market, relative earnings and human capital formation.

6. The UK announced a new policy for support of £1.5m to individual artists at the end of 1999. See Chapter 7.

7. The other side of the story in more ways than one, is entertainingly told by Bender and Sampliner (1997). It is a tale, as so often in the analysis of copyright and, indeed, of cultural policy, of unintended consequences. In order to encourage the development of an American literature (and reject ties with the old colonial power), copyright was granted to American nationals but not to foreign authors, in order to foster an American literature. However, publishers, looking to their profits rather than cultural ideals, preferred to publish works by English authors to whom they did not have to pay royalties, enabling them to charge lower prices for books, than publishers who published American authors who *did* receive royalties. Eventually, it was American authors who pressed for equal treatment of foreign authors in their own (American) interests! According to Plant (1934) and Breyer (1970), however, American publishers voluntarily paid royalties at least to some English authors.

8. The doctrine is known as fair dealing in the UK; in the USA and the UK exceptions and limitations are judged in the context of the case. In other countries they are specified by statute (see, for example for Netherlands, Holzhauer, 1999).

9. Liebowitz and Margolis (1995) have argued in opposition to Menell, however, that the concepts of market failure and network effects are considerably overrated.

10. Their argument as outlined above was about works in the public domain; they also deal with the related issue of derivative works (Landes and Posner, 1989). The economic logic is the same but applied to distinct legal doctrines.

11. Plant (1934) is a notable exception to this.

12. It does not exist in the Netherlands nor the UK, which in 2000, strenuously resisted adopting an EU Directive that aimed to harmonise its provision throughout Europe because of pressure from art market interests.

2. The cultural industries, copyright and cultural economics

INTRODUCTION

The twentieth century saw the growth of cultural industries delivering information, mass entertainment, 'low' and 'high' culture to a global market. Their development was made possible by successive technical discoveries of sound recording, film, radio, television, photocopying, laser printing, digitalisation and the Internet. They have transformed the production and consumption worldwide of the arts, entertainment and education – cultural goods and services – as well as altering other economic behaviours and fundamentally changing social and political life. These new media have had an enormous impact on artists' labour markets. The backbone of the cultural industries, like the arts, is the labour of creative men and women, artists of all kinds – writers, composers, visual artists, actors, musicians, craftspeople and the rest. They produce cultural content that embodies some spark of creativity, talent or novelty; this content is delivered to audiences, art-lovers, consumers – the public – by the firms in the cultural industries. Both content and delivery are protected by copyright law, which, as argued in Chapter 1, is adapting to new technologies. Most firms in the cultural industries are for-profit, market-based firms, some are huge multinational corporations, some are small-time enterprises; some are subsidised or regulated by governments. They all want the state to protect their property rights by copyright and other intellectual property law. Thus copyright becomes a *de facto* part of cultural policy through the cultural industries. That is now stated policy in the UK, and copyright features in the cultural policy of other countries, for example, the USA, Japan and Australia.

Interest in the economics of cultural industries has recently sprung to life; even a few years ago, this was not a well-established area of cultural economics, nor even a widely accepted one. That may have reflected the lack of interest in the cultural industries, indeed their negative image, in cultural policy circles (Bennett, 1991; O'Connor and Wynne, 1992). This view changed quite suddenly in the UK with the new Labour government, which adopted the term the 'creative industries' to encompass the 'traditional' arts in a broader definition of cultural industries. The

Department of Culture, Media and Sport's *Mapping Document* (DCMS, 1998) of UK creative industries covers advertising, architecture, the art and antiques market, crafts, design, designer fashion, film, interactive leisure software, music, the performing arts (that is, theatre, opera, dance, live music, mime, circus), publishing, software and television and radio (broadcasting). In this chapter, I discuss the development of this interest, the question of definitions, the economic analysis of these industries and policy on cultural industries and review work on them over the last few years in the UK and in the Netherlands.

DEFINING THE CULTURAL INDUSTRIES

The first champion of the cultural industries as part of cultural policy was Girard, a senior figure in French cultural administration (Girard, 1981). As is well known, the term 'cultural industry' was introduced by Horkheimer and Adorno in *Dialektik der Aufklärung* in 1947 in a pejorative way to suggest the erosion of the arts by mass culture. Girard took a more pragmatic stance, arguing the case for inclusion of the cultural industries in cultural policy-making in a 1972 paper for UNESCO (Girard, 1972). However, this plea was still being repeated in 1981 in the *Journal of Cultural Economics*. As he memorably wrote:

> those responsible for cultural policies have persistently turned a blind eye to the growing importance of these industries in people's leisure time ... The conclusion that inevitably springs from this observation is that far more is being done to democratize and decentralize culture with the industrial products on the market than with the 'products' subsidised by the public authorities. (Girard, 1981, p. 25)

Girard's list of French cultural industries was broadcasting, publishing, music ('records') and films; he considered whether newspapers and magazines should be included as 'cultural' products and also the inclusion of advertising; thus his list is the same as that of the UK Ministry 30 years later, minus the 'high' arts. His primary concern was that of the cultural policy-maker; that, on the one hand, these industries were already increasingly satisfying people's demand for the arts and entertainment through the 'democratization of the market' – for many with a higher quality product than could be obtained in live performance outside major cities – and, on the other hand, they are private enterprise, market-orientated industries whose purpose is to sell copies rather than to worry about cultural content, which, of course, cultural policy could not determine. (The significant exception to this at the time was broadcasting, since radio and TV were under some form of state ownership throughout Europe.) Girard identified a range of financial, fiscal and regulatory measures available to policy-makers for achieving public policy objectives in the cultural industries as in the arts, that is, he proposed an integrated cultural policy. These measures included quotas on foreign (usually American and English language) TV and film imports, the latter eventually to cause major problems for France and Canada in the Uruguay Round of GATT in the 1990s (see Acheson and Maule, 1999).

In the 1980s, cultural accounting, that is, the collection of statistics on a wide range of arts and cultural industries, began to be done, stimulated initially by UNESCO and supported in western Europe by the Council of Europe. From the diversity of data that emerged from this process, it became obvious that one country's 'cultural industry' was another's 'subsidised art' sector. Every attempt to compile internationally comparable statistics required expert knowledge of each participating country's cultural perceptions and policies; so, for instance, the newspaper industry was subsidised in France, while the 'freedom of the press' in the UK required it to be totally independent of government. In 1981 in France, municipalities with over 10 000 inhabitants spent nearly 200 million francs (out of a total of 8 billion) on the press; from 1981 to 1984, the Ministry of Culture in France increased its expenditure on cinema and 'audio-visuals' fourfold, from 1 to 4 per cent of its total spending, during which time the total budget rose by 300 per cent. In 1981, the central government in Italy spent 15 per cent of its cultural expenditure on the cultural industries (press publishing, broadcasting and cinema); central government in Sweden spent 22 per cent on newspapers and magazines alone; the Austrian Federal government spent 7 per cent on press, film and broadcasting; even the UK spent 5 per cent of its arts budget on film (Myerscough, 1984). Different countries took different views about how much and for which reasons they subsidised their cultural industries, if at all. The French concern with its distinctive culture and language and the desire to fend off Americanisation and the spread of English had defence of its language as a prime motive for subsidy of film, publishing and broadcasting. So do many other countries. Figures for the Netherlands offer an instance of this: the Dutch language share of book titles was held to around two-thirds from 1970 to 1988, while broadcast product in Dutch was around 70 per cent, due to the assistance of the Development Fund for Dutch Cultural Broadcasting Productions, which in 1993 had a budget of Nfl.30 million (Myerscough, 1994). Even in the UK, with its huge advantage of the English language and the economies of scale in publishing, film, TV production and so on that that allows, some aspects of publishing, for example, poetry, are subsided, as are Welsh and Gaelic language TV.

The question of how to define cultural industries, therefore, cannot be answered independently of the specific issues and objectives of cultural policy. Attempts to solve the problem by recourse to using state subsidy as a guide are doomed to failure; it simply is not possible to draw a line based on what cultural products are subsidised and view one side of the line as 'art' and the other as 'mass entertainment' supplied by cultural industries. That approach somewhat dogged UNESCO's and the Council of Europe's early efforts at cultural accounting. Those efforts have been rewarded, however, by vastly improved (though still far from perfect) cultural statistics in European countries as witnessed by the Council of Europe's national reports on France, Sweden and the Netherlands and by individual national governments' own attempts to estimate the value of the arts and cultural industries in Gross National Product.

MEASURING THE VALUE OF THE CULTURAL SECTOR

Two related motives underlay what could be dubbed the move from cultural accounting to national income accounting for the cultural industries in the 1980s. One was the understanding prompted by international comparative work on cultural accounting, not only, as argued above, that perceptions and practice vary in different countries, but also that the subsidised arts and the cultural industries are heavily intertwined on both the production and consumption sides. Studies of artists' labour markets and of the use of artists' time were particularly instrumental in demonstrating this. This was, for example one of the findings of my enquiry into the market for classically-trained singers (Towse, 1993). The second motive was what could be called 'facts for advocacy' – the, to an economist, curious belief that policy can be influenced simply by the presentation of facts about that for which support is sought. This belief (which, one has to say, seems to have been vindicated in the UK, at least by its results) rests on the notion that 'size counts' – the bigger the item under investigation, the more it counts politically. The cultural industries, initially sneered at by the 'pure' arts lobby, conveniently boosted the figures and added weight to the size and value of the cultural sector. Thus they gained a sort of back door admission to a newly conceived integrated cultural sector. And the exercise subtly changed from being a positive one of fact-finding to normative study of the economic importance and impact of the arts, broadly defined now to include the arts aspects of the cultural industries (Myerscough, 1988).

Where does economics come into this picture? Indeed, where did *economists* come in?

As one who was partially involved, these are interesting issues to review with the benefit of hindsight. One problem was that the pioneers of economic impact or economic importance of the arts studies were often non-economists who did not (or chose not to) fully understand the hazards of double counting and the aggregation problem in national income accounting. What they did choose to understand, however, was the multiplier effect, which was wonderful: not just was the sector large, it could be increased by the application of a proper economic idea! But even when economists were responsible and able to control measurement, they often found their results hijacked and blown up out of all proportion (Puffelen, 1996). In retrospect, we should have seen it coming: certainly the Council of Europe's cultural accounting work was already headed in that direction; the use of statistics for advocacy was emphasised in the opening and closing sessions of the 1984 conference in Munich (reported in Myerscough, 1984) and again in the Council of Europe conference on European Arts Statistics in Lisbon in 1986. The size of the cultural sector was increased by including the cultural industries and by ascribing tourism to the presence of arts and heritage facilities. When economists criticised economic impact and other such studies as contravening basic economic logic and Ministries of Finance, such as the UK Treasury, dismissed them as unsound and anyway inappropriate as advocacy, arts lobbyists were both shocked and angry as they believed they had done the right thing by taking economists on board.[1]

An example of this type of advocacy was Myerscough's (1988) study of the economic importance of the arts in Britain. This was in fact a concoction of nationally available data and three local studies. The local studies followed a well-established pattern of economic impact studies in the late 1970s and the early 1980s in the USA, where the National Endowment for the Arts sponsored surveys of several US cities and, most successful of all, the New York–New Jersey metropolitan region study published in 1983 (see Heilbrun and Gray, 1993, chapter 15 for a convenient summary and references). The proliferation of these studies had already prompted economists to question both procedures and the economics utilised in them (Seaman, 1987). However, Myerscough went even further than these studies by attempting to aggregate the local results over the whole of Great Britain, oblivious of the fact that the supposedly marginal nature of the analysis makes it untenable at the national level – that one locality's exports must be another's imports. Moreover, as one is looking for value-*added*, and not value, additionality must be established since consumers and producers have alternative uses for their resources – put at its simplest, that people would eat anyway even if they did not go to the theatre and have supper nearby!

Notwithstanding the problems of this and other economic importance or impact studies (and amazingly enough, they continue to be produced, as I discuss below), they stimulated an interest in gathering data on the arts and on the cultural industries and on employment in the cultural sector as a whole. The process had begun in the UK with Nissel's *Facts About the Arts*

(Nissel, 1983), a pioneering and exemplary publication of statistics on the arts and cultural industries in the UK, which for the first time gave an objective overview of the sector. However, it took the supercharged context of advocacy to knee-jerk widespread interest in fact-finding exercises of this kind.

The facts that were summarised in the Myerscough *Economic Importance* volume showed that in 1985 in the UK, of the total of £3992 million ascribed to the so-called arts sector, £3057 million came from what we would now call the cultural industries, that is, broadcasting, film, video and cinemas, publishing, the art trade, the music business (recording) and crafts (the last named contributing £77 million). Therefore, the cultural industries by far dominated the cultural sector as a whole, a fact much remarked on at the time by critics of the study on one (or both) of two counts, that they were not 'high culture' and that they grossly inflated the 'true' figure. The benefits to trade bodies and the like of data-as-advocacy were thus established and we now see the cultural industries similarly displaying themselves in the hope of political favours. In the late 1990s, we saw exactly the same process of data-for-advocacy taking place with the cultural industries as happened a decade before with the subsidised arts. The difference was that the subsidised arts sought government financial support whereas the cultural industries seek government protection through copyright law.

Despite the universal condemnation of national economic impact studies by cultural economists and the indifference to them in the UK by the Treasury, another such exercise was undertaken in Britain in the 1990s. Entitled *Culture as Commodity?* (Casey et al., 1996), this was another data-as-advocacy exercise. At bottom, what it did was to repeat the Myerscough study minus the multiplier (or, as an economist might prefer to put it, it assumed the multiplier was one – which is close to the supposed national value of it), while attempting to distance itself from that work's overt embellishment. The criterion for inclusion in the study adopted by Casey et al. was that there had to be some subsidy to the industry; so, included as 'the media industries' were film, video, multimedia, broadcasting (TV and radio) and book publishing. On this basis, the total 'value' of subsidised culture in the UK was £2.25 billion, with £60–70 million in the media industries; these are turnover figures, however, as the authors appear not to have understood the concept of value-added.[2] However, according to this criterion, the music business was left out because it was unsubsidised. But by doing so, Casey et al. ignored the cross-subsidisation that others had demonstrated to exist, say, between live performance of a piece of classical music and a recording of it. This completely missed the point of the main criticisms of Myerscough's study, namely that cultural economics has established the presence of some public goods characteristics and externalities of both production and consumption and any proper economic study of the cultural sector would attempt to measure them (Hughes, 1989; Brosio, 1994).

There are, however, some differences between the subsidised sector and the cultural industries in respect of the availability of statistics about them: while the subsidised arts are publicly accountable, the cultural industries are not and, short of some juridical intervention, such as an enquiry by the anti-monopoly authorities or other regulatory process, it is difficult to obtain verifiable data unless firms in the industry agree to provide them. They have the incentive to do this only when they believe something is to be gained thereby. At the end of the day, it is really only governments that have sufficient resources and powers to do proper national income accounting in the cultural sector and that is what the UK *Creative Industries Mapping Document* (DCMS, 1998) is. However, this is not yet part of the regular process of national data collection and, so far, was a one-off exercise undertaken under the supervision of the DCMS (Department of Culture, Media and Sport) rather than by the Office of National Statistics. Moreover, the publication is not one of dry data but is loaded with normative comments and observations, while it lacks standard statistical conventions, such as the year to which the data relate. Despite these shortcomings, this represents the most reliable source of statistics to date on value-added in the arts and cultural industries in the UK. Definitional issues still need to be ironed out and primary data collection needs improving, though, especially of employment and self-employment when the exercise is repeated. Table 2.1 summarises the key statistics on the UK creative industries.

It will be noted that the large total figure (size counts to the DCMS too) is revenue not value-added. In 1995, value-added in creative industries was £25 billion, 4 per cent of UK Gross Domestic Product – bigger, as is stated, than any manufacturing industry! For even this official government exercise is tainted with the motive of propaganda. The opening pages of the publication state:

> The creative industries occupy an increasingly important place within the national economy. However their importance is not yet widely recognised. Nor has there traditionally been any formal co-ordination across Government of policies designed to promote them, which are the responsibility of several government departments. The Creative Industries Task Force was established in June 1997, with the aim of providing a forum in which Government Ministers could come together with a few senior industry figures to assess the value of the creative industries, analyse their needs in terms of Government policies and identify ways of maximising their economic impact. (DCMS, 1998:3)

What is the value of these studies and mapping exercises and do they contribute anything to the study of cultural economics? The Myerscough and the Casey et al. studies were self-confessedly concerned to establish the

Table 2.1   UK creative industries: revenue, exports and employment, 1997[a]

	Estimated revenues £m	Exports £m	Employment
Advertising	>4 000	565	96 000
Architecture	1 500	250	30 000
Arts and antiques market	2 200	1 300	39 700
Crafts	400	40	25 000
Design	12 000	350	23 000
Designer fashion	600	350	11 500
Film	900	522	33 000
Interactive leisure software	1 200	417	27 000
Music	3 600	1 500	160 000
Performing arts	900	>75	60 000
Publishing	16 300	1 900	125 000
Software[b]	7 500	n.a.	272 000
Television and radio	6 400	234	63 500
Total	>£57bn	£7.5bn	*c.* 1m

Notes:
a.   I assume the year is 1997 in the absence of that information.
b.   No figures available for exports.

Source: *Creative Industries Mapping Document* (DCMS, 1998).

importance of subsidy to the arts and cultural industries. However, most of the cultural industries, as noted by Girard in 1972, are independent private enterprises. There is a fundamental confusion at the base of the attempt to demonstrate the economic importance (that is, measured size) of an art form or cultural industry. If it is so big and important and therefore, according to this way of thinking successful, it should not need subsidy! If it needs subsidy, it must be a lame duck industry. That is a matter for industrial rather than cultural policy. We subsidise the arts and culture for their cultural not their economic significance; why, then, make the case on the basis of size and economic success?

Where size does matter to an economist is in respect of firm size within an industry; the industrial structure (microeconomics) is more significant than macro share of GDP. The question of regulation, particularly of global media corporations, depends far more on the size of firms within the industry than on the size of the industry per se. And that is an important problem for cultural economics.

INTERNATIONAL TRADE, GLOBALISATION AND THE CULTURAL INDUSTRIES

Despite a very promising start by Seaman (1992), the study of international trade in cultural goods has been a relatively neglected area in cultural economics until recently (see Mas-Colell, 1999; Schulze, 1999). Specific commodities for which trade is restricted, such as the export of art and artefacts and cultural content restrictions in imports of film and TV have attracted interest (Giardina and Rizzo, 1994; Acheson and Maule, 1999). But there are few general restrictions, other than those connected to copyright, in the trade of goods produced by the cultural industries, though immigration laws often restrict free movement of artistic labour (work permits are typically needed for performers' services, usually at the behest of national trade unions, such as Actors' Equity). Most cultural products and many artists serve global markets and globalisation is widely believed to be a feature of the information age. However, that is not easy to test as evidence is inadequate; this is another area of cultural economics that calls for basic data collection and analysis. Schulze (1999) provides a useful summary of International Monetary Fund (IMF) trade statistics for standard industrial classifications of the art trade, sound recordings and publishing; the total (for 154 countries) was US$3587 billion averaged over the years 1990–94. Schulze also looked at import:export ratios and, for sound recordings (51 per cent of total trade), identified 10 countries that were net exporters. Surprisingly, this did not include the UK or Sweden (though it included the Netherlands), countries that have made much of the importance of their music businesses as a source of foreign exchange earnings as net exporters. In 1997, according to the DCMS *Mapping Document*, the UK had 7 per cent of world sales, in fourth place to the USA, Japan and Germany (the Netherlands had 1.6 per cent and Sweden 1 per cent); in 1993, the UK had net earnings of £324m from sound recording (and £571m including all music business items, that is, music publishing and instruments (the latter a net import), performance income and musical theatre (DCMS, 1998)). The differences between these results demonstrate yet again that cultural statistics are still too poor for accurate comparisons.

EMPLOYMENT IN THE CULTURAL INDUSTRIES

There has been increasing interest in artists' labour markets in cultural economics over the last 20 years but apart from the USA, where the large population allows detailed census classification that enables analysis to be done from published official statistics, most of the work on artists and craftspeople in other countries has been based on surveys. Problems of defining and identifying artists (as well as the perpetual problem of low response rates to questionnaires) have been a feature of this work (see Chapter 3). Concern about unemployment and changing labour market institutions in many sections of the economy and the growing importance of information-based industries have combined to stimulate official interest in employment in the cultural industries and arts in several individual European countries and on the part of the European Commission. Table 2.2 summarises the picture for the European Union as a whole.

Comparison between Table 2.1 and Table 2.2 for the UK shows a considerable disparity; the European Commission figure is half that of the Creative Industries Taskforce's *Mapping Document* (DCMS, 1998) and the gap cannot be explained just by the difference in year. A different definition of cultural industries has been used; for example, the EU document does not include the art market. On the other side, the DCMS document does not include heritage, which is a large employer (depending on what is included in heritage). There is, of course, no correct way to define these industries, as we saw earlier. It is just a matter of arbitrary decision and adopting a standard for the whole of Europe and internationally.

The other problem with the figures in Table 2.2 is that they relate to persons not to jobs and include part-time as well as full-time workers. They seem to include self-employed workers in the cultural industries, who dominate crafts and visual art production and are increasingly to be found in the performing arts (where in several countries the performer can choose her employment status) and in film and television programme production. Again, this is a matter of adopting a standard definition. Whether artists and cultural workers are employed regularly, full-time or part-time, on short-term contracts or occasionally depends upon industrial structure and finance as well as institutional labour market regulations in individual countries. Work by O'Brien and Feist (1995 and 1997), by Casey et al. (1996) and by Pratt (1997) has sought to unravel these difficulties in official UK statistics. A more detailed account of the problems of UK statistics on the labour force in the cultural industries is provided in the appendix at the end of this chapter.

Finally in this section, we can compare the figures from Great Britain with those of France in the performing arts and the audio-visual industries in Benhamou (1999). The growth of employment (employees only) in the French cultural industries was 73 per cent from 1982–90 and 36 per cent for equivalent industries in Britain. For cultural occupations, the figures were France 48 per cent, Britain 25 per cent, reflecting, among other things the considerable difference in the economic climate of the arts under Mitterand and Thatcher. These selected figures and those in the appendix give a flavour of the problems to be solved before confident statements can be made about

Table 2.2 Number of persons* directly employed in the cultural sector in the European Union, 1995

Country	Total	Performing arts	Heritage and education	Cinema and audio-visual	Publishing and recording	Press	Crafts
Germany	1 000 760	100 000	80 000	200 760	170 000	–	450 000
Austria	3 681			3 681			
Belgium	57 653	12 400	10 970	20 889	6 485	–	6 909
Denmark	17 599		2 900	14 699			
Spain[a]	257 113	42 400	21 930[b]	88 523	32 260	–	72 000
Finland	33 566	9 060	8 560	7 025	1 971	–	6 950
France[c]	745 158	160 000	96 400	177 108	95 180	66 470	150 000
Greece	10 134			10 134		–	
Ireland	31 536	6 150	1 500	6 086	1 800	–	16 000
Italy[c]	495 583	104 000	36 413[b]	144 023	64 201	63 946	83 000
Luxembourg	2 320			2 320			
Netherlands	151 647	35 000	15 961	57 186	22 500	–	21 000
Portugal	35 918	12 000	4 000	8 918	2 500	–	8 500
United Kingdom[c]	511 743	90 000	71 600	198 543	25 400	101 100	25 000
Sweden	60 907	33 000	3 500	10 907	3 500	–	10 000
Total	3 415 318	604 111	353 734	950 802	425 797	231 516	849 359

Notes:
*The figures given are estimates derived from diverse sources. They relate to the number of people working in the cultural sector regardless of status (full-time or part-time).
a. To this total the Spanish add the graphic arts and related activities, audio-visual equipment, manufacture of musical instruments, photographic and cinema laboratories (87 970 jobs in all).
b. Excluding art teaching but including architecture.
c. Including the press.

Source: European Commission (1998).

employment at any one time in the cultural industries and about the growth of the employment they provide, however defined.

COPYRIGHT AS THE BASIS FOR DEFINING THE CULTURAL INDUSTRIES

A unifying feature of the cultural industries is that at their core is creativity protected by copyright. This has been explicitly recognised in the UK where copyright is now viewed as the organising principle of the creative industries. The Creative Industries Task Force set up to review cultural policy took as its definition:

> those activities which have their origin in individual creativity, skill and talent and which have a potential for wealth and job creation through the generation and exploitation of intellectual property. (DCMS, 1998, p.1)

The centrality of the individual creator is captured in Figure 2.1, a figure that was used by the Task Force. All but the outside layer 'Tools of the Trade' are activities that are protected by intellectual property law.

Given this broader approach to cultural policy, it is appropriate that the Department for Culture, Media and Sport rather than the Department of Trade and Industry (DTI), previously responsible for policy in relation to some of these industries, should have the creative industries under its remit; copyright, however, is still dealt with by the Patent Office under the DTI. In Australia, matters have been taken further with the formation of the Department of Communications, Information Technology and the Arts, which is responsible for IP as well as cultural policy.[3] By contrast, cultural industries in the Netherlands are not perceived as part of cultural policy. Though it is clear from policy statements of the Ministry of Education, Culture and Science (1998) in the Netherlands that copyright is important for cultural policy, and even though media policy is administered by the same ministry, the two are viewed as separate entities. There is not the same emphasis on the cultural industries having common cause with the traditional subsidised arts nor an appreciation that copyright is a binding force; copyright policy seems to be divorced from cultural policy and is handled by the Ministry of Justice.

There have been successive studies done by SEO, the Foundation for Economic Research of the University of Amsterdam, which demonstrate the growth of these industries in the Netherlands between 1982 and 1994, reported here in Table 2.3 (Booij, 1993; Van Asselt et al., 1997). It can be seen from Table 2.3 that the list for the Netherlands is similar to but not the same as that of the UK Task Force list in Table 2.1. The Dutch figures include engineering

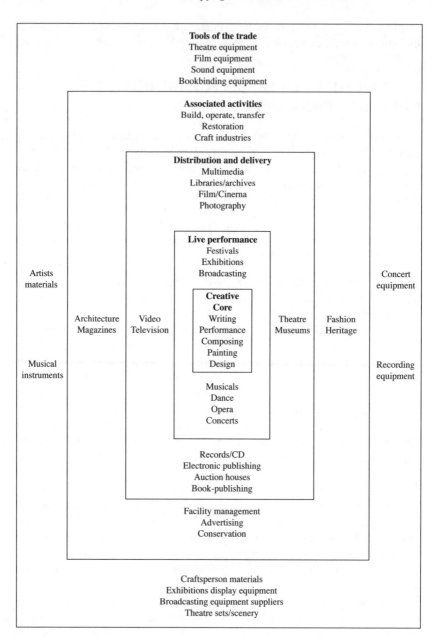

Figure 2.1   The creative industries

Source: Creigh-Tyte (1998).

consultants and researchers, most of whom are academics; a novelty is that only that part of advertising is included (40 per cent) that is deemed to be creative work. Value-added by all cultural industries was 4.5 per cent of GDP in 1989 and that had grown to 5.23 per cent in 1994, a growth rate of 6.4 per cent which much exceeded the growth of GDP in the Netherlands over that period. The fastest growing industries are multi-media, software and broadcasting – 'information age' industries. The growth of value-added is mirrored in the growth of employment in these sectors.

Other countries have made estimates of the economic importance of copyright. How accurate they are depends upon the breakdown of national income accounts as well as on the definition of the industries themselves. Some caution has to be exercised in making comparisons between countries in case they have different copyright coverage (for example, performers have fewer economic rights in the USA than in the UK and the UK does not have a blank tape levy as does the Netherlands). The same reasons advise caution in making intertemporal comparisons, at least over long periods, because copyright law is forever being extended and that could affect the measured size of the protected industries. A final point is that, like the studies of the economic importance of the arts, the true cultural value of copyright cannot be fully captured by measuring value-added in the cultural industries, however accurate those measures are, because there are external benefits that are not priced through the market place; the national culture, a creative environment and freedom of expression are examples of non-appropriable benefits. Copyright law, however, embodies the power to alter the balance between what is private and public, what must be paid for and what is freely available (see the discussion of fair use in Chapter 8). The working of markets is framed and regulated by copyright law and there is a constant tension between economic realties and legal doctrine that is played out in the arena of the cultural industries. This becomes more important in the information age with all the uncertainties about the effects of digitalisation on copyright and markets. The interaction between culture, copyright and the economy in the creative industries should be at the heart of the cultural economists' approach to cultural policy.

CULTURAL ECONOMICS AND THE CULTURAL INDUSTRIES

What was the response of cultural economists to Girard's *crie de coeur* about the cultural industries? In fact, the same issue of the *Journal of Cultural Economics* contained a major article by Garvin on the economics of 'mass entertainment' with references to a modest literature on film, video, television

Table 2.3 Copyright industries in the Netherlands, 1994

Cultural industry	Value-added output in millions of guilders	Percentage of GDP	Percentage average annual growth of value-added 1989–94	Employment	Percentage of employment	Percentage growth of employment (in FT equivalents)
Press and literature	11 093	2.01	6.1	122 713	1.83	1.1
Design	5 355	0.97	4.9	62 296	0.93	5.8
Software	4 445	0.77	11.6	51 285	0.77	15.3
Research[a]	3 021	0.55	5.0	47 388	0.71	6.0
Broadcasting	2 488	0.45	9.5	31 290	0.24	14.2
Music and theatre	1 496	0.27	5.9	15 947	0.47	–2.1
Film and video	544	0.10	0.3	15 410	0.17	8.4
Photography	129	0.02	–3.9	11 341	0.06	4.2
Multi-media	116	0.02	20.0	4 105	0.02	18.9
Visual arts	109	0.02	–14.2	1 203	0.23	–4.4
Copyright and administration	55	0.01	3.4	611	0.01	1.9
Total	28 851	5.23	6.4	296 332	5.43	4.5

Note: a. Universities and research organisations.

Source: Van Asselt et al. (1997).

and book publishing (Garvin, 1981), demonstrating that there was already some limited interest in the field.

In 1984 an important article by Hilda and William Baumol was published (reprinted in Towse,1997a); the article was a response to the criticism of Baumol and Bowen's (1966) unbalanced growth hypothesis and the 'cost disease' in the performing arts. Critics had made the point that mass media (cultural industry) production of the arts could overcome the tendency to cost and price rises above the rate of inflation. The Baumols showed that the cost of making TV programmes and movies in the USA was, like live performance, eventually subject to the cost disease, though they also pointed out that these high fixed costs could be spread over many performances of the programme or film. This dismal prognosis seems to have had a discouraging influence on economists studying the cultural industries.

The immediate response of the cultural economics profession was a conference on the performing arts and the audio-visual sector (organised under the auspices of Girard and the French Ministry of Culture) which resulted in a publication *Bach and the Box: The Impact of Television on the Live Arts* (Hendon et al., 1986). As the title indicates, the question on the agenda was: how can TV and other media help spread and finance the live arts? That is an important question in cultural policy. Policy-makers are increasingly aware that high quality live performed arts, for example, cannot be made easily accessible without very large subsidies and look to TV and other media to assist in increasing the availability of the arts. However, there is clearly far more to television and other media than as a purveyor of high culture on the cheap! The output of the cultural industries at that time apparently was not recognised as inherently interesting and culturally important in its own right. Through the 1980s, cultural economics began to move away from its earlier dominant concerns about the role of subsidy to the high arts and the wider macroeconomic aspects, such as the economic impact of the arts discussed earlier, towards microeconomic studies of cultural organisations and institutions, for example, theatre, opera, orchestras and art markets in the 'traditional' arts sector and the economics of the film and music industries in the commercial cultural sector. This gathered force during the 1990s.[4] Now, interest has shifted to the problems of global markets, multinational ownership within and across media and the impact of the Internet and digitalisation on cultural production.

The cultural industries, like other information industries, are characterised by two inter-related features: within the firm, high fixed costs and low (or even zero) marginal costs – the conditions for natural monopoly – and, at the industry level, the concentration of economic power dominated by a few oligopolistic firms. The music industry is typical of this structure, where five multinational record companies are owned by giant globalised holding companies (Bettig, 1996). There are also substantial network economies (Shapiro and Varian, 1999) and economies of scope, leading to a tendency to cross-media ownership.[5] These supply-side features are reinforced on the demand side by consumers' preferences for superstars (see Chapter 4). Another economic feature of the creative industries is pervasive risk, even radical uncertainty, about markets and products (Caves, 2000). This exacerbates the effect of high sunk costs as firms strive to achieve success with a few titles (books, records, films), which cross-subsidise the inevitable failures. This leads to over-supply; Kretschmer et al. (1999a) see the combination of network economies, uncertainty about markets and over-supply of creative output as the defining features of the cultural industries. These features not only determine industrial organisation, they also increase demands for copyright protection to reduce free-riding.

All these economic factors add up to a matter of great concern for cultural policy, that cultural diversity will be lost in homogeneity and globalisation. For the last 50 years, cultural sociologists have debated Adorno and Horkheimer's prognosis without, however, reaching a consensus. There is also controversy within economics about the case for cultural subsidy and regulation to combat the outcomes of these market features. Cowen (1998) offers an economic history of cultural production over the last 500 years, arguing that our artistic heritage is almost entirely due to the private enterprise cultural industries of the past. He sets out the view that the capitalist market economy successfully nurtured artistic creativity and developed consumers' cultural tastes and considers why the view that the market inevitably corrupts culture – cultural pessimism – prevails. He presents histories of the book publishing and music industries and the production of art in Florence, Amsterdam and Paris at different times as evidence for his case that the market rather than state subsidy has been the basis of the growth of culture. The case for adopting free market policies is argued by Acheson and Maule (1999) in another context, of protectionism in Canada in its trade disputes with the USA over cultural content in the film, broadcasting and publishing industries.

The creative industries lend themselves well to the information age paradigm of the distinction between content and delivery of the core of creative input and the periphery of related or derivative economic activity that is the means of delivery (what Caves calls 'humdrum' activities). In Figure 2.1, humdrum 'Tools of the trade' are on the outer rim: for example, CD production – the sound carrier – is distinguished from the creation of the master tape, the depository of the information content of composition, performance and sound engineering. This image corresponds to the economic characteristics of the production process and of value-added by each stage. It also highlights the content areas that are most vulnerable to free-riding by illegal copiers and hence where copyright protection plays its greatest role.

There is huge technical change taking place with digitalisation and the Internet, the delivery of content and in methods of transaction, such as licensing, franchising and a host of other means of exploiting information goods and services. As digitalisation progresses and becomes more widely disseminated, more and more information goods will be delivered into people's homes. Thus the output of the cultural industries can be downloaded by households, charged for and paid electronically. Whether these services will be delivered by computer, TV or radio sets or mobile telephones depends on how markets develop and are allowed to develop by government regulators. These changes will no doubt give rise to similar discussions in the new century about the threat the Internet poses to mass culture as those which took place during the middle of the twentieth century about the threat of the 'industrialisation' of culture to the live arts and to 'high' culture.

CULTURAL INDUSTRIES AND CULTURAL POLICY FOR THE INFORMATION AGE

The forgoing analysis suggests that policies for the global cultural industries in the information age are likely to be very different from the type of national cultural policy that was concerned with state subsidy to the traditional arts in the mid to late twentieth century. Policy must be multi-faceted; it must be national and global; micro and macroeconomic, protectionist and free trade. It is argued in this book that copyright law will have to become an instrument of cultural policy. The globalisation of copyright as a means of regulating cultural industries is as significant as the globalisation of their ownership and of their cultural content. Decisions about the scope of copyright and about its enforcement are made at the supranational level by bodies such as the European Union, the World Intellectual Property Organisation (WIPO) and the World Trade Organisation. It is perhaps only at this level that the cultural industry conglomerates can be regulated.

These developments obviously have important implications for national cultural policy. Whatever the economic merits of one type of policy or the other, though, the enormous capacity for cultural change bound up with them must be very seriously considered, and allowed to override private economic benefits. Cultural goals of society – the social benefits – range from preserving language, heritage and institutions to ensuring that every child learns to use IT. Governments need the whole gamut of regulatory and economic instruments to protect national culture, to enable markets to function and to restrict unwanted outcomes; these include decency laws, IP law, anti-monopoly/competition law, financial guarantees, subsidy and state ownership. Moreover, economic policy, for example, the encouragement of competition, must not conflict with cultural policy, for example, strengthening IP laws. This is a massive and difficult balancing act for government policy and it may well be the case, as Cowen and Acheson and Maule have argued, that the freer the market, the better. My opinion is that like the physical health of a nation, its cultural health cannot be left entirely to market forces simply because markets cannot be relied on to work unaided. Cultural economists should be able to play an important role in analysing cultural policy for the information age, as they have done in the last 30 years, by understanding those market forces in the cultural industries as they evolve.

APPENDIX

Problems of Artist Labour Force Statistics in the UK

There are several different sources of official statistics in the UK on employment. The 1991 decennial Census of Population (known as the Census for short) is the most reliable source of official data on Great Britain (that is, excluding Northern Ireland). Completion is compulsory and requires the whole population over the age of 16 to return a self-completed questionnaire, which includes demographic questions and ones about economic activity, industry, place of work and qualifications; it does not, however, include earnings. O'Brien and Feist (1995) used tabulations on artists and the cultural industries commissioned from the Office of Population Census and Surveys. The Census asks for information on employment status, hours worked, (main) occupation and the industry in which it occurs; the latter are backed up by questions on job description to enable a Standard Occupational Classification to be made in a Standard Industrial Classification (SOC and SIC). The crux of this investigation by O'Brien and Feist hinged on the intersection of SOC and SIC, that is, having an artistic or cultural occupation and working in a cultural sector industry, which enabled estimation of employment in the sector and also a comparison of trends in the 10 years between censuses and with other official statistics on employment.

The Census of Employment is a statutory census of employees covering nearly everyone, though it only surveys workplaces with fewer than 25 employees; it excludes the self-employed and unemployed (that is, those not employed in Census week). As many artists and craftspeople are self-employed or work in small enterprises, the Census of Employment is therefore unsatisfactory. Another problem is that the UK Census, like the US Census, asks only about the person's main occupation in census week; it does not seek information on multiple job-holding, seasonal working and so on, which we know to be important characteristics of artists' labour markets (Chapter 3).

The Labour Force Survey is a quarterly survey of households by voluntary interview of an effective sample size of 60 000 people; it includes more – and more detailed – questions than the Census but does not ask for earnings and, being smaller scale, it has relatively few persons in some categories which makes analysis of artistic occupations difficult; for example, in replies to several questions the sample size of musicians dropped to below 40 and it never exceeded 160. It is, of course, part of the problem that there is no total figure; a cross-check, known to be a considerable overestimate of professional musicians, is membership of the Musicians' Union, which is around 35 000.

The other survey analysed by O'Brien and Feist (1997) is the New Earnings Survey, a sample survey of 1 per cent of employees in employment earning enough to be in the pay-as-you-earn tax scheme and to pay National Insurance contributions; this yields very small numbers in artistic occupations and, of course, like the Census of Employment excludes the self-employed, casual and piece workers, the unemployed and, in addition, the very low paid.

The figures reported in the text are from the two sets used by O'Brien and Feist (1995 and 1997), as these conveniently coincide with those of DCMS (1998). Comparing a selection of cultural occupations (SOCs) in the 1992 Labour Force Survey with the 1991 Census of Population, the former counts 307 800 and the latter 281 800. Comparing the Census of Employment with the Census of Population for selected cultural industries (SICs) in 1991 gives figures of 232 700 and 322 000 respectively. A ballpark figure is therefore plus or minus 300 000. A final figure from O'Brien and Feist (1995) is that, using the Census of Population data to do a longitudinal analysis, they found that roughly half those with a cultural occupation were still in the same one from 1981 to 1991 (that is, half left, retired, moved jobs, became unemployed, migrated and so on) and that a quarter of the 1991 figure were young people under the age of 16 in 1981. Pratt (1997), working with Office of National Statistics data found a growth of 3.7 per cent of what he defined as the production sector of the cultural industries, which is roughly equivalent to O'Brien and Feist's 1995 categories.

The employment figures in Casey et al. (1996) are from the 1994 April Labour Force Survey. They chose a broader definition of the cultural sector to include libraries and heritage and so included a broader range of occupations appropriate to that choice. As there is no external standard according to which either SIC or SOC should be selected, such differences are par for the course. As their figures include heritage, they may be compared to those of the European Commission (1998) documented here as Table 2.2.

The problems with using official statistics to analyse artists' supply behaviour have caused researchers to undertake their own surveys of artists' labour markets. The difficulties inherent in these surveys are documented in Chapter 3.

NOTES

1. Alan Peacock has memorably called this the economist as 'hired gun'. When we do not come up with the 'right' answer – a case in point was his path-breaking work testing Baumol's cost disease in the UK in the 1970s (see chapter 20 of Towse, 1997a) – economists are regarded as a menace.
2. See Towse (1997c). Having myself taken part in aspects of these studies, I find it very depressing how often authors fail to acknowledge the discipline of cultural economics and feel free to ignore those who try to explain its basic ideas. I know I am not the only one who has experienced this (see Puffelen, 1996). Cultural economics still has a long way to go in establishing itself.
3. See www.dcita.gov.au/ip. An interesting example of this joint policy is the PAML (Performing Arts Multimedia Library) pilot project, which combines IP information and advice for performing arts organisations. See www.cinemedia.net/PAML.
4. The economics of the film industry have been studied by Wallace et al. (1993), Prag and Casavant (1994), Acheson and Maule (1994/95), Hoskyns et al. (1997), Albert (1998, 1999), Sedgwick and Pokorny (1999), Bagella (1995), Bagella and Becchetti (1999) and Vany and Walls (1999). Topics covered are film finance and the search for indicators of the success of film titles. Cameron (1986, 1988, 1990) and Fernández Blanco and Baños Pino (1997) have analysed the demand for cinema and Frank (1994) considered the decision to release film titles in video format. The music industry has been studied by Belinfante and Johnson (1982), Murph (1984), Baker (1991), Alexander (1994), Burke (1994, 1996a,b), Cox et al. (1995), Rutten (1996), Kretschmer et al. (1999b) and Strobl and Tucker (2000). Despite all this, some areas have been neglected; there have been very few economic analyses of the publishing industry, though it is one of the largest of the cultural industries; Szenberg and Lee (1994) and Greco (1999) have looked at US publishing and Hjorth-Andersen (2000) provides an econometric study of the publishing industry in Denmark. The path-breaking work on the economics of broadcasting and government policy was by Coase (1966) in the US; Peacock (1986) on broadcasting finance in the UK; Withers (1983) on the cultural influence of public broadcasting and Papandrea (1999) on the regulation of commercial TV in Australia.
5. See Doyle (2000) on cross-media ownership in press and TV in the UK.

PART II

Rewards to artists

3. Economics of artists' labour markets*

INTRODUCTION

The primary aim of this chapter is to review research undertaken on the economic characteristics of artists. This area of investigation is fraught with problems of definition, as are so many issues in the area of arts policy. Because of this, the chapter begins with a brief discussion of the ways used to define who is and who is not an artist. (The term 'artist' is used here to include a range of creative and performing artists and craftspeople). Section 2 examines how labour markets work in the arts. Section 3 looks at what is known about artists' earnings from various surveys and Section 4 contains a short summary of the role of institutional arrangements such as grants for artists, and taxation. Research on the contribution that training makes to artists' earnings is outlined in Section 5. Section 6 discusses the findings of this body of work.

2. GENERAL ISSUES IN LABOUR MARKETS FOR ARTISTS

The Definition of Artists

At the conceptual level, who is and who is not an artist is as complex as the question, what is art? Frey and Pommerehne in their book *Muses and Markets* (1989, p. 47) identify eight criteria that may be applied in order to determine who is an artist:

1. The amount of *time* spent on artistic work;
2. The amount of *income* derived from artistic activities;
3. The *reputation* as an artist among the general public;
4. *Recognition* among other artists;
5. The *quality* of artistic work produced (which means that artistic 'quality' must be defined somehow);
6. *Membership* of a professional artists' group or association;
7. A professional *qualification* in the arts;
8. The subjective *self-evaluation* of being an artist.

Criteria 1 and 2 are objective criteria and may be measured from survey data; data on criterion 6 are easily obtained but may involve external assessment if membership is selectively conferred; criteria 3, 4 and 5 are inherently difficult to apply in practice; data on criterion 7 can be obtained, though with difficulty, and with the proviso that possession of a qualification does not always lead to practice as an artist. The last criterion, that of self-definition, has, perhaps surprisingly, been adopted in most surveys of artists' labour markets. As we shall see, however, different studies of artists have utilised all of these criteria to a greater or lesser extent, as well as more general labour market surveys or censuses. UNESCO has defined an artist as:

> any person who creates or gives creative expression to, or recreates works of art, who considers his [sic] artistic creation to be an essential part of his life, who contributes in this way to the development of art and culture and who is or asks to be recognised as an artist, whether or not he is bound by any relations of employment or association. (UNESCO, 1980, p. 5)

This may be termed the self-definition model of the artist, the last of Frey and Pommerehne's criteria, and the view is essentially the same as that taken by the authors of *A Creative Future* who represented the various bodies subsidising the English arts, crafts and media sector (Arts Council of Great Britain, 1993a, chapter 1). It clearly seeks to avoid problems of elitism and any 'official' designation of the arts and artists, and in so doing it applies only the standard of self-assessment. Several studies have utilised this definition: Brighton et al.'s (1985) survey of visual artists concentrated on specific geographical locations and built in a 'snowball' method of collecting lists of names of artists. My study of artists of all kinds in Devon, including craftspeople, used a list compiled by the Beaford Centre that included many self-defined artists (see Towse, 1991b). Joan Jeffri's study of visual artists in New York combined both self-assessed and externally-assessed definitional criteria (Jeffri et al., 1991). Wassall and Alper (1985) included self-defined artists in their survey of artists of all kinds in New England, USA, as did Mitchell and Karttunen (1992) in their survey of Finnish writers. These latter two studies compared self-defined artists with externally-assessed definitions of artists, showing the effects that different definitions have on research findings about employment characteristics and earnings.

External assessment of artists entails several different criteria as listed by Frey and Pommerehne (1989): the 'market place' criterion relating to income generation from work in the arts, membership of professional associations or trade unions, a training qualification in the arts, and peer group assessment. Clearly these criteria can overlap, with some artists falling into all four categories (and self-definition too). Jeffri, a sociologist, was interested in defining professionalism, and the focus of her work was on both self-assessment and on peer assessment. Visual artists were asked to specify the most important reasons for defining both themselves and someone else as a professional artist. The survey results showed that 'inner drive' was the highest ranking choice (Jeffri and Throsby, 1994).

Economists, perhaps predictably, have tended to adopt a market place criterion concentrating on the first and second of Frey and Pommerehne's (1989) criteria (time allotted to artists' work and income). Throsby and Mills (1989) in their survey of Australian artists, which covered performing and creative artists and craftspeople, started by compiling lists that included self-defined artists as well as members of trade unions and professional associations and other 'externally' defined artists, and then at the first stage of the survey, they used telephone interviews to eliminate artists who had not practised (that is sold, performed, published, commissioned and so on) their art in the previous five years. This was a liberal interpretation of the market place criterion in that it did not require the artist to be *currently* practising. Filer (1986) subscribed to the most rigorous market place test of all, according to which only those who succeed in a strict financial sense (the market test) count as artists. His study used US Census data, again for the whole range of artistic occupations, which are compiled by asking people in the Census week what their occupation was in which they spent the most time earning money. This method of identifying the artist population, similar to the one adopted in the British Census of Population, has been shown by Wassall and Alper (1992) to eliminate people who would by other criteria be counted as artists.[1]

The survey by Knott (1994) for the Crafts Council and an earlier survey by Bruce and Filmer (1983) made strenuous efforts to include as many different types of maker by contacting a wide range of organisations and outlets for lists of names and addresses, and also by sending out calling cards. The authors succeeded in reaching full-time, part-time and occasional craftspeople suggesting that they would conform to several definitions; a market test, peer and external assessment, and self-definition (see Knott, 1994; Appendix A gives details of the survey base). The survey of artists in Wales (Towse, 1992a) and a more recent Scottish study (Scottish Arts Council, 1995) utilised a variety of sources for obtaining the relevant artist population: membership of artists' associations and trade unions, Arts Council lists and, in the case of the latter, recent graduates of art, drama and music colleges.

Membership of professional associations and trade unions, Frey and Pommerehne's seventh criterion for defining an artist, may or may not imply a market test or peer assessment. It all depends on how members are admitted. Performers who are full members of Equity have passed a market test, because in order to obtain full membership they must have worked a set number of weeks at the recommended Equity minimum rate of pay. Provisional Equity membership, however, is conferred automatically for two years on actors, dancers, stage managers and so on who have trained at accredited schools. The Jackson et al. (1994) survey of dancers and actors used Equity membership lists for actors and they supplemented them with lists of dancers from other sources. Other professional associations have a range of different criteria for membership. Membership of the Musicians' Union, for example, is open to all and therefore includes self-defined musicians, as well as those who would pass any test of being professional. The Incorporated Society of Musicians, however, only admits members with recognised professional training.

To sum up the question of the definition of the artist population, various criteria may be used and there is no one 'correct' definition. The main point is that whichever definition is used is bound to produce different research findings, which may in turn lead to different policy implications.

General Characteristics of Artists' Labour Markets

There are two sides to transactions in a labour market, the *supply of labour*, that is, the hours offered at various rates of pay by workers, and the *demand for labour*, how many artists or hours of their work are hired. We could speak in general terms about the labour market for artists of all kinds or of a specific labour market, say for singers, or even more specifically, of the market for classically trained singers. Here the term is being used in a general sense. This however does not imply that the supply of artists' services is homogeneous (nor that demand is for 'high culture' or commercial purposes). It is useful to make a distinction between creative artists and craftspeople on the one hand, and performing artists on the other, for the purpose of analysing survey results. Creative artists can be taken to include composers, writers, visual artists, film-makers and choreographers; performing artists are actors, singers, dancers, instrumental musicians, mime artists and so on. By and large, performing artists sell their services to promoting organisations and those services are labour itself, whereas creative artists produce by their labour something more tangible (a work of art, a book, a score, a play, a choreographed dance) which is bought or commissioned by some intermediate organisation (an art dealer, a patron, a publisher, an orchestra, a dance company). Some work is sold directly to the public, especially, but not only, the work of visual artists and craftspeople. For some artists, however, the distinction between creative and performing artists is not valid, because their work falls into both categories.

To speak of artists' labour markets, however, is to imply that there are economic features common to all artistic activities. Is this so? After all, different groups of artists and craftspeople reach the final consumer in different ways, and the timing of work and payment for work varies. Creative artists and craftspeople mostly have to finance the period of production themselves, whereas performing artists are mostly paid as they rehearse and perform. There are exceptions in both cases: some visual artists are paid salaries as artists-in-residence; some visual artists, authors and composers receive an advance from publishers or on commissioned work; solo singers are only paid for performances, not during the rehearsal period and have to finance themselves while they learn roles. What all artists have in common, though, is that they sell their accumulated skill and intellectual property in one way or another. In general, work is exchanged for payment via the labour market. How different artist labour markets work is discussed further below.

Depending on how the artist population is defined, various characteristics of the supply of artists may be identified. Clearly, for practical purposes, all research must start with a list of artists before work can begin, and that list inevitably introduces some bias into the findings. This particularly affects data on earnings, as shown most notably by the work of Mitchell and Karttunen (1992) and Wassall and Alper (1992). But it may also affect other economic and social characteristics; for example, a strict market place criterion for inclusion would tend to systematically eliminate younger, less established artists who have not yet begun to earn much from their *principal artistic activity* (PAO).

It can be seen from the number of studies cited above that quite a lot of research has taken place on different types of artists, and it is therefore possible to generalise about the economic and social characteristics of artists as a group; gender, age, education and training qualifications, hours worked in arts and non-arts occupations, and so on. There seems to be little relationship between earnings and age or experience; many established artists have similar earnings to less-established artists. Evidence from pay scales in the performing arts shows that there is little progression in rates of pay to reward experience, to support a career structure, or indeed, to stimulate career development. These points are discussed in more detail below and in Sections 3 and 5.

The surveys that have been done all tend to show that artists are younger than the workforce in general, they are better educated in the sense of having higher educational attainment, and they have longer periods of training or higher education than the average member of the workforce. Some occupations tend to be dominated by one sex; dancers are predominantly female, conductors male. Most artists tend to be self-employed; this may mean that it is in the nature of their occupation to work independently, or that they work for others on a series of short-term contracts (a high proportion of performing artists in the UK fall into the latter category). Because of this pattern of work, it is difficult to make statements about unemployment or under-employment (working less than they would like to) of artists; generally, though, most research findings suggest that artists do not do as much paid work in the arts as they would like. As noted above, many, though not the majority, are active in non-arts as well as arts work. The survey of artists in

Wales found that performing artists did less arts work than they would have liked because work was not available, and creative artists spent less time on their arts work than they would have liked to because they had insufficient time left over from other income-earning work (Towse, 1992a). Surveys have shown that, on average, artists and craftspeople work more hours a week in total than other comparable workers. And, in general, artists earn less in total than other comparable professionals. The one exception to this finding is Filer's (1986) mentioned above.

On the demand side, artists' services are purchased by a wide range of subsidised and commercial organisations, and artists often work in several sectors. Take the case of singers. Classically trained singers work live in choirs and choruses, opera, oratorio, musicals and as recitalists, and in recorded work in sound recording, radio and TV as well as in commercials, jingles and suchlike (Towse, 1993). The same is true of actors, dancers and instrumental musicians. Markets are often organised by go-betweens: agents, fixers (approved musical contractors), art dealers and galleries. Creative artists' transactions are often with commercial organisations or individuals. Surveys of artists' employment and earnings do not discriminate between the commercial and subsidised sectors; they may identify which sector provides the most work and pay but they mostly have not been confined to analysing one or the other sector (though the Scottish Arts Council survey (1995) concentrated on artists of particular interest to them).

Having identified the general characteristics of artists' labour markets, we now turn to analysing how they work.

How Artists' Labour Markets Work

The interaction of supply and demand, in aggregate, determines the amount of employment and the distribution of earnings in a sector of the economy. Supply and demand are the outcome of individual decisions to offer hours of work and to purchase labour services at various rates of pay. Ultimately, the result determines the size of the artistic population, artistic income and output.

Different factors affect the supply side and the demand side of the equation. In this section, those factors are discussed, and related to the level of employment of artists. Section 3 deals with artists' earnings.

What is meant by employment?
First, it is necessary to clarify what is meant by 'the level of employment' and its converse, unemployment, with respect to the arts. This is particularly difficult in the arts for a number of reasons: the occupational structure of most arts and crafts activities is such that there are relatively few regular jobs. Only a few artists have full-time, long-term contracts. Creative artists and

craftspeople are mostly self-employed, and many performing artists work freelance (and may be self-employed for tax and other such purposes). The significance in this context is first, that the level of employment cannot be measured by the number of jobs, nor can unemployment be measured by the gap between jobs and vacancies; and second, self-employed people cannot, from an official point of view, be unemployed. Self-employment is viewed as being a business activity that either yields sufficient income for the 'firm' to survive or results in it closing down.

Indeed, in a number of ways many artists are like businesses. They must invest resources in preparing whatever it is they supply (developing skills, practising, rehearsing, making sketches and so on). They spend time and money promoting themselves, going to auditions, showing their work, approaching agents, dealers and publishers. Only some of these expenses are tax deductible. Artists who are employed, whether on short or long-term contracts, may not be able to get recognition by the tax authorities for their outlay of time and other resources (see Section 4).

If employment is defined by hours of paid work, such preparatory and promotional activities do not constitute hours of employment. Many surveys of artists have obtained information both on the number of hours spent on artistic activity and on paid employment. They also ask respondents about periods of unemployment. What emerges is that many artists, in effect, are *under-employed*. That means that they are unable to obtain as many hours of paid work as they would be willing to do at the going rate of pay. A different but related issue is multiple job-holding, that is work in arts-related or non-arts occupations because insufficient income is earned from the principal artistic occupation. Summaries of findings from various surveys dealing with these issues are including in this chapter.

What determines supply and demand for artists' services?

The demand side In every art form, demand for artists' services depends upon demand for the final product. This relation is direct for those visual artists and craftspeople who produce works for sale to the public but tends to be indirect (derived) in other cases. Turning first to the performing arts, casting for a play, musical, film and so on depends upon both the type of character in the script and the director's interpretation. Thomas (1992) showed that female Equity members are less likely to be employed in the mechanical media because the type of script that is most frequently used calls for fewer female than male actors. In ballet, though, the reverse is the case; there is more employment for women in the performed repertoire and this in turn is reflected in the gender composition of companies. The demand for any individual's labour is derived from the demand for the work itself. The demand for solo trumpeters is generally determined by the public's taste for trumpet concertos. If the trumpeter is Wynton Marsalis, the public may demand more performances of trumpet concertos. Star artists are a draw for audiences and demand focuses on them. Promoters can raise prices and accordingly pay them more. Substitutes cannot easily be found and that raises their bargaining power, but rank and file orchestral musicians, for instance, can be substituted more easily. The public's demand is for the orchestra not for its individual players (and matters are complicated on the demand side by the taste for the works performed, the conductor, the venue and so on). The demand for artists, as for other workers, is determined mainly by consumers' tastes for the goods and services they produce. And like other workers, artists are subject to technological developments in the means of production.

The overall level of demand for artists' services, however, is also determined by the level of public subsidy to the arts. It is not market forces alone which determine the size of the arts sector in the economy. The level of public funding for the arts, and its distribution by art form, influences the prices at which the products of artists' services reach the public via arts organisations.

To put the above in economic language: demand for artists' services is derived from the demand for the 'product', and this is determined by the level of demand for the product; the cost of the labour embodied in it and the price of alternatives: alternative artists' services, alternative ways of producing the product, and alternative art works or events. This is just as true when the 'product' is a performance, that is the artistic service itself, or a physical work of art embodying the artist's labour.

The supply side   The 'supply' of artistic labour is the flow of artists' services offered at various rates of pay. Artists decide how many hours they are willing or able to devote to their artistic work, that is, their labour supply. Questions about that flow of supply cannot be answered by estimating the stock of artists (that is, the size of the artist population), because many artists, however they are defined (whether by self-assessment, by training criteria, or by membership of trades unions and professional associations), do not work full-time on their chosen principal artistic occupation. Nor can the flow of supply be identified with the numbers of students graduating from arts courses in universities, art and music colleges and dance and drama schools. On the one hand, not all of them seek work as artists, and on the other, a proportion are trained outside those institutions.

Figures of membership of trades unions and professional associations are a useful indicator of the size of the artist labour force. However, for the very reasons identified above, they may either underestimate or overestimate the size of the 'true' artistic population. Indeed, a realistic figure for visual artists cannot be provided in this manner, since artists are famous for not joining anything. The population of visual artists is estimated to be in the region of 95 000 (O'Brien and Feist, 1995), though membership of the National Artists' Association is approximately 500. The Crafts Council survey estimated the number of professional craftspeople to be over 20 000 (Knott, 1994). Equity, the trade union of performing artists, includes directors and stage managers (but not film or recording technicians). Membership of Equity is conferred after 13 weeks of work at the agreed minimum rate of pay. Some working professional dancers are not eligible because they are paid below the Equity minimum (see Jackson et al., 1994, p. 160). The membership figure of 43 000 is therefore an underestimate of the total population of performing artists, although again one has to be careful over assumptions in this area. Equity membership also includes a proportion of 'resting' and former actors. The Musicians' Union membership figure of 33 000, in 1994, by contrast, includes many who seek only part-time work in music. The Writers' Guild (1800 in 1994) and the Society of Authors (5000 in 1994) have to some extent an overlapping membership.

These figures do not, however, tell us about the supply of labour. Many professional artists are unable or unwilling to work full-time in the arts. Until a comprehensive survey of artists' labour market behaviour is undertaken in the UK, it is not possibly to analyse the relation between the time artists spend on their principal artistic occupation, hereafter called PAO, and their earnings from artistic work.[2] The surveys of artists in Devon and Wales (Towse, 1991b; 1992a) and the Scottish Arts Council study (1995) provide a partial picture of artists' time allocation, earnings and the reasons for working less than they desire to in their chosen PAO. Both studies produced broadly similar results and for simplicity, only those from the Wales survey are reported in detail here.

The average weekly hours worked for all artists responding to the Wales survey was 36, with male artists working 40 hours and females 31 hours; approximately two-thirds of that time was spent on PAO work and the remainder on other income-producing work (either arts-related or non-arts work). In Scotland, artists worked 46 hours a week on artistic and related work when in work, with a further average 12 hours on teaching. In the Crafts Council survey, 70 per cent of all respondents worked over 40 hours a week (Knott, 1994). Artists in Wales would have liked to spend more time on arts work, but were under-employed either because work was not available or because they had insufficient time left over after undertaking work in their other income earning activities (see Table 3.1). For women artists, domestic responsibilities were also an important reason for not working as much as they would have liked to on arts work.

Table 3.1 shows that approximately 40 per cent of all artists surveyed in

Rewards to artists

Table 3.1   Under-employment of artists in Wales (%)

	All	Males	Females	Creative artists	Performing artists
Worked less than 26 weeks full-time in PAO in reference year	42	38	50	38	45
Worked less than 26 weeks any days in PAO in reference year	40	39	41	36	48
Main reasons (a) and (b)					
Work not available	43	44	40	21	70
Insufficient time left over after other income earning activities	42	43	40	56	24
Domestic responsibilities	23	17	36	22	23

Notes:
(a)   Multiple reasons could be given by respondents, hence totals do not add up to 100. See original report for full details of other reasons given.
(b)   Percentages refer to all respondents.

Source: Towse (1992a) Tables VI: 4, 5, 6.

Wales were under-employed. The figures support the point made earlier that performing artists rely more than creative artists on being offered work but that the main problem for creative artists is that they cannot earn enough from their PAO and so have to seek other kinds of work to support themselves. In Scotland, over half of those surveyed felt they did not spend enough time on their artistic activity, and that was true for those who worked full-time. For women with dependants, the figure was 75 per cent (Scottish Arts Council, 1995, p. 13).

What is clear, therefore, is that to understand artists' labour supply decisions, account must be taken of earnings in both the arts and non-arts sectors. Throsby (1994, 1997) has estimated 'labour supply functions' for artists in Australia. A supply function shows hours of work offered increasing with rates of pay. For artists who divide their time between arts and non-arts work, hours of arts work undertaken depend on both arts and non-arts rates of pay. Throsby found that artists spend more time in both arts and non-arts work as rates of remuneration rise. In other words they respond to economic incentives, *but* they have a marked preference for arts work and only spend time on non-arts work up to the point at which they can earn enough to support their chosen PAO. The more they can earn *per hour* outside the arts, the less time they spend on non-arts work and the more on arts work.

As we shall see in the next section on earnings, many artists endure relatively low incomes because of their strong preference for pursuing their chosen artistic career. In Wales, half of all the respondents did no non-arts work and 38 per cent were satisfied with the amount of time they spent working in the arts. In Scotland, 37 per cent said that their artistic activity was their main occupation (Scottish Arts Council, 1995). Jeffri et al. (1991) found that 70 per cent of visual artists surveyed in the USA had on more than one occasion turned down lucrative opportunities that were not artistically fulfilling. It would therefore be wrong to conclude that all artists are dissatisfied with their choice of career. Many people in all sectors of the economy prefer to be self-employed and earn less than they could working for others. Two-thirds of the respondents to the Craft Council survey regarded 'being their own boss' as being very important and the same proportion valued the chance to explore their own ideas (Knott, 1994).

These are the non-economic benefits to artists and craftspeople, sometimes called psychic income. Psychic income may be regarded as a measure of the importance artists and others attach to their chosen career but it also measures the cost of that commitment. While the concept of psychic income can be used to rationalise career choice, it lays artists open to possible exploitation. Withers (1985) has argued that artists themselves provide a significant subsidy to the arts via psychic income by working at rates of pay that are lower than they could earn in other occupations.

The survey results noted above, however, are all based on cross-sections of the artist population at a given point in time, and such surveys cannot tell us what happens over time. Without longitudinal studies that follow the course of artists' careers over a period of time, we cannot say how many people give up careers in the arts because of lack of work and income.

One final point about artists' labour supply. In the performing arts, all sectors of the labour market are dominated by negotiated agreements on minimum rates of payment. This is discussed in more detail below. The result is that the supply decision that many performing artists have to make is just how much work to accept at the going rate, since few organisations seem to pay above minimum rates. Under these circumstances, the only way artists can raise their arts income is by working longer hours. The Scottish Arts Council study found that dancers and actors worked an average of 55 to 60 hours a week when in work.

Over-supply of artists

In many developed countries, it is widely believed that there is an over-supply of artists, though the concept of over-supply is very difficult to define (ILO, 1992). While in everyday usage the term implies that there is a general excess of supply over demand, over-supply has no economic meaning unless it is defined at particular prices or wage rates. For the sake of argument, would there be over-supply at zero rates of reward? Clearly not.[3] As we saw above, artists often work outside the arts to earn a living; artists appear to have a 'reservation wage' below which they do not supply labour to the arts. What does seem to be the case is that the reservation wage is very low in comparison to other wage rates in the economy (see Section 3). It also seems to be the case that artists are willing to take considerable risks in relation to income. I have argued that this risk-taking behaviour is the cause of over-supply. It comes about because artists overestimate their (average) chances of success prior to entering the labour market (Towse, 1992b, see Chapter 4). Creative artists and craftspeople, being for the most part self-employed, decide whether or not to continue to work in their chosen field according to their realised net profits or incomes. Over-supply of the works they produce for sale would result in low prices but if they are willing to accept low incomes, they can continue in full-time work. This over-supply cannot be defined at any given price, but for performing artists, over-supply can be defined in relation to going negotiated rates of pay. The considerable under-employment and unemployment of performing artists can be interpreted as an indication of over-supply at those wage rates.

Concern about over-supply of artists has often led to moves to restrict the number of places offered in the higher education system to trainee artists.[4] However, demand for such places is strong and it is argued that in the interests of equality of opportunity, such moves should be resisted. It can be claimed that it is not in the interests of society at large to turn away potential artists because training 'excess' numbers maximises the pool of potential talent for consumers of the arts. This in turn ensures a high number of excellent artists in years to come. If young people are prepared to face the rigours of the market place, we should, some would argue, not prevent them from doing so. Sadly, of course, few have sufficient information on which to base their decision to train as artists and this in turn has possibly contributed to artists overestimating their chance of succeeding (see above). One of the most frequent criticisms of art, music, dance and drama schools and colleges is that students are inadequately prepared for the world of work (see, for example, Jackson et al., 1994, chapters 3 and 5). This is discussed further in Section 5.

The role of trade unions and professional associations in artists' labour markets

Artists' labour markets in the performing arts are significantly affected by trade unions and professional associations of both employees and employers. Minimum rates of pay and conditions of work are agreed by collective agreements. The structure of these agreements is complex and cannot be discussed in detail here.[5] Such agreements affect both the demand and the supply side of the market. Conditions of work, which include restrictive practices, are mostly designed to protect artists from exploitation, overwork and danger at work. Overwork could lead in various art forms to long-term physical damage that would prevent the artist from working again. There is a huge array of agreements on working conditions in the performing arts, which have implications for the amount of work offered to performers and for their earnings. For example, overtime rates of pay must be paid after agreed basic hours are exceeded. Particularly in recorded work, agreements are designed to restore levels of employment for performers who would otherwise suffer technological displacement.[6] Conditions of work, therefore, while protecting the health and safety of performers also affect demand.

Supply is affected because, in practice, few non-union performing artists are employed by voluntary agreement. Associations of creative artists and craftspeople, however, do not have such binding collective agreements, concentrating rather on advice on contracts and so on, and on recommended rates of remuneration for specific types of work. Creative artists, particularly visual artists, are much less likely to join a professional association. Even so, the Exhibition Payment Right was negotiated by agreement between the National Artists' Association and the subsidised public art galleries (see Miller, 1988). In general, the market power of trades unions is limited by the fact that there is not enough work to keep all their members in full-time employment. A survey undertaken for Equity in 1989 showed that 11 per cent of the sample had been unemployed for the whole year, and nearly half those who did work, worked for 15 weeks or less in the year (King, 1989). This is evidence of over-supply, and it is that which restricts the unions' market power in determining rates of pay.

Promotion of work

One of the effects of the over-supply of artists and its concomitant, under-employment, is that artists spend a considerable amount of time and effort searching for work. This search process is expensive in terms of lost working hours as well as because of direct expenses of outlays on travel and so on. Performing artists attend numerous auditions, some being arranged by their agents but in many cases it is the performer herself who has to obtain information about available work and auditions. In the singing profession, for example, only a very few trained singers would have an agent at the point at which they begin to look for professional work. Most agents will only consider taking on performing artists who already have work experience (see Jackson et al., 1994, chapter 6). In the Wales survey, only 21 per cent of all performing artists had an agent, with 58 per cent promoting themselves.[7]

In the case of craftspeople, searching for outlets may be regarded as the marketing activity typical of any business enterprise. Knott (1994) analyses this in detail; she reports that over half of all respondents experienced problems in selling work. Brighton et al. (1985) describe the markets in which visual artists sell in considerable detail and it is clear from this evidence that most creative artists are effectively business people.

Only one quarter of all creative artists in the Wales survey reported having an agent, gallery or publisher promoting their work; 60 per cent promoted their own work (62 per cent of male and 53 per cent of female artists), and only half of all respondents were satisfied with the promotion of their work.

When it comes to the question of the *structure* of artists' careers, there is little information to go on. All of the studies quoted above are cross-sectional, that is, they use survey or census findings from a particular moment in time. Little, if any, true longitudinal research has been done charting the progress of a sample of artists over time. Throsby (1997) has repeated his survey of Australian artists, thus developing a picture of a sample over five years, no doubt including some of the same individuals in each survey. Repeated analysis has been done in the USA of Census data and, again, presumably some of the same individuals have cropped up successively. Filer (1987) did an interesting analysis following the subsequent careers of a sample of artists who had left the arts and changed to non-arts occupations. None of these studies, however, monitor the career paths of a sample of artists. Biographies of artists, of course, provide some insight into the career development of an individual but these are only written about a handful of stars, and anyway they are not systematic in their treatment. Furthermore, biographies do not normally explore the artists' financial details. As Jackson and his colleagues point out, longitudinal studies of students leaving college and their subsequent careers would provide vital information on career development and the value of training (Jackson et al., 1994, chapter 2).

Unemployment

Only employed persons can register as unemployed. To be eligible for unemployment benefit in the UK (now called Jobseekers' Allowance), a worker must have paid Class 1 (employed) National Insurance contributions. Self-employed workers cannot, by definition, be unemployed, and so cannot claim unemployment benefit. In the Wales survey, 80 per cent of creative artists were self-employed or freelance, as were 61 per cent of performing artists. Half of all respondents had Schedule D tax status but some would be eligible for unemployment benefit; 10 per cent of creative artists and 22 per cent of performing artists had claimed unemployment benefit or income support. The official definition of unemployment, however, is not the one that most people mean when they speak of unemployment among artists. But, in the absence of official data and a national survey of artists, the only empirical evidence available is from the partial surveys reported above. The position of artists with respect to social security is discussed again in Section 4.

In Scotland, one-third of all respondents had been registered as unemployed during 1993, for an average of 22 weeks (Scottish Arts Council, 1995, pp. 14–15). Unemployment was reported as declining with age, suggesting that artists leave the artistic labour market if they do not get enough work nor income from their PAO.

Summary

Many artists seem to be able to pursue a career to their own satisfaction but many more would like to devote more time to work in the arts. That they are unable to do so is a reflection of economic conditions. The supply of artistic time would increase if they could earn more from arts work but it would also rise if they had higher hourly earnings in non-arts work, enabling them to supply more arts labour time. This means that there is significant under-employment of artists, particularly of performing artists, who generally have to rely on others to provide employment. People have a strong vocation to work as artists and this contributes to over-supply. Even though trades unions are relatively strong in the performing arts, their bargaining power is restricted by market conditions. For creative artists and craftspeople the problem manifests itself in low prices and profits. We know very little about the career development of artists because few studies have been undertaken of artists' career development over time.

3. ARTISTS' EARNINGS

What Determines Earnings?

If labour markets work freely, rates of payment are determined by the interaction of supply and demand. Prices for works of art are determined in the same way. The higher demand is in relation to supply, the higher we would expect prices and rates of pay to be. In many areas of the arts, labour markets do not work freely because there are negotiated agreements between employers (theatre managers, record and film companies, subsidised art galleries) and artists' organisations, but ultimately agreed rates of pay reflect the relative forces of supply and demand, since they are what determines bargaining power. Furthermore, if negotiated rates were far out of line with market conditions, there would be a tendency to undercut minimum agreed rates. It may well be the case that negotiated rates of pay assist the working of the market by obviating arguments between artists and managers and between artists themselves, which would be damaging to team work. It is, of course, open to those who demand artists' services to offer payments above the negotiated minimum and this obviously happens in the case of star artists, whose fees are usually negotiated by their agents. But anecdotal evidence suggests that the 'typical' artist is paid the minimum rate and, overall, there are few cases where higher rates are paid.[8] This means that what chiefly determines artists' earnings is the amount of work they do.

In labour markets in general, earnings rise with age and experience. Age-earnings profiles, mapping the relationships between earnings and age (age acts as a proxy for experience) rise up to a certain point (typically around the age of 50) and then begin to fall off somewhat. Earnings also rise with educational attainment. Filer (1990) used 1980 US Census data to analyse the effect of age and education on artists' earnings by comparing predicted earnings of high-school leavers with those of college graduates. He found that earnings did rise with age, and in some cases, with higher additional education, but that the effect of education was much weaker for artists than for other professional and managerial workers. Indeed, for some groups, notably dancers and choreographers, musicians and composers, those with more formal education earned less until later in life. Higher education made virtually no difference to the earnings of visual artists and sculptors. The relation between training and earnings is discussed again in Section 5.

Filer's work suffers from two drawbacks: the Census data he used did not distinguish earnings from arts and non-arts sources; and the designation of workers is done according to the occupation in which most working hours were spent in the week of the Census (which amounts to the so-called 'market test', described in Section 1). Wassall and Alper (1992), using their own survey of US artists as a basis for comparison with Census data, showed that by avoiding this market test and separating out non-arts from arts earnings, artists earned less from arts work than other workers in comparable occupations, and education was not positively correlated with income. US artists' non-arts earnings, however, did rise with educational attainment.

Wassall and Alper's results were confirmed by Throsby's work for the Australia Council for the Arts. Throsby (1997) estimated 'earnings functions' for both creative and performing artists, using 1981 data from his large-scale survey of Australian artists. To date his study represents the most reliable and detailed analysis of artists' labour markets. An 'earnings function' shows earnings as the relationship between function of hours of work and other variables, such as age and length of training. As with the labour supply function, earnings and hours of work were divided into arts and non-arts work. Besides the (small) effect of age and education on artists' earnings, Throsby produced numerical results for the effect of gender on earnings; income from both arts and non-arts work was lower for female artists, even after all other sources of variation (hours worked, age, education attainment and so on) were accounted for. The gender effects on arts income were considerably stronger for creative artists than for performing artists, suggesting that females were less discriminated against in the performing arts in Australia than in other sectors of the arts economy.[9] I also estimated an earnings function using data from the Wales survey (Towse, 1992a) using the same specification as Throsby. The only statistically significant influence on arts earnings was the time artists (of all types) spent on arts work. Neither how established and experienced artists were, nor gender nor level of education apparently exerted any influence on arts earnings. The advantage of this type of analysis is that it becomes possible to use the numerical values from the estimated relationship to predict the effect of changes. For example, the earnings function of artists in Wales showed that if artists were to spend 1 per cent more time on artistic work, their earnings from artistic work would rise by 0.5 per cent. This kind of information is obviously useful in assessing policy on support for artists.

Evidence on Artists' Earnings in the UK

Over the last 10 years, a number of surveys of artists have been carried out in the UK, either covering different geographic areas (Scotland, Wales, Devon) or different occupations (actors, dancers, craftspeople and so on). Table 3.2 summarises the results of a number of surveys and compares them with an appropriate figure for all income earners.

Trends in the earnings of artists
Most of the surveys summarised in Table 3.2 are cross-section ones which do not allow comparisons to be made of earnings over time. The Crafts Council survey does, however, compare Knott's (1994) findings with those of an earlier survey by Bruce and Filmer (1983). A comparison of the two in equivalent terms shows that craftspeople's incomes rose in real terms between 1981 and 1992, and the gap between male and female incomes narrowed quite conspicuously. Allen (1990) also compared the position of musicians in Welsh National Opera between 1975/76 and 1988/89. Over that period they had become worse off in real terms. In 1975/76, they earned 14 per cent more than non-manual men in Great Britain, but earned 3 per cent less by 1988/89. The study by Peacock et al. (1982) of the effect of inflation in the 1970s on the

Table 3.2 Summary of data on artists' earnings by group surveyed

	Year of reported income	Average/median total income (£)			Average/median gross arts earnings (£)			Comparator (£)	
		All	Males	Females	All	Males	Females	Males	Females
Artists in Devon (Towse, 1991b)	1989/90	8344[a] 6900[m]	–	–	5881[a,b] 2100[m,b]	–	–	15371[c]	10478[c]
Artists in Wales (Towse, 1992a)	1990/91	10269[b]	11754[a,b]	6665[a,b]	2565[m]	7775[a]	5789[a]	15922[d]	10036[d]
Artists in Scotland (Scottish Arts Council, 1995)	1993/94	0–10000	–	–	0–5000[m]	–	–	–	–
Equity members (King, 1989; Thomas, 1992)	1987/88	–	–	–	0–5000[m]	–	–	–	–
Welsh National Opera (Allen, 1990)	1988/89	Na	Na	Na	12116–32500[e] 12668[f]	–	–	15922[d]	10036[d]
Opera choruses (all) (Towse, 1993)	1991/92	Na	Na	Na	10019–15392	–	–	16583[g]	11565[g]
Private music teachers (Gibbs, 1993)	1990/91	Na	Na	Na	8460	–	–	–	–
Craftspeople (Knott, 1994)	1992	Na	Na	Na	Na	11856	8141	–	–

Notes:

-	=	not given	b	=	net of expenses
m	=	median	c	=	average adult earnings 1990
Na	=	not applicable	d	=	average non-manual earnings in Wales 1990/91
a	=	average			

e	=	orchestra players
f	=	chorister
g	=	GB average earnings full-time 1991

performing arts showed that performers' earnings fell in real terms during the decade, though other costs, including those of non-artistic labour, rose above the Retail Price Index.[10]

Other sources of income

It is worth asking, in view of the picture of relatively low earnings and under/unemployment painted earlier, how indeed do artists survive financially? For even when account is taken of non-arts income, many have total incomes that are significantly below the average for all workers in the UK. Apart from grants, which are discussed in Section 4, artists rely on several other sources of income for support, such as parents, partners' earnings and state benefits. Knott (1994) found that only 3 per cent of all the Crafts Council survey respondents had received state benefits during 1992, whereas 40 per cent of full-time female artists and 20 per cent of full-time male artists had support from parents or a partner. In the Devon survey, 20 per cent of respondents were in receipt of state benefits (including retirement pensions). In Wales, 15 per cent of all artists claimed unemployment benefit or income support (the UK welfare payment). In view of their lower earnings it was surprising that the same percentage of women as men claimed these benefits. In both surveys, respondents were asked about their partners' incomes. In Wales, partners of male artists earned on average £6658 per annum whereas those of female artists earned £16 659. The Crafts Council survey found that 20 per cent of full-time craftsmen and 41 per cent of full-time craftswomen had support from 'others in your house'. It would seem that artists' partners provide essential financial support to the arts.

Unpaid artists

Almost one fifth (18 per cent) of respondents to the survey of Devon had received no payment for their arts work over the last three years. Their replies were analysed to see if they differed considerably from paid artists. Apart from the fact that they were slightly older (11 per cent were retired) and had begun work in their PAO a little later, they shared other characteristics with respondents who were in receipt of PAO income. Nearly half described themselves as established artists and they worked the same hours on their PAO as paid artists; they also were as well qualified as paid artists. Two-thirds said they had insufficient time left over from other income earning activities to devote themselves to arts work but only one-quarter were working outside the arts.

Summary

The survey evidence presented above shows that artists on average earn less than average earnings for comparable workers in Britain. Some groups of artists, for example, performers working in the media and musicians in several orchestras, do better than average. Some female artists in certain arts occupations (for example, opera choruses) earn more than the average female working in the UK (see Table 3.2). There are few data on trends in artists' earnings over time. Research shows craftspeople are now better off than in the past, but other artists appear to be worse off in real terms. We have to be wary of all these figures, however, for two reasons: one is that surveys, particularly those which cover the sensitive area of earnings, may not paint the total picture; the findings are based on what respondents report. Second, the distribution of artists' earnings is so uneven that average figures are not representative; even the median which is a better representation of the 'typical' survey respondent, is not necessarily a reliable statistic with a very skewed distribution.[11] Some artists do earn high incomes from artistic activity but they are a minority. The majority earn considerably less than they would outside the arts, and the sums involved frequently fluctuate from year to year.

4.   SUPPORT FOR ARTISTS

Several of the surveys reported here sought information on grants to artists from Arts Councils and other official bodies, and canvassed their opinion on the purpose of such grants. Questions were also asked in the surveys of artists in Devon and Wales about pensions and taxation.

Grants to individual artists in Wales and Scotland were typically between £2000 and £3000. In Wales, one in five respondents to the survey had received a grant; in Scotland, the figure was 16 per cent, surprisingly low in view of the fact that the survey favoured Scottish Arts Council funded individuals. The single most important purposes of grants to artists, in the opinion of respondents in Wales, was for maintaining income or 'buying time', with study grants coming second.

Grants to artists raise their income for arts work and affect the supply decision. Most artists want grants so that they can 'buy time' for artistic activity by reducing the time they spend earning income from non-arts work. It seems very unlikely, however, that the funding bodies in the arts, media and crafts will substantially increase direct financial support to individual artists, though that is what artists most want. Other forms of support, such as assistance with promotion and marketing, and the purchase of equipment and materials could also increase the supply of artists' output and earnings.

Tax, pension and National Insurance issues also affect the labour market for artists. Under the government's 'Common Approach', workers are classed as employed or self-employed consistently for income taxation and National

Insurance purposes. Employed workers pay tax under Schedule E (PAYE) and so cannot count expenses such as travel to work as tax-deductible, but they are entitled to unemployment benefit. Self-employed workers are not entitled to unemployment benefit but are able to deduct a range of work-related expenses from taxable income. Entitlement to unemployment benefit is important to many artists, particularly performing artists, who, as was shown in Section 2 above, typically experience periods of unemployment.

In the survey of artists in Wales, half were taxed under Schedule D (self-employed). Only one-third were in a pension scheme (the figure was one-quarter for artists in Devon).

5. TRAINING AND ARTISTS' LABOUR MARKETS

Training is frequently advocated as the solution for a whole range of economic and social problems. Training more people certainly reduces unemployment levels, at least temporarily, and people undoubtedly benefit in terms of personal development from training and higher education. But what is the economic effect of more training and higher education: is the considerable expense to the individual and to society justifiable as an investment in human capital? The economic role of training and higher education has been studied for the last 40 years by economists, and in this section the main issues discussed in that literature are summarised. Also presented are the findings from various surveys of artists on the perceived value of training and higher education in the arts and crafts. No attempt has been made to survey training provision itself nor to discuss its merits. Rather observations focus on the economic role training plays in artists' labour markets.

Formal and Informal Training

In discussing the training of artists it is important to distinguish between formal, informal and on-the-job training. Formal training is mostly provided through the subsidised higher education system; however, some training, such as that of dancers and actors, takes place outside that system in institutions of further education, some of which are publicly funded, but others of which are private, non-profit organisations (see Jackson et al., 1994). In those professions where a start in childhood is essential, mainly music and dance, vital initial training is often undertaken privately, though there is also some public sector provision. Formal training is usually vocational but that does not mean that it is valued only in a specific occupation. Evidence suggests that qualifications, such as a degree or its equivalent, are accepted by employers in the labour market regardless of the subject studied. But, however much formal training is undertaken and however good is its quality, what is sought by those who employ the services of artists is talent and the ability to use it in specific contexts. Thus informal and on-the-job training are necessary complements to formal training.

Informal and on-the-job training may simply take the form of learning from experience or it may be more structured; in crafts occupations, 63 per cent of men over the age of 45 had followed a craft apprenticeship (Knott, 1994). Workshops and the like are widely available for artists of all kinds. These are often privately provided and offer a halfway house between formal and informal training. In opera there has been a long-running debate about the need to formalise on-the-job training for singers; the Arts Council conducted a national review of open training to consider ways in which this might be organised (Arts Council of Great Britain, 1993b).

The economist's approach to the question of the value of training is to look at the role it plays in the labour market. The economics of education provides an analytical framework for studying this interaction. Several economists of the arts have applied this theory specifically to arts labour markets (Filer, 1990; Towse, 1993; Throsby, 1994). Training is viewed as investment in human capital but it also provides a 'filter' which allows employers to use qualifications to screen potential employees. This is discussed in more detail below.

The provision of formal training
There have been several reports over the last 30 years on the provision of artists' training.[12] Here the economic aspects of that provision are considered. The chief criticism that has been made about the institutions that provide training is that too many students are admitted for the market to absorb and this leads to an over-supply of artists. It is clear that in many countries there is a considerable demand on the part of students for training in the arts, and that the supply of places responds to that demand. This is not surprising where training is provided privately, as private institutions obviously have a financial incentive to offer places. What is not so well understood is that state-funded institutions also have a financial incentive to do so. Indeed, the government has encouraged the higher education system to expand places for students in all fields by setting the level of fees above the marginal cost, the cost of training an extra student. This is discussed in detail in relation to the training of singers in (Towse, 1993, chapter 2). There has been a dramatic increase in the number of students undertaking courses in the performing arts and art and design as part of the recent expansion of higher education. Although public funding per student has fallen somewhat in these fields (and in the case of music, student places have been marginally reduced), total expenditure on arts training rose significantly in the 1990s (see Towse, 1996).

Rates of return to training

What then is the economic argument for subsidies to training? The economic test of this hypothesis is the market place one: does training raise earnings by a sufficient margin to cover the cost of the investment? This question may be posed on an individual level and with respect to society as a whole. The 'private rate of return' to training measures the economic benefit to the individual and the 'social rate of return' measures it for society at large. If all training were privately funded, the only economic issue would be the private rate of return; students would calculate the expected increase in lifetime earnings due to training, the extra earnings that they stand to receive over what they would have earned without the training, and the cost of training. The benefit side is measured by age–earnings profiles which compare the earnings of people with various educational qualifications – say, a degree with the earnings of people with advanced ('A') levels.[13] Costs of training are measured by the direct costs (fees, maintenance, books and other materials) and by the indirect costs, the earnings that are forgone during the training period. For example, what a school leaver with 'A' levels would earn between 18 and 21 years of age is the indirect cost for a student entering a three-year college course at 18 (for a fuller explanation and application to the training of singers see Towse, 1993, chapter 6 and appendix 2). The individual's decision would rest on the expected private rate of return on the investment of training. One way of thinking of this is to imagine that students have to borrow a capital sum from a bank to finance their training; the rate of return to training must exceed the rate of interest charged by the bank for the investment to be worthwhile financially.

The social rate of return measures the net benefit to society. Because education is subsidised by the state via taxes, the whole of society bears the cost of its provision. While students are out of the labour market studying they do not pay taxes on income, and most receive student grants (albeit means tested on their parents' incomes), and the cost of the place is financed by direct central government subsidy.[14] The benefits of training to society are both pecuniary and non-pecuniary. Pecuniary benefits are that higher incomes yield higher tax receipts in the future. Non-pecuniary benefits are those that society in general gains from having a lively culture, creativity, national pride, social cohesion and other such factors. The social rate of return to training in the case of artists must be compared to those from training other workers, or to other types of government expenditure, such as health care, transport and so on.

Attempts have been made by economists to measure both private and social rates of return and to measure age–earnings profiles of artists. These are reported in Towse (1993). Filer's (1990) analysis of artists' age–earnings profiles in the USA were reported in Section 2. However, his data on artists' earnings from the US Census were biased upwards (see Section 1). The problem of measuring rates of return is that artists' earnings data are not sufficiently systematic in the way in which they are collected and it is therefore difficult to draw any conclusions from this work.

Informal and on-the-job training is much more difficult to assess in these terms because they cannot easily be disentangled from experience. Throsby (1997) found that experience had little influence on the earnings of artists in Australia. Until better data on artists' earnings and training are collected, it is not possible to establish the economic value of training in Britain using rates of return.

Equity and efficiency of subsidies to training
The justification for subsidising the training of artists is, of course, not only an economic one. Society has other objectives than economic efficiency for doing so. One of the chief social objectives in education in general is equality of opportunity. If government policy is to enrol one-third of all people of student age in institutions of higher education so that all have an equal chance, the question of whether or not the social rate of return is reasonably high is not necessarily important. What is important is that equality of access is maintained across the sector. Nevertheless, there are economic consequences of such a policy and these can be analysed. Subsidies to training artists have the effect that they encourage more students to enter artistic occupations. Given that most artistic professions are already overcrowded, this leads to concern about the pressure of over-supply on pay and employment and possible consequences for the status of artists (see ILO, 1992; and Irjala, 1992).

Over-supply of artists has a considerable human cost; peoples' expectations of success are raised by getting a place to train and they work hard to learn skills which they may well not be able to translate into a financially viable career. Though society at large may benefit from any over-supply of artists because it may well raise the quality of artists, some young people are disappointed and disillusioned if they fail to make a living entirely from working in the arts (see Towse, 1993, conclusions).

The labour market and training: human capital formation or screening?
Economists of education have put forward two conflicting hypotheses about the role of formal training in labour markets: one is that it raises productivity by forming human capital; the other is that it is an elaborate screening device for sorting students within the labour market. Employers use educational qualifications as an indication of students' ability to 'jump through the hoops' set by successive levels of achievement ('A' levels, degrees and so on), but these do not test the ability to perform skills but rather they test other factors, such as hard work, innate ability, socialisation and the like. For their part,

students use educational qualifications to signal these attributes to employers. The prediction that this theory makes is that where the screening function of training is dominant, there will be over-investment, because students have an incentive to 'out-signal' others by taking more years of training or extra exams, that is to say, students will over-qualify beyond learning the skills necessary for the work they want to undertake. This has been aptly labelled the 'Diploma Disease', and it is easy to see, if one accepts the screening hypothesis, that a self-perpetuating momentum can develop.[15]

Another aspect is what has come to be called 'credentialism'. Because employers place so much emphasis on paper qualifications they require the system to accredit certain courses over others. If all students have degrees, the problem employers face is to select those which are most appropriate to their needs. Selecting employees is a costly process of searching which employers prefer, if they can, to pass on to others. If educational institutions can be persuaded to do this on their behalf, employers save on search costs. Accreditation also benefits parents and students by providing them with information about standards, and it is arguably also useful to local education authorities who support students (and indirectly institutions). Accreditation exists in arts training in specific sectors, notably dance and drama (see Jackson et al., 1994), and also through the industry lead body, the Arts and Entertainment Training Council.

Screening by paper qualifications, however, does not appear to be very successful in arts labour markets. Neither performing nor creative artists get work on the basis of their educational record alone, except in teaching or similar educational work, though, of course, it may help them to get initial interviews or auditions. Selection is normally done by audition in the performing arts and by practical demonstration of their abilities, say a portfolio of art work or compositions, in creative arts fields. Thus the costs of searching for workers are borne by employers or their equivalent in the arts (theatre managements, art dealers, publishers and suchlike) from which it must be concluded that the education system does not fulfil a screening role in this sector beyond indicating those individuals who have undertaken training.

Is the explanation for such widespread training in the arts, then, that it raises productivity, that is, that it forms human capital? This is perhaps the more attractive option because it suggests that worthwhile skills are imparted during the training period, whereas the screening hypothesis implies a cynical view of any inherent value to training. The problem with accepting the human capital model is that, as we saw in Section 3, artists' earnings simply are not raised by training; the market apparently does not place an economic value on training. Nor as we show below, do many artists believe that their training contributed to their professional success.

Artists' training in Britain

Finally in this section the survey evidence on training is summarised. The Crafts Council (Knott, 1994) survey, the Jackson et al. (1994) survey on dance and drama training and the surveys of artists in Devon, Wales and Scotland (Towse, 1991b; 1992a; Scottish Arts Council, 1995) all collected information about artists' training. This is discussed in detail below.

The Crafts Council survey found that over half of all craftsmen and craftswomen were mainly self-taught. However, 11 per cent of them who gave that response had done both a foundation course and a higher level course at an art college or university. As Knott says:

> If more than one in ten of those who, despite having graduated from a higher level art or craft course become independent craftspeople in a discipline for which they rely heavily on self-instruction, some questions should perhaps be raised about the way subject choices are made within the art or craft departments of colleges and universities. (Knott, 1994, p. 67)

In all, 38 per cent of craftswomen and 48 per cent of craftsmen had no craft qualifications whatsoever, 40 per cent of the women and 31 per cent of the men had a degree or diploma from a university or college. Thus, women were more likely to be qualified than men, though on average they earned less, a finding that is replicated in other studies.

Turning now to the surveys of artists in Devon and Wales. In Devon, two-thirds of female respondents and half of the male respondents had obtained a formal qualification in their chosen art form; over half of all artists had been in higher education.[16] In Wales, 32 per cent of male artists and 16 per cent of female artists had no arts training qualifications. Performing artists were less well formally qualified than creative artists. Two-thirds of all respondents had received their arts training in university, music, drama or art school and half of them had a degree or diploma; 40 per cent had undertaken other types of training (note that they could do both). In both surveys over one-quarter of respondents had less than three years' training and, given the percentage who had not obtained a formal qualification even though they attended college, one should probably conclude that they had dropped out.

The survey of Scottish artists, in line with other surveys, found that artists sampled were generally very highly qualified; 23 per cent had postgraduate qualifications and 61 per cent were educated to first degree or diploma level. However, for half of the sample their qualification was not related to the arts. Half the artists in the survey thought that their arts training contributed to their professional success, though there was considerable variation as between different types of artists (Scottish Arts Council, 1995, p. 112). However, the survey showed a negative relationship between length of training and earnings from artistic activity, with postgraduate degree holders earning half of that earned by those with no degree or other higher education. Those with a first degree or diploma earned around three-quarters of the estimated artistic earnings of those with no degree, or other qualification.

One other result of interest in this context is the age of starting professional work. In Wales, one-third of performing artists (and 9 per cent of creative artists) had started before the age of 21; one-quarter of creative artists (and 14 per cent of performing artists) had started over the age of 30. In Devon, 15 per cent of all respondents started professional work before the age of 21, with 15 per cent starting over the age of 40. Given the different methods of defining the artist population in the two surveys, it seems likely that the Wales result is more representative of professional artists. What is actually meant by the expression 'starting work' is however unclear. A partial or occasional professional involvement may be very different from full-time engagement at an early age.

It is useful to compare these findings to the Jackson et al. survey of dancers and actors. The findings revealed that about 30 per cent of all respondents had 'other training only', that is, they did not attend one of the 23 schools accredited by the Council for Dance Education and Training, but they were not asked the age at which they started working professionally (presumably fairly young for dancers). The majority of respondents professionally active in drama (86 per cent) had received formal training, with over 30 per cent receiving 'other training only'. As far as the finance of training was concerned, 65 per cent of dancers and 70 per cent of those working in drama had received a mandatory or discretionary grant that covered fees, and 30 per cent of dancers and 40 per cent of those working in drama had received a local authority maintenance grant (see Jackson et al., 1994, chapters 3 and 5). In Devon, 62 per cent of women and 44 per cent of men had received a grant for their PAO training.

These figures on training reveal, in some sectors at least, how misleading it would be to equate the supply of performing artists with the output of recognised educational institutions. Clearly there are significant numbers of artists who have not had any formal or recognised training or who have trained privately. This statement itself needs to be tempered by an understanding that the 'stock' of the artistic labour force is a function of training provision over an extended period of time. The spread of higher qualifications and training opportunities during the last two to three decades has probably induced an 'age' effect, whereby younger artists are more likely to have received formal training than older artists.

Summary

To sum up the economic role of training, the majority of artists (but a minority of craftspeople) have formal training and qualifications in their artistic occupation; more women artists have formal qualifications than men. Most received some form of state subsidy to train (women did better than men in this respect). The economic value of training to the individual can really only be tested in the labour market but there are some 'external' benefits to society at large. Non-economic factors, such as equality of opportunity, are important considerations for policy-making.

To an economist the issue is how artists' labour markets react to these qualifications. It appears that they do not do so favourably. Earnings from arts work seem not to be raised by increased training, indeed some evidence points to the opposite (Towse, 1996). It has to be concluded, therefore, that training is not the panacea some claim it is. Neither the screening hypothesis nor the human capital model appear to provide a satisfactory economic explanation for the market response to training in the arts. In this respect, artists' labour markets function differently from those in other sectors of the economy. In non-arts work, however, artists' earnings are raised in the expected way by training and higher education.

6. CONCLUSION

By now, a certain amount of work has been done on artists' labour markets in the UK and elsewhere. While we do not fully understand the economic motivation of artists, economists can make useful observations, and in many areas, there is a remarkable consistency in the results of all the surveys; of artists in Wales and Scotland; craftspeople, dancers and actors throughout this country and of the artist populations in the USA, Australia and Canada. These surveys have produced a mass of statistical data about time allocation between artistic work and income work in the non-arts sector, about unemployment, about earnings and about social characteristics. They have also gathered information about artists' attitudes: satisfaction or otherwise with the promotion of their work; why they work less than they would like at their chosen artistic occupation; what support they would like from the funding bodies and so on.

But all surveys have limitations. A survey is a survey, not a census, and there is always the possibility of bias in the results. The survey of Wales may have been representative of Welsh artists but one cannot be sure that it would be representative of the whole UK. Moreover, all these surveys are cross-sections at a point in time. What is now needed is a longitudinal survey of a cohort of students undergoing different types of training in different fields of the arts to see how they fare when they begin to work and, say, five and ten years later.

Perhaps the most difficult finding common to the surveys is that concerning the relation of artists' training and income. Though it is widely accepted that formal training and higher education raise earnings in most sectors of the economy, the relationship appears to be weak in the labour market for artists. Possible reasons for this were discussed above. On the basis of the evidence so far, it has to be concluded that on strictly economic grounds, an extension of formal provision for training artists would not seem automatically to have the desired result of raising the earnings or status of artists. Moreover, it is not just economists who have reservations about training; as we saw earlier, those responsible for specialist art training in a number of European countries, as well as artists' trades unions, are concerned about excess supply of artists of all kinds. The problem is this: on the one hand, they are concerned with the status of the present generation of artists, most of whom do not fare as well in the labour market as it is believed they should; on the other, they support the social goal of equality of opportunity, which, given the pressure of demand on the part of young (and even not so young) people wanting places to train as artists, cannot be met fully. So there is a dilemma: too many artists and not enough work to allow them all to make a decent living in the arts. From the economist's point of view, the problem may be put as follows: because there is no shortage of artists, there is no case for subsidising training for artists so as to increase supply; there is always a shortage of truly gifted artists, but talent probably cannot be taught, only sought out by spending money.

However, there are very real equity problems in restricting the training of artists or limiting the subsidy; for example, why should it be more difficult for an actress to get a student grant and a place in an institution of higher education than for a divinity student to do so? There are no economic answers to such a question; all that we can do is to point out the true resource costs of different policies.

Economists specialise in understanding how markets work and why markets develop. Those working in the field of the economics of the arts (or cultural economics as it has come to be known) are sensitive to the view that the arts are different from other types of productive activity and that artists are not just another type of worker. Artists' labour markets do not work quite like other labour markets, but neither are they so different that nothing can be said. My own experience of talking to artists about the economic side to their lives suggests that many are very hard-headed and well-informed about the business side of their art form. The help that artists need from 'the system' is practical: negotiating better tax and social security arrangements; ensuring that property rights are properly established; assistance with getting loans and insurance; advice and assistance with promoting and marketing their work. All these things would assist the working of the market. Artists would like more grants for 'buying time'; I believe that short-term grants for specific innovative purposes to both performers and creative artists are justified on economic grounds; the analysis of artists' supply functions suggests that such grants could be cost-effective.

Finally, what may ultimately aid artists most is the fact that the UK economy, like that in other countries, is increasingly moving away from full-time employment to more casual work and self-employment. In the past, artists did not easily 'fit in' with the institutional arrangements designed for a workforce that was employed 'nine to five', as it used to be known. But they do much more easily fit into a labour market in which many people work from home, undertake a range of work for different employers and rely on their intellectual property to earn them a living. The changing nature of the UK labour force and the implications for social policy of issues such as pensions, benefits, and taxation, as well as on training, are documented in the Commission on Social Justice (1994). Their proposals, and those of other bodies involved in present day discussions about the future of the welfare state, will not only affect artists as members of the workforce but may be well of particular benefit to them as a group.

POSTSCRIPT

This chapter was substantially written before the results of the analysis of the 1991 Census were published by Jane O'Brien and Andy Feist (1995). It is now possible to compare some of the survey findings with the Census data on artists (see Chapter 2, Appendix). O'Brien and Feist have adopted a much broader definition of the relevant population than did the surveys of Devon, Wales and Scotland, and therefore direct comparisons cannot be made. With such a high proportion of artists and cultural workers being located in London and the surrounding regions, those surveys dealt with comparatively small groups of artists; that is not a problem, however, as long as they are a representative sample of the whole population.

Surveys seem to have picked up somewhat higher proportions of women and slightly older artists on average than the Census reports. That could be due to the fact that surveys deal with different definition of artists. On the whole, though, the results on hours of work, employment status, training and qualifications appear to be consistent. Incidentally, figures on trades union membership (in Appendix D of O'Brien and Feist) show that it has declined over the last ten years, and this has implications for surveys which are conducted via the trades unions.

Census data do not include earnings and surveys will continue to be an important source of information on artists' incomes. With such high proportions of the artist labour force being self-employed it is almost impossible to use government statistics to obtain that information at present.

NOTES

* This paper was commissioned in 1995 by the Policy, Research and Planning Department of the Arts Council of England. It has been reduced somewhat for publication here, but otherwise left unamended. I was asked to summarise recent research in the economics of the arts on artists' labour markets and to report on the results of previous work commissioned by the former Arts Council of Great Britain, South West Arts and the former Welsh Arts Council. I have attempted to do so objectively but my own opinions and interpretations inevitably inform the presentation. They do not represent those of any of the organisations concerned. I am most grateful to those organisations and to many individuals too numerous to acknowledge for their help and interest over the last few years. I am first and foremost an economist, albeit one with a considerable appetite for the arts and with some limited personal experience of work in the arts. Economists necessarily see the world from a certain viewpoint which is often not to the taste of many inside or outside the arts. Both the arts and economics thrive on controversy and that is always a good thing. I have not sought to be controversial but hope that this paper will lead, as intended, to better-informed discussion of the issues it raises.

Finally, I would like to express my thanks to Andy Feist (Senior Policy Analyst), Dr Jane O'Brien (Senior Policy Researcher) and Sara Benn of the Arts Council of England for their valuable comments, criticisms, editing and improvement of the manuscript. Errors of judgement and content are, of course, mine.

1. The British Census of Population simply asks the individual to categorise the *main job* undertaken in the week before Census night. How the respondent determines what this constitutes is open to question.
2. In 1991, I was commissioned by the Arts Council of Great Britain to consider the feasibility of such a survey (Towse, 1991a). The study of artists in Devon was originally intended as the pilot for a national survey (Towse, 1991b).
3. There are, though, many amateur artists who do not seek to earn money for their time spent in artistic activity. They often pay for the privilege, frequently by hiring professional assistance. See Hutchison and Feist (1991) for a study of amateur arts.
4. An early example is Jenkins (1965) and there has been a steady stream of such reports over the last 30 years.
5. For details in the UK, see Cotterell (1993) and for a general description of conditions of work in other countries, see ILO (1992).
6. See Peacock and Weir (1975, chapter 4).
7. Of the remaining 21 per cent, half were promoted by a teacher or employer, and the other either felt the question did not apply to them or did not know.
8. In the labour market for singers, there was a strong evidence of this (see Towse 1993, chapter 5).
9. In this context it is worth noting that in most developed countries, on average women earn one-third less than men.
10. It would be timely to repeat this study; besides providing information about trends in costs, along the way it also provided important information about the relative costs of labour, materials and administration.
11. The Wales survey demonstrates the point: for example, visual artists' maximum income was £60 000, the minimum was zero, average £4475 and the median £1000; for writers, the equivalent figures were £33 000, zero, £4346 and the median £100. (The median is the midpoint of the distribution.)
12. Recent reviews are to be found in Jackson et al. (1994) on dance and drama, and Towse, (1993) on singers.
13. Advanced level is the final school examination in England and Wales.

14. This was written before the introduction of fees in UK higher education. Students now obtain loans at a rate of interest below the market rate. Student grants are available to low income families and the government subsidises the cost of the place since fees do not cover the full cost.
15. The screening hypothesis is explained in detail in the International Encyclopedia of Education, the article by Winkler (1985). See also Dore (1976) on the 'Diploma Disease'.
16. In the Devon survey, tests were run to see if artists who had received payment in the last five years for their work had different profiles from those who had not; 61 per cent of those who had been paid had a formal qualification in their PAO compared to 50 per cent of those who were unpaid.

4. The earnings of singers: an economic analysis*

INTRODUCTION

This chapter is based on my study of the singing profession in Britain, which deals with classically trained singers. As far as I know, this is the only study of the market for singers, though singers' earnings have been separately identified in studies by Throsby (1986) and Santos (1976). The earnings of artists of all types have been the subject of important national studies by Filer (1986) in the USA and Throsby (1986) in Australia; these and other earnings studies have shown that there is considerable variance in artists' earnings, as indeed there is in other professions. What I do in this chapter is to review explanations of the variation in earnings and relate these specifically to the singing profession in Britain, looking at the role of institutional factors; in particular, the 'superstar' theory is considered and I attempt to offer an alternative explanation of skewness in the distribution of singers' earnings, which better fits the real world workings of the labour market for singers.

EXPLANATIONS OF SKEWNESS IN THE DISTRIBUTION OF EARNINGS

In Book 1, Chapter 10 of *The Wealth of Nations*, Adam Smith addressed the question of why earnings vary between different occupations. In a famous passage on 'the exorbitant rewards of players, opera-singers, opera-dancers etc.' he suggested that the rarity of talent and the discredit of employing them in 'public prostitution' accounted for their high earnings, predicting (wrongly, as it has turned out) that if public opinion with respect to the discredit of such occupations should ever alter, 'their pecuniary recompense would quickly diminish' (Smith, 1776, p. 107).[1] Rarity of talent has persisted, but as Smith also wrote: 'in a profession where twenty fail for one that succeeds, that one ought to gain all that should have been gained by the unsuccessful twenty', implying that the earnings distribution would be skewed and that risk is an aspect of the story. Indeed, he emphasized the role of risk in relation to the 'lottery of the law' in which 'the chance of gain is naturally over-valued',

leading more people to enter the profession than could ever hope to succeed.
For as he rightly observed, 'the contempt of risk and the presumptuous hope
of success are in no period of life more active than at the age at which young
people choose their professions' (ibid., p. 126). The singing profession is
undoubtedly such a lottery, and over-supply is likely to be part of the reason
for low average earnings. So is the presence of psychic rewards again
identified by Smith as 'publick admiration':

> To excel in any profession, in which but few arrive at mediocrity, is the most
> decisive mark of what is called genius or superior talents. The publick admiration
> which attends upon such distinguished abilities makes always a part of their reward;
> a greater or smaller in proportion as it is higher or lower in degree. (Ibid., pp.
> 122–3).

Thus Smith suggests that earnings will be skewed with differences in talent
and attitudes to non-pecuniary rewards and risk being relevant factors.

Superstar Theories

The role of talent in causing earnings distributions to be skewed by the
presence of high earning superstars was one feature of Rosen (1981) in his
seminal paper on 'The Economics of Superstars' and was the subject of a
subsequent article by Adler (1985). MacDonald (1988) looked to the role of
over-supply in explaining the skewness of earnings in superstar dominated
professions, such as the arts and entertainment. Rosen offers an explanation
that revolves around two features: (1) the development of media technology –
TV, recordings and the like – which considerably increases economies of scale
on the supply side; and (2) consumption costs on the demand side which arise
from the imperfect substitutability between suppliers – 'lesser talent is often a
poor substitute for greater talent'. This second feature is an aspect of a more
general information problem in the demand for the arts. Adler (1985) showed
that economising on consumption capital leads consumers to prefer the
services of superstars, even if there are no perceived differences in talent
between suppliers, and MacDonald (1988) showed how information gained
from successive market exposure leads young entrants to performing
professions to assess their chances in the market. Both models confirm the
skewness of the resulting distribution of earnings.

Superstars, according to Rosen's definition, are people who 'earn enormous
amounts of money and dominate the activities in which they engage'; they are
highly talented and highly rewarded for their talents; talent can be scaled, its
distribution is assumed to be fixed and it is costlessly observable to all
economic agents, who, *ceteris paribus* prefer greater to lesser talent. Rosen
shows that net revenue earned from talent is a convex function and this leads

to small differences in talent being magnified in larger earnings differences. There is, by definition of the problem, imperfect substitution between sellers with different talents and this would, in and of itself, provide a general explanation of skewed earnings distributions. But, Rosen argues, preferences alone cannot explain the other feature of superstars, namely the marked concentration of output on a few sellers who have the most talent. This second feature is explained by the use of mass media technology which allows joint consumption. As the performer needs to put in the same effort whether 10 or 1000 people show up in the audience or whether one or one million people buy a record, the implied economies of scale of this joint consumption technology allow relatively few sellers to service the entire market. The combination of the joint consumption technology and consumer preferences leads to talented people commanding very large markets and very large incomes.

MacDonald in 'The Economics of Rising Stars' (1988) addresses the process whereby superstars get started with a model that deals with the dynamics of supply. He explains skewness in the distribution of performers' earnings by the presence of numerous young hopefuls with low earnings (less than their opportunity cost outside the artistic profession), who are gaining performing experience as a way of finding out their chances of a professional performing career. At each stage some drop out, says MacDonald, when their performance is unfavourably reviewed, leaving only a few successful older performers still in the profession earning increasingly higher net returns performing to relatively larger audiences. It is their higher earnings that cause the skewness at the top of the earnings distribution. This explanation is clearly close to Smith's 'one who succeeds for twenty that fail'.

Adler in his article 'Stardom and Talent' (1985) takes up the point made by Rosen that consumers minimise their consumption costs. He develops a behavioural model which explains why consumers would choose the same stars thereby causing the market to concentrate on a few superstars. In doing so, he also avoids Rosen's completely unrealistic assumption that talent is costlessly observable to all economic agents, a point I shall discuss below. Consumers develop consumption capital by investing time in acquiring specialised knowledge; they do this by both engaging in the activity itself, say, going to the opera, and by discussing it with other people who know about it. A consumer is better off patronising the same artist as others do because that maximises the possibility of learning about the artist. As Adler puts it 'stardom is a market device to economise on learning costs in activities where "the more you know the more you enjoy"'. Clearly, consumers' equilibrium will then lead to only one performer being chosen; as in addictive behaviour, which performer will be chosen by any one consumer then depends upon others' choices. Adler likens the process of the public adopting a particular performer as the star to the acceptance of one money as currency; once one performer has a few more consumers 'voting' for him or her, this will quickly snowball into market dominance. There is room for more than one star (unlike money), because some consumers have invested in acquiring knowledge about the 'wrong' performer and it is costly to change; in addition, performers might charge different prices such that price differentials are greater than the savings in search costs.

The advantage of Adler's model is that it avoids a major question hanging over Rosen's approach which is how do we identify talent? Adler gets his result independent of talent; performers could be of equal talent in his model, or even be equally untalented! In beginning to develop consumption capital, consumers pick a performer at random, believing that all performers have an equal chance of stardom. As time goes by, they learn from discussion with other consumers what their choice was and so the ball begins to gain momentum. This hypothesis is appealing since it provides an explanation for several things we observe in the real world. People who know very little about opera will buy a record by a singer 'they've heard of', in order to avoid disappointment; opera houses can always fill seats by performing 'war horses', and so on. As there are many more people with a little knowledge, this explains why superstars have much bigger markets.

In the course of this debate, it can be seen that the emphasis has subtly changed from the role of talent and risk in explaining skewness in earnings to the question of the cost of information about them. Whatever we think talent is, there is a very considerable information problem associated with it, one that Rosen assumes away by saying it is costlessly observable to all economic agents, while MacDonald displays a touching faith in the credibility of critics! (Most singers will tell you they never read reviews anyway – though they usually find out what is in them!) Adler has very perceptively avoided this problem and is clearly on to something with his idea of talent as currency and the snowballing of one particular performer into superstardom. However, in the real world of singing we know that this does not happen at random; there is such a thing as identifiable talent, something, at least, that is enough for the snowball to get started. We also know that it is very expensive to acquire information about it.

Search and Information Costs in the Market for Singers

There are various sorts of search and information costs in the market for singers; those who would employ them search for talented singers and gain information about the type and quality of the services they have to offer, consumers build up their consumption capital and singers search for work. Because all this takes time it imposes costs. The market solution to this problem is 'middlemen' in the form of promoters and agents whose activities economise on search and information costs. As opera houses are quantitatively the most important employers of singers in Britain, I shall discuss this question with reference to opera.

Opera in Britain is organised on a mixture of the *stagione* and repertory systems. Apart from a few principals who are on an annual contract and the opera choruses of the five permanent opera companies, all other singers in Britain are hired for the run of the opera. Space does not permit a detailed account of the organisation of the market here. A full description is in Towse (1993). Opera houses' search costs take the form of labour time and the direct costs of auditioning singers at home and in going to performances throughout the world to hear singers perform. Even relatively small provincial opera houses in Britain audition large numbers of singers; figures of 300–400 per company per year were typically quoted to me in interviews with opera managements. A large opera company has three or four casting staff regularly travelling abroad to hear singers and they also pay singers' expenses to come to audition for them. Of course, superstars do not have to audition – information about them is public knowledge – and this saves promoters' search costs. Opera houses' own search costs are lowered to some extent by the activities of singers' agents; they provide information about their clients (what roles they sing, where they may be heard and so on) and singers pay for this through their commission fees. It is very striking how well organised the information network is and how the grapevine works, starting at the level of the music colleges and going all the way up. Because the market is largely freelance and opera companies put on several different operas a year (from 9–19 in the permanent British companies in 1988) with several principal roles in each opera, they are hiring around 300 principals a year. Taking account of the seasonal opera companies, that figure would rise to about 400. I quote these statistics to give an indication of the size of the search and information problem of opera companies. In addition, other types of promoters, such as orchestras, will also have similar information problems. Being a highly personalised market in which sellers are certainly not homogeneous, this is what you would expect.

The fact that opera houses and other promoters engage in this search process means that they cut down consumers' search and information costs to a considerable extent. So far from promoters' activities being 'trivial', as MacDonald holds them to be, they go a long way to solving the consumer's information problem. How does a consumer know how good a singer is? 'She must be good if she's singing at the Royal Opera House.' This can be applied to recording as well as live performance; a TV broadcast 'from the Royal Opera House' again establishes a stamp of approval of the quality of the singer's performance.[2]

On the supply side of the labour market, singers equally have a problem of getting known and bear high costs in doing so. One solution to the problem is to enter competitions or take part in public master classes. Developing a repertoire for these purposes and for auditions is expensive as are time and travel costs. It could cost a young singer around £1000 in accompanists' and singing teachers' fees, travel and entry fees to enter one of the big singing competitions. Music college opera productions, and particularly those of the National Opera Studio (Britain's specialised postgraduate training centre for opera singers) are an important showcase for graduating singers as they are attended by professional talent scouts, such as agents and opera company officials. Otherwise young singers spend considerable amounts of time and money preparing for and attending auditions.

We see now why Rosen's assumption that information about talent is costlessly observable to all economic agents is unrealistic. MacDonald is equally unrealistic in suggesting that would-be singers will decide whether or not to proceed with a career on the strength of reviews of their early performances (that is like saying that if your first article is rejected you would never write again!). Singers' biographies are full of horror stories of auditions they failed! The problem is that reviews are not accurate information. If there were such a thing the process would be cut short before it began; music colleges could provide the correct certification and the graduate could show his or her grade to future employers as in economics or plumbing. But opera houses do not take notice of or even ask about music college certificates; they rely entirely on what they hear and see in auditions. Nor is it just a question of talent; the promoter may be looking for someone to sing a specific role that does not suit some singers; they may want someone short and the singer is tall! Some singers take a long time to really 'find their voice' and until they do they may fail in auditions while being encouraged to continue studying (see, for example, the biography of Joan Sutherland by Major, 1987). Moreover, opinions differ about almost every aspect of singing technique and performance, and everyone knows this. Few audition panels are willing to tell a young singer to forget it. Furthermore, even if they were repeatedly told they are wasting their time, many singers would not believe it.

The search and information process, therefore, is highly organised, if not necessarily infallible. It starts with the music colleges, progresses through the National Opera Studio to auditions for opera choruses and small parts, to work experience with the smaller touring companies, such as Opera 80 and Glyndebourne Touring Opera, and eventually with the provincial opera companies, then the national companies and finally, for the real stars, to work in the international opera houses. Promoters will be watching them at all stages, monitoring their development as performers. The less talented will either fail to make a start or will drop by the wayside.

Since search and information costs are so high, strong incentives exist to

minimise them. We have seen how audiences (consumers) solve ~
by opting for superstar performances. My contribution to this debate
suggest that singers and those who hire them use the performance fee as a
signal of talent.

The Performance Fee as an Index of Talent

Like Adler, I believe that talent is largely socially determined. Yes, there has
to be something to set the ball rolling but many singers have that. In fact, a
singer represents a bundle of services – voice, voice type, stage presence,
physical appearance, musicianship, ability to work with others – and a
'talented' singer is one with the right combination at the right time. The
demand for singers is anyway derived from the demand for particular works
and also depends on current taste or fashion for particular types of
performance (buxom Mimi's are no longer acceptable). In Adler's model the
motive for conformity of taste is economising on consumption capital and that
implies interdependence of consumer's utility functions. This immediately
suggests the presence of 'Bandwagon' and 'Veblenesque' effects in consumer
behaviour, to use terms coined by Leibenstein (1950). The Bandwagon effect
explains the snowballing of demand for a particular singer's services, because
the more people demand to hear him or her, the more popular he or she
becomes. The Veblen effect or conspicuous consumption, is where consumers
judge quality by price; this is clearly a possibility in a joint consumption
situation as envisaged by Rosen; since one 'consumes' a singer's performance
with others present, there is an immediate gain in utility from the knowledge
that others share your tastes. Demand curves for Veblenesque goods and
services are upward sloping; the higher the price the more the good or service
is demanded, at least up to a point. Where both Bandwagon and Veblenesque
effects are at work, they can reinforce each other and this could well be the
case with singers' fees.

The focus of the bargain between the promoter and the singer is the pro rata
performance fee. This is as true of concert and sessions singers working for the
Equity minimum rate as for the top opera stars (see Towse, 1993 for details).
The fee establishes a singer's rank. It is fixed in a highly competitive market
in which fee bargains are frequently struck. Concert promoters and opera
houses want to hire popular singers and the easiest way of judging a singer's
popularity is the market test of what fee they can command. They put up ticket
prices when a superstar is billed and this suggests to audiences that a better
quality performance is being offered for which they are prepared to pay more;
thus the promoter can afford to pay the star a higher fee. For their part, singers
will also invoke the accepted ranking of opera houses in the fee bargain;
having sung at La Scala or Covent Garden acknowledges their talent and so

raises the fee. All singers have a notion of their minimum fee and will not accept work below it as this would spoil their image and hence their bargaining power. Singers do sometimes, in fact, work at a lower fee if it is something they particularly want to do, say, take on a new role, but, by and large, they will withhold their services to preserve their position in the rank order. Lowering the fee would signal to the market that a singer's popularity was waning, and this brings us to the second point, that the fee is a signal of rising or falling demand for their services. At the bottom end of the market the result is that struggling singers cannot increase the demand for their services by lowering their fees, since all that indicates is that they are struggling! Instead of a lower fee stimulating demand, it will depress it.

Media Technology and the Singing Profession

So far, the role of talent has been discussed at length but Rosen's other point, that the development of media technology has been responsible for the emergence of superstars has not been considered. This is not so unreasonable when one recognises that in singing, superstardom is hardly a twentieth-century phenomenon; there have, after all, always been superstars in the singing profession since the inception of opera in the late sixteenth century; such was their fame that we can still name some of them and information about their fabulous fees has been gathered from contemporary sources (see Rosselli, 1984 and Christiansen, 1984). For example, the prima donna Pasta was paid a fee of £2365 for the 1827 summer season (which probably lasted about eight weeks); in that same season other soloists earned as little as £75 or £100.[3] This is roughly the equivalent at 1990 prices of £650 000; as compared to £2000 a ratio of approximately 30:1. If, as is rumoured, Domingo commands a fee of £15 000 per performance at Covent Garden (in 1990), the same ratio implies other soloists getting £500 a performance, which is feasible and consistent with other information I have about singers' earnings. So, in live performance it is conceivable that the superstars' dominance of the earnings distribution of the singing profession as a whole has changed little.

But Domingo, unlike Pasta, has earnings from recordings as well. Not all his recordings are of the same repertoire that he would perform live and some are distinctly aimed at the popular market, catering for audiences of people who would never step inside an opera house or concert hall. Mass media technology has, in fact, allowed superstar singers to serve two distinct markets, the more traditional live opera and concert market and the mass popular market, and this has clearly increased singers' market sizes, as Rosen argued. The mass market consists of people with a low investment in consumption capital and there are simply many more of them! This market for recordings may well offer economies of large scale production[4] and it is this market that is dominated by a few superstars. While the demand for home entertainment continues to increase, it seems likely that superstar singers' earnings from records, TV, videos and film will continue to rise and we might reasonably expect that variance in the cross-section earnings distribution will accordingly increase successively over time, causing greater skewness in the future.

That is not the end of the story, however, because there is a flourishing market in live performances, particularly of opera, which seems to be growing worldwide. Indeed, it may be stimulated by records and broadcasts of opera, the two sides of the market being complements rather than substitutes. In the world of live opera and recitals there are technological limitations on both the scale of performance and on the number of performances that any one singer can give in a year. The result is that, while mass media technology has allowed the market to concentrate on a few superstars, many less starry singers continue to be hired in live performances. The technology of live performance militates against market domination by a few star singers. Live performance imposes a number of technical limits on the size of the market that individual singers can serve.

The most obvious limit is the size of performance venues; opera houses usually seat about 2000 people; venue sizes for concerts are more flexible. However, performance in such venues is subject to consumption dis-economies, because the quality of the service is diluted by what Rosen calls 'crowding', the need for microphones, and such like.

Live performance also imposes constraints on the number of performances that a singer can give. Because live performance is fixed in time and place, the number of different opera houses that a freelance singer can serve is limited by travel time between them. (This, of course, has itself been subject to technical change; the advent of jet travel allowed singers to reach international audiences with greater ease.) In addition, opera singers are contracted to rehearse productions in advance of a run of performances; in Britain in the 1990s this was typically 4–6 weeks for a new production and 2–3 weeks for a revival. Besides such constraints of time and place, there is also the question of how often a singer can sing a major role, because there are technical vocal constraints; most singers would not undertake to sing a major role more than two or three times a week and opera houses take account of this in scheduling operas. These technical constraints of live performance make it difficult for even very busy singers to do more than 80–100 performances a year. At the height of their careers, Domingo and Sutherland were giving respectively around 80 and 50 live performances a year (see Domingo, 1983 and Major, 1987). It is interesting to note that so far no star singer has emerged (to my knowledge) from recording only; all the top singers work live as well as doing recordings. Undoubtedly, some singers have made their reputation through recording rather than on stage but they nevertheless do live performances. Possibly there is an economic explanation for this, but I do not have one.

CONCLUDING REMARKS

Several explanations have been put forward for extreme skewness in the distribution of earnings. In this chapter I have concentrated on singers and drawn on my study of the market for singers in Britain, but clearly these explanations have a wider relevance to any artistic profession and, indeed, to other occupations in which workers are self-employed and where people wanting to use their services have to assess the quality of their work. The explanations divide into those which emphasise the costs of information (Adler, 1985; MacDonald, 1988; and my own, see Towse, 1993) as opposed to the role of mass media technology (Rosen, 1981). Perhaps all are right in their own way because in fact each protagonist deals with a slightly different problem. It is not inconsistent to regard that part of a superstar's income which comes from recording work as due to advances in media technology, while believing that the superstar's talent is just that he or she is 'famous for being famous'.[5] I wish I could conclude this chapter by devising a decisive test that would discriminate between the different hypotheses. Rosen's hypothesis could be construed to predict that the variance in earnings between the superstars and the rest of the profession will increase over time as developments in mass media technology take place; MacDonald's that, as more young singers train and enter the profession, the distribution of earnings will become more skewed; Adler's explanation suggests a prediction that as incomes rise, people will have higher costs of forming consumption capital and so the market will concentrate more and more on superstars; and my explanation predicts that opera companies and the like will spend less on search costs, rather using the market-determined performance fee as an index of quality instead. At least these predictions are testable in principle, though I would not personally want to conduct the tests!

NOTES

* This chapter is based on a two year research project undertaken at the London School of Economics between 1988 and 1990 with financial support from the Leverhulme Trust. The chapter was first published in Towse, R. and A. Khakee (eds), 1992, *Cultural Economics*, Springer, Heidelberg.
1. I now see that this is ambiguous. The view of singers has certainly changed since Smith's day but his predictions about earnings have been borne out.
2. Since consumers' fixed costs of consumption, to use Rosen's term, depend upon lost working time measured by the wage rate, this may explain why rich consumers favour certain opera

houses which are therefore able to charge higher prices, and less rich consumers attend lower ranking houses, for example, Royal Opera House rather than the English National Opera. Sometimes consumers could see the same singer in the same opera at either house but at different ticket prices. Consumers' different wage rates are the explanation.

3. See Christiansen (1984) p. 94.
4. Baumol and Baumol (1984) have shown that the cost disease applies to film and broadcasting as much as to live performed arts; however, they offer no evidence on the recording industry which they say is possibly exempt. Casual evidence of TV, video and film productions of opera suggests that they do not benefit from economies of scale; it seems reasonable to assume that they do apply in the field of opera records, however.
5. See Cowen (2000) for an economic analysis of fame.

PART III

Copyright incentives and rewards

5.   The value of performers' rights: an economic analysis*

With Millie Taylor

1.   INTRODUCTION

Copyright law provides the institutional framework within which the exchange of intellectual property takes place in the cultural sector of the economy. Since the Statute of Anne in 1709, copyright law has been adapted to accommodate changes in technology (which have influenced both the creation and the means of exploitation of ideas) and changes in social and economic organisation. This has been a two-way process, with changes in law being both cause and result of new forms of social and economic exchanges. Copyright is, in fact, a bundle of rights to prohibit and authorise a number of different acts and new rights have evolved over time to accommodate new acts. From an initial concern with publishing the written word, the principles of copyright law have been gradually extended to other media for the creation and dissemination of ideas. With the development of sound recording, film, broadcasting and electronic media, the protection of 'authorship' has been extended to include choreographers, film directors and performers (actors, dancers, musicians and so on), as well as record, film and broadcasting companies.

Various changes to copyright have recently been made as part of the harmonisation programme of the European Union and these include new and extended rights for performers. These changes were brought about by Directives agreed by the EC Council of Ministers and member state governments to alter their existing law to establish conformity; in the UK that law is mostly based upon the 1988 Copyright, Designs and Patents Act. We are concerned here with a Council Directive 'on rental and lending rights and on certain rights related to copyright in the field of intellectual property' (EC Directive, 1992), which was implemented in the UK by Statutory Instrument (SI 1996/2967) *The Copyright and Related Rights Regulations 1996*. The SI came into force on 1 December 1996. Implementation had been delayed well beyond the scheduled date in 1994 because of a long and contentious consultative process, during which various bodies representing performers maintained that the first draft of the SI not only did not fulfil the spirit of the Rental Directive, but that it would leave performers in the UK disadvantaged in relation to other performers in Europe.

Our research looks at the economic effects of the changes to performers' rights, mainly in the UK, and mostly in the music industry. It is expected that these rights are valuable to performers but the question of 'what are they worth?' is an empirical one that no one has attempted to answer. To do so, we must ask which performers are more likely to benefit, the stars or the average backing artist? Underlying these questions is the fact that market outcomes determine the value of the commercial exploitation of performers' work, over which they mostly have little control even though their royalty earnings depend on it.

Copyright clearly has symbolic value to artists of all kinds, creators and performers, as they seek to improve their status as professionals and seek greater recognition of their role in society, but the law provides only the institutional framework for market transactions; it does not control rates of payment. Within the cultural sector, most rights are traded either by individual contract or by standard agreements between representative organisations. The introduction of new rights does not automatically increase earnings, rather contracts and negotiated agreements are likely to change in accordance with statutory requirements. The intention is to improve artists' bargaining power but market forces could conceivably reduce the sum of money over which the bargain takes place. The economic approach to these questions is to ask who gains or loses financially from changes in the law.

In this present case of changes to performers' rights, we also ask who will pay for any improvements in the financial position of performers – the artists, the firm that promotes their work or consumers in the form of higher product prices? In addition, we consider the fact that the collection of royalty and other payments, including any remuneration from these new rights, is a complex and costly process, for which someone – and it is often the performer – must pay.

Section 2 of this chapter outlines the 'pay-for-use' principle, which is the underlying rationale of the system. In Section 3 the operation of the music industry collecting societies is explained; it is through them that the new rights are administered. Section 4 deals with the new rights contained in the Statutory Instrument. In Sections 5 and 6 we consider how the new rights are likely to be exercised in practice, including a discussion of their value and the costs of collection. In Section 7 we ask the question of who will pay for them. Section 8 contains a tentative assessment of whether performers are likely to benefit as a result of these new rights and Section 9 offers some concluding remarks.

Though the empirical evidence presented here relates to the UK, similar changes to performers' rights are taking place throughout Europe and some comparisons are made with the situation in Denmark and Sweden. Implementation of international policy by national legislation is at the root of the debate over implementation in the UK and the detailed discussion of matters in the UK highlights this wider issue. Besides, all countries that are signatories to the Rome Convention agreed to national treatment for performers in the performance of sound recordings and so are experiencing changes, as will non-signatories through changes in the balance of world trade. In particular, the position in relation to US performers may change, as the USA, the world's biggest exporter of cultural product (films, TV and recorded music), has not signed the Rome Convention. There is also a new protocol to the Rome Convention currently under discussion at WIPO (World Intellectual Property Organisation), which will introduce rental rights beyond Europe. Our topic, therefore, is relevant in many countries. Although our detailed research findings relate mostly to the UK, the strength of our work lies in the combination of institutional detail with an economic approach. We hope that this research will stimulate similar work by others elsewhere.

2. THE 'PAY-FOR-USE' PRINCIPLE IN MUSIC

The collection and distribution of royalties and other payments due to copyright holders is a complex matter. Different arrangements exist in different branches of the cultural sector. Literary publishing is perhaps the most straightforward and well-known case; an author has a contract with the publisher, which assigns the publication right to the publisher and lays down the royalty rate (a percentage of the price of the book) and any advance on future royalties that will be paid to the author. The contract also covers a host of other items, such as film and translation rights. The publisher keeps account of how many copies of the book are sold and every so often sends the author a royalty statement and a cheque. The purchase price of the book includes the author's royalty.[1]

The same principle of the user paying applies in the music business in the UK, but the situation is more complex. Composers usually assign the copyright of a work to the music publisher; they are contractually entitled to royalties whenever their works are sold (as printed copies or as recordings) and performed (whether live or recorded). In order to ensure that they are paid for each performance, all performances must be monitored and due payments collected according to the amount of use and the size of the audience. This is the so-called 'pay-for-use' principle.

The pay-for-use principle applies also to performers in sound recordings, though the situation is even more complex. Named (featured) artists have a contract with the record company and receive royalties from record sales from the company. Backing artists (session musicians) are also often involved in the recording sessions, but they have different contractual arrangements and are usually paid a fee per session with no royalty for record sales. This is a buy-out of the reproduction and distribution rights.[2] When recordings are publicly performed, that is, used in broadcasting and in a host of public venues, performers as well as composers are entitled to remuneration. The pay-for-use principle requires that each and every use of each and every copyright owners' work be identified and paid for. Monitoring use and collecting composers' and performers' royalties is an enormous task that is undertaken by collecting societies in the music industry.[3]

3. COLLECTING SOCIETIES

Collecting societies have developed over the last 100 years to administer rights on behalf of copyright owners. They are non-profitmaking organisations controlled by their members on whose behalf they issue individual as well as collective or blanket licences. Collecting societies have three main functions:

1. To license the works in which they hold the copyright for specific uses;
2. To monitor use and collect revenues;
3. To distribute the revenue as royalties to members of the society.

The societies referred to in this chapter are mainly those which operate in the record industry. They are: the Performing Right Society (PRS), to which is assigned the performing and broadcasting right in works by composers and music publishers; whenever a piece of music is performed or broadcast a royalty is paid to the composer and/or publisher of that piece; and the Mechanical Copyright Protection Society (MCPS) which licenses the mechanical right (the right to record) on behalf of composers and lyricists; anyone wanting to record a piece of music must obtain a licence from MCPS and pay royalties on the sale of the recordings. The third society in the record industry is Phonographic Performance Limited (PPL), whose members are record companies; it licenses the performing and broadcasting right (that is, the right to play records in public or broadcast recordings) of the record companies, who are the owners of the copyright in sound recordings, and it collects licence fee income.[4] Until the SI, PPL distributed its income to three groups; 67.5 per cent to record companies, 20 per cent to featured artists and 12.5 per cent to the Musicians' Union (MU) for the other performers (non-featured sessions players). This was a voluntary (*ex gratia*) arrangement between the record companies, PPL and the MU which has formed the basis of contractual obligations (between record companies and featured artists) and negotiated agreements (between the record companies and the MU).[5] Figure 5.1 illustrates the process.

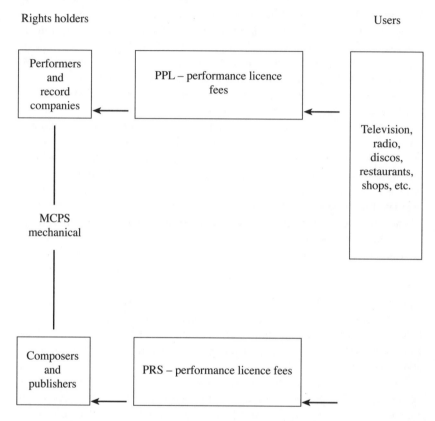

Figure 5.1   Flow of payment for the performing right in music and records

Collective administration has developed with the proliferation of rights and of the markets in which they are traded. Through collective action the costs of extensive administrative networks are spread, making the monitoring and collection of even small sums feasible for individual rights holders. Collecting societies also reduce the costs to users of obtaining all the necessary permissions from a large number of rights holders by issuing blanket licences that give access to a wide repertoire of works. For example, permission is needed for every single recording a radio station might want to play, not only from the composer, but also from the record company. This applies equally to discos, restaurants, shops and every other public place in which music is played. Blanket licensing cuts out this time-consuming and expensive process; users simply buy a licence from PRS and/or PPL which entitles them to use the whole repertoire of works whose copyright has been assigned to the societies. In addition, there are reciprocal agreements with overseas collecting societies and also international conventions, so that use of foreign copyright repertoire is also licensed at the same time. In the absence of reciprocal agreement between national collecting societies, international agreements entitle individuals to national treatment in countries who are also members of the appropriate Convention (Berne for composers, Rome for performers).

The pay-for-use principle is implemented via the collecting societies. Licence fee income is allocated to individual copyright owners by various methods. Some uses are logged in detail by the user, for example, radio and TV stations; others are monitored on a sample basis, and still others use a combination of these methods.[6] Whatever method is used, the licence fee takes into account audience size, that is, how many people hear the music. Income is then distributed by the collecting society to its members according to the estimated use made of their works.

The transaction costs of these activities are quite high, however, and are mostly borne by the creators of intellectual property. In 1994, MCPS charged commission to the member at an average of 7.1 per cent of royalty payments (MPA and MCPS, 1994, p.16). PPL charged about 13 per cent of gross income for administration costs deducted before payment is made to record companies and artists (PPL, 1994, p. 13). PRS's administration costs averaged 17.2 per cent of gross revenue (26 per cent on domestic licensing revenue), deducted before payment is made to authors and publishers (PRS, 1995, p. 12). These figures are not unusually high when compared to similar societies in Europe and America.[7]

Despite the fact that in Britain, as in most other countries, each collecting society operates as a monopoly, the Monopolies and Mergers Commission has found that this is not against the public interest. The natural monopoly is recognised as beneficial on the grounds that it reduces the costs to both user and copyright holder.

4.   NEW AND EXTENDED PERFORMERS' RIGHTS

The Statutory Instrument introduces new and extended performers' rights in the UK. These come under two headings:

1. *Performers' rights (non-property)*, which cannot be licensed or assigned, include the right to equitable remuneration for the performance of sound recordings.

2. *Performers' property rights* (similar to neighbouring rights in some continental European countries) include a reproduction right, distribution right and rental and lending right. In the UK they are to be treated in many respects as copyright, for example, they are assignable in whole or in part, they may be licensed and are regulated by the Copyright Tribunal. The rental right can be licensed collectively and administered by a collecting society.

In this chapter we concentrate on the right to equitable remuneration for the performance of sound recordings and on the rental right, as they are the ones that are expected to be most valuable to performers. These rights relate to any fixation of the individual's performance – on film, video, sound recording and so on. There is a presumption that the performer's rental right is transferred to the producer and, as compensation, the performer is entitled to equitable remuneration from the copyright owner, that is, the record company or film producer. The Rental Directive stipulates that these rights be made unwaivable.

National governments and the EU have attempted to build on past practice to implement the harmonisation programme. This creates problems because existing legislation, practice and the operation of the markets are different in member states. The harmonisation programme, implemented through national legislation and building on existing agreements, has highlighted national differences. It was the clear intention of the authors of the Rental Directive specifically to increase the bargaining power of performers *vis-à-vis* producers (Reinbothe and von Lewinski, 1993) by making the right to equitable remuneration unwaivable. The Directive makes the user responsible for payments of equitable remuneration for the performance of sound recordings. However, the UK SI makes the owner of copyright (that is, the record company), rather than the user, responsible for remuneration to performers in accordance with existing UK practice. That violates the pay-for-use principle and reinforces the unequal balance between performer and producer. In Denmark and Sweden, for example, performers and producers work together to administer, collect and distribute income from this right (which is due from the user), thus giving an equal balance of power between performers and producers. In the UK, what is 'equitable' has to be bargained for with the producer, or, if that fails, determined by the Copyright Tribunal, while elsewhere in Europe, equal rights have meant equal shares of income from the user.

The Directive also states that a single payment, that is, a fee instead of a royalty, can be equitable. Judging by existing practice this is more likely to be relevant to the rental right and will be discussed later. It was left to national governments to determine the person responsible for payment of the rental right and, in the case of the UK, this is 'the person to whom copyright has been transferred'. However, the only permitted assignment of the performer's right to equitable remuneration is to a collecting society and not to the record or film producer, so the right cannot be bought out. This may or may not require the formation of a new society for performers in the UK; either way, the role of collecting societies is clearly boosted.

5. EXERCISING THE NEW PERFORMERS' RIGHTS IN PRACTICE: PERFORMERS' RIGHTS IN SOUND RECORDINGS

In this section, we look at the practical aspects of exercising the new and extended performers' right to equitable remuneration for exploitation of sound recordings and discuss the main concerns aired during the consultation process preceding the Statutory Instrument. In Section 6, we do the same for the rental right.

Performers have had some statutory protection against unauthorised copying of their performances since 1925,[8] and recording contracts have long since specified conditions and payments for the exploitation of the recording, including the performance and broadcast of sound recordings. Under the new legislation performers acquire a statutory right to equitable remuneration for the use of their sound recordings in broadcasts and other public performances; in many cases this may simply reinforce the existing contractual position. However, as the new right is an individual one, this necessitates some changes in the collection, monitoring and distribution of performers' royalties. The system of distributing remuneration must be changed to take account of the individual performers' contribution to the recording, and to make the split between the various parties equitable. The debate about the draft SI in the UK focused on the interpretation of the word 'equitable', which elsewhere in Europe has been established as a 50/50 split of post-tax profits between performers and record companies, and about the entitlement of the performer to this income from the producer rather than the user. In the event, PPL voluntarily agreed to change its *ex gratia* arrangement to a 50/50 split. This is not the statutory requirement that exists elsewhere and that UK performers were seeking. The SI also only allows the performer to claim this income from the producer and not jointly with the producer from the user, as happens elsewhere in Europe. This reinforces the imbalance of power between producer and performer, the effects of which are discussed below.

The Performing Artists' Media Rights Association (PAMRA) has been set up by (among others) Equity, the MU, the Incorporated Society of Musicians (ISM) and Re-Pro (representative of sound engineers) to act as a collecting society for all performers.[9] Three issues must be decided:

1. The appropriate sum to be divided;
2. The appropriate reciprocal agreements to make to gain access to funds from foreign collecting societies;
3. How to administer the right of performers in the performance of sound recordings.

The first two points are considered in this section. The third point is discussed in Section 7.

The Appropriate Sum to be Divided

Although PPL has agreed to give performers a 50/50 share, there is some confusion as to what totals are to be divided. Representatives of PAMRA argue for 50 per cent of the gross licence fee income received by PPL. PAMRA will then pay some administration costs to PPL for the licensing and collecting service that PPL provides. However PPL has argued that performers are only entitled to 50 per cent of the revenue from the use of their own recordings.[10] This means that rather than a split of the amounts collected, which would then be allocated by each society to its members by ratio, the amount paid to PAMRA would not include the earnings of non-qualifying performers (such as US performers)[11] nor those of non-members of PAMRA. This point can be illustrated as follows: the 1994 PPL distribution after administration and combating piracy costs are deducted was £30.6 million. The actual shares are shown in Figure 5.2.

The performers' share was £9.4 million: £6.1 million to named performers and £3.3 million to session players. A 50/50 split would have given performers £15.3 million. If UK performers had played on only one-third of the tracks performed by PPL's licensees (a figure which is the MU's estimate for current radio play) and UK performers allocated 50 per cent of the use of recordings on which they performed, the amount paid to UK performers would have been only £5.1 million. Thus the total amounts earned by UK performers as a group may be reduced as a consequence of the new arrangements. This is illustrated in Table 5.1.

In comparison, in Denmark where performers and producers each have an equal right against the user, GRAMEX (Denmark), which represents both performers and producers, splits gross income from users 50/50. They argue that their tariffs to users are set at a level only to license the performances of Rome Convention nationals and that there is no unclaimed balance for non-qualifying performers to be argued over. Distribution costs are then deducted; each party's costs are not equal because of the greater number of performers, but the appropriate balances are then divided by ratio according to use.

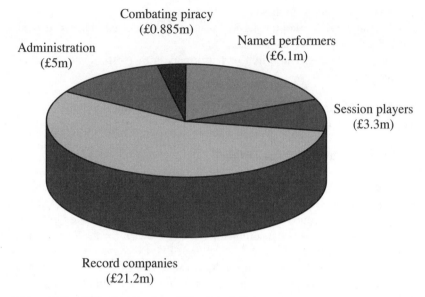

Combating piracy
(£0.885m)

Administration
(£5m)

Named performers
(£6.1m)

Session players
(£3.3m)

Record companies
(£21.2m)

Figure 5.2   PPL distribution of income, 1994

This shows that the way that the Directive has been implemented differs
between countries and does not give the same entitlement to net income. In
order to identify how much should be paid to each individual performer in the
UK, each amount that is paid to PPL in licence fees from use in TV, radio,
discos, shops, restaurants and wherever else records are played in public must
be accounted for on a track-played basis. PPL at present receives some of this
information in statements of use by licensees as well as from sampling and

Table 5.1   PPL distribution, 1994 (£ million)

	Actual split	50/50 split	50/50 split to UK performers only (assuming one-third of play is UK recordings)
Record companies	21.2	15.3	25.5?*
UK performers	9.4	15.3	5.1
Total	30.6	30.6	30.6

Note: *The balance of the total is hypothetically allocated to record companies; some of this
would be distributed to non-UK named performers and to foreign collecting societies.

monitoring; that is how it allocates income to the appropriate record company. However, the breakdown currently only goes as far as identifying the label of the recording used. The information will now have to be broken down even further to identify every performer on every track.

With the track-by-track breakdown, PPL will pay PAMRA the money due to its members but it will also pay all performers who are not PAMRA members directly, arguing that this will be easier and cheaper (and incidentally, that it would obviate the need for PAMRA, see PPL, 1996). Whatever route the money takes to the performer, this track-by-track breakdown is now necessary and will require new databases and registration procedures which will be expensive and time-consuming to set up but should facilitate the allocation of income according to use.[12] This is necessary not only as a result of the Directive but because of legal decisions, such as the Phil Collins case, which have found that the earnings of performers from the performance of recordings should be allocated according to use.[13]

Remuneration from Foreign Collecting Societies

Britain is a net exporter of recorded music, thus gaining access to income from the broadcast and performance of recordings overseas through reciprocal agreements must be advantageous to British performers. On the other hand, income due to foreign session players cannot always be distributed to them. The illustration in Table 5.1 shows that licence income from foreign recordings was paid to UK performers in 1994 because no mechanism existed to separate it out. The sum paid to UK performers was 32.5 per cent of the PPL net licence income from the performance in the UK of all recordings, including those of non-UK performers. No system existed either for payment of non-UK session players (although featured artists may have had contractual arrangements), or for remuneration to UK session players from performance of sound recordings abroad. In effect there was an unofficial 'reciprocal agreement' whereby collecting societies in each country kept the funds earned from performance of recordings to recompense use elsewhere (such agreements when formal are known as B agreements).

When income is collected in a way that enables the exchange of licence income for performance of sound recordings (A agreements), performers acquire access to earnings from broadcast and other performances of their recordings in the European Economic Area (EEA) and Rome Convention countries. In 1997, PAMRA had begun negotiations with several European collecting societies and had submitted some members' returns to GVL, the German performers' society.[14] Of course, performers are entitled to claim from all other societies in Rome Convention countries as individuals in the absence of reciprocal agreements. While this is time-consuming and costly, it is possible for featured artists, but for session players who are not identified on the recording it may be more difficult. However, in 1996 an agreement had been reached with the French performers' collecting society ADAMI, which was holding money for British artists that was a combination of a blank tape levy and public performance revenue tax collected from broadcasters (Equity, 1996b). The sum involved was expected to exceed £1 million.

How much UK performers stand to gain overall from access to foreign licence income now that the new performers' rights have been introduced depends on the balance of trade between the UK and countries that have performers' rights and reciprocal agreements. It is possible to gain some idea of the potential earnings for performers from the use of UK records by looking at PRS figures on earnings of composers from public performance income, as PRS does have reciprocal agreements with other countries. Using that as a basis, we roughly calculate that overseas earnings for PPL could be of the order of £20 million. However, it has been estimated by Dane (1995, p. 3) on the basis of pop chart information that UK performers' share of the world market is declining because of the growth of domestic repertoire throughout the world. This is corroborated by British Invisibles who chart a decline in UK performers' share of record sales from 23 per cent in 1989 to 18 per cent in 1993 (British Invisibles, 1995: 31). Nevertheless, the UK record industry in general is in a healthy state. The value of trade shipments in 1994 increased by 16.8 per cent (Dane, 1995, p. 2), while profits increased by 83 per cent to £121.5 million (Dane, 1995, p. 10).

Figures also suggest that the income stream from licensing in the UK is growing faster than income generated through sales. Performance income collected over the eight years from 1988 to 1996 rose by 270 per cent as compared to the increase in UK record sales revenue of 174 per cent. This can be explained partly as a result of the growth of the independent radio network in the UK (Dane, 1995, p. 222). However, collecting societies throughout Europe also record growth, both through greater enforcement of rights and through the development of new consumers, such as aerobic centres and shopping malls.

Thus, overall, with the addition of new performance income from overseas due to reciprocal agreements and growing markets for all areas of the music industry in Asia and South America (partly because of the success of the campaign against piracy and because of Trade Related Intellectual Properties – TRIPS), UK performers' remuneration from abroad is likely to grow. PAMRA intends to collect the money generated in the UK for performers from all countries with similar rights, in order to gain access to the income generated for UK performers from licence fees collected in those countries.[15]

There are several unresolved difficulties to do with reciprocal agreements. While these are not direct results of the Directive and its implementation, the move towards harmonisation has highlighted differences and potential difficulties. One is identifying whether a recording is entitled to national treatment. While the Berne Convention stipulates that the rights of composers are protected according to the place of publication (which includes simultaneous publication in other states within 30 days), there is no equivalent international agreement on performers' rights. Some states use the nationality or place of residence of the producer to determine whether national treatment is appropriate (Sweden); the UK uses the term 'qualifying performance', which is a performance by a British or EEA resident or made in the UK or other EEA state. Unless and until the protocol to the Rome Convention clarifies matters, such differences will remain. Changes in the technology also pose problems: digital and interactive technology on the World Wide Web now enables a recording to be made with perhaps a bass player in the USA, a guitarist in Germany and singers in the UK and it may be published on the Web. It is not clear which is the country of fixation or publication, and what would constitute a qualifying performance. These changes have implications for establishing national treatment and therefore where, or even whether, performers' rights exist in the work and how they should be administered. Such problems will proliferate with the increasing globalisation of the music industry.

Another issue is the question of cultural deductions – the use of funds by collecting societies or unions for communal benevolent purposes – brought into question by the Phil Collins decision. The Monopolies and Mergers Commission in 1988 forced the British Musicians' Union to distribute funds to individual musicians rather than using the 12 per cent it received from PPL for general purposes. This contrasts with some European countries where cultural deductions are included in agreements and legislation. Certainly they are regarded as beneficial and are used to provide excellent facilities for local musicians and to promote national music. However, there remains some question as to whether they will be legal following the decision, which maintained that Phil Collins was entitled to all of the income earned by his recorded performances in Germany (and, it follows, in any EU country) under the Treaty of Rome.

6. EXERCISING THE NEW PERFORMERS' RIGHTS IN PRACTICE: THE RENTAL RIGHT

There is no commercial rental of sound recordings in the UK; video is the only rental market.[16]

One of the most curious of our research findings was that no arrangements had been made by 1997 for collecting performers' remuneration from the new rental right. Economic logic suggests that either the right has no potential financial value (which seems unlikely) or it would be so costly to collect that there would be no net value.[17] One explanation is that the rental right may be deemed to be already covered under existing arrangements (Equity, 1996a).[18]

Most payments by film and TV producers to performers are negotiated in agreements between the representative organisations, the Musicians' Union (MU), Equity and the Producers' Alliance for Cinema and Television (PACT), and are made to the performers directly or through their agents. These agreements use a system of residual payments, that is, payments related to the original fee, for whatever rights the producer chooses to buy.[19] For example, an actor receives a fee for the filming period, another payment of 50 per cent of that fee buys the theatrical rights (for showing the film in a cinema) for the USA and Canada and a further 50 per cent buys the rights for the rest of the world. A 25 per cent residual payment buys the videogram rights (currently applied to sales of videos) and there are other residual payments agreed for further exploitation (Equity, 1993, p. 16). There is a similar buy-out clause for musicians called the 'combined-use-fee' (MU/PACT, 1996, pp. 11 and 16). Some film producers have started inserting a contractual clause stating that 'the total guaranteed minimum payment constitutes equitable and adequate consideration for the assignment of rental and lending rights and cable retransmission rights' (Equity, 1996a), assuming the right to be already equitably remunerated under existing arrangements. Whether this is legally acceptable remains to be seen. Alternatively, performers could lay claim to a separate residual payment for the right, which would be easy to implement, being in line with existing practice, or they could claim a percentage of the income of the producer from exploitation of the rental right.

Producers acquired a rental right in the 1988 Copyright, Designs and Patents Act, which is exercised through licences. Film producers sell the rights for video rental to distributors who then sell films in video format to video outlets. The payment received by the producer confers a licence to rent the video to the public.[20] Under the new regulations, performers have a right to equitable remuneration exercisable against 'the person to whom copyright has been transferred' in exchange for the 'obligatory presumption of transfer' of the exclusive right (that is, the right to authorise or prohibit) which allows the producer to exploit the film. In effect, this is a form of compulsory licence. It could mean that performers are entitled to a portion of the price at which the video rental rights are sold or a portion of the earnings of the distributor depending on whether the rights are assigned or licensed. In Denmark and Sweden, where performers have been remunerated for rentals under collective agreements for some years, they receive a percentage of the income of the producer from exploitation of the film through both rental and broadcast.

The fear of performers' unions is that there may be no visible amount to which performers can make a claim because of vertical integration;[21] unless this trade in rights is transparent, it may prove difficult to assess the sums to which performers might make a claim. The Statutory Instrument has addressed this concern by stipulating that the rental right is only assignable to a collecting society and anticipates a scheme being introduced for licensing performers' property rights (Regulation 22). If the producer sells the rights to a distributor at a price that is less than fair, the performer has individual access to the Copyright Tribunal for redress, though a collecting society or trade union would be in a better position to achieve negotiated agreements with producer organisations and to appeal to the Copyright Tribunal.

If film companies have to pay a new licence fee or royalty as equitable remuneration for performers, producers may raise the price of videos to the rental market, which in turn, video rental outlets might pass on to their customers. The market might not withstand such increases. The spread of digitalisation via cable and satellite distribution and its many film channels, and the arrival of video-on-demand are all strong competition for video rentals, which fell by almost one-third between 1989 and 1995 (BVA, 1996).

It remains to be seen how valuable this new right is to performers and how it will be implemented, but the point argued here is that the new rights do not necessarily increase earnings.

7.   ADMINISTERING PERFORMERS' RIGHTS IN SOUND RECORDING: WHO WILL PAY?

Four aspects of administration are common to all copyright and related rights: a record must be made of the use or sale of the work; payments must be collected; all rights holders must be identified by name and address so that they can be paid what is due to them; and the royalty or licence income must be divided between rights holders on the basis of each individual's contribution. In the case of the performer's right to remuneration from the exploitation of sound recordings, licence fee income must be allocated to individual performers on the basis of their contribution to each track, making it necessary to identify use of the track, the individual's contribution to the recorded performance and then the percentage of income due. While this is fairly straightforward for a string quartet, it is rather more complicated when, for example, a solo singer employs a collection of session players and singers in a different combination on each track, and perhaps there is an additional quartet featured on some tracks and the London Symphony Orchestra or a penny whistle on others. The contribution of each artist must be logged by either the producer or the sound engineer and while all this is possible, it is expensive.[22] In 1996, PPL had no system of working out the weighting of the contribution of each performer to the track to allocate the royalties. This further breakdown on both existing and new recordings must be undertaken by either PAMRA or the record companies. That will add an unknown extra amount to administration costs. GRAMEX (Denmark) estimates that it takes two hours, at a cost of £80–£100 simply to register the requisite information for each new CD with each performer allocated a number of points according to her contribution.

In 1997, PPL was setting up a computer system to identify use of and allocate royalties to each track on a disc; they expected it to increase their administration costs, which were at the time just under 13 per cent, by 2 per cent.[23] PPL was also exploring the possibility of links with either MCPS or PRS (although the last attempt was the PROMS[24] disaster), with whom it could share information on use of records. MCPS holds a national discography set up in 1987, a database of recordings with links to societies throughout Europe. This might be extended to contain the information on the individual contributions of all composers, performers and other creators required by both PPL and PRS.[25]

All the collecting societies are promoting the use of International Standard Recording Code (ISRC), which is implanted in the recording during production and contains the necessary information about all rights holders. It is said this would cost in the region of £150–£200 per release and the cost would presumably fall on the producer. Each user would then need the appropriate hardware so that every time the recording was played, the use would be automatically logged. This would be expensive to set up as everyone who broadcasts or plays sound recordings in public would have to buy the hardware for the system to be effective.[26] However, this could be linked to an international performers' database (such as that at SAMI in Sweden), which would distribute income. Such a direct link would reduce the cost of sampling and monitoring (costs which fall on some users, and on the collecting societies) and the costs of collecting and distributing licence fee income, a cost which falls on the collecting society and hence on the performer. These systems are expensive to set up but enable information to be shared out at low cost once they are established.

Whatever improvements can be made to ways of monitoring, collecting and distributing income due to performers, overall revenues must exceed costs for these changes to be worthwhile and, one way or another, someone has to pay.

In the short run, administrative costs will increase and a larger share of incomes should go to performers (this includes non-UK performers through reciprocal agreements); in sound recording they now have 50 per cent of the income from the use of their recordings rather than the previous 37.5 per cent of licence fee income. If performers do gain at the expense of producers, film and record companies may accept a reduction in profits or try to raise prices to maintain existing profits. However, whether the income of performers will rise overall depends on the financial prospects of the industries concerned.

In Section 5, we estimated that the cost to record companies of a straight 50/50 split of PPL licence income would have been £6 million in 1994. That represents less than 1 per cent of the record companies' income using Dane's (1995) figures. Given the upward trend in both record sales and licence fee income from the public performance of sound recording, record companies could tolerate the reduction in profits; however, there are several ways in which they might seek to counteract any such reduction. One option would be to offer smaller advances to named performers.[27] It is debatable whether record companies can do this and maintain the quality of the recordings (and accompanying videos), since the advance on royalties finances the artists' outlay on recording. Alternatively, companies might become more cautious in their choice of artists, taking fewer risks on whom they sign, which would be detrimental to consumer choice.

Perhaps a more likely consequence of the legislation is that record companies could insert a clause into artists' contracts to use their public performance licence income along with other royalty payments for recouping advances.[28] Usually, the recording costs are paid by the artist only out of royalty income from sales; income from public performance of the recording goes to the artist via PPL.

Finally, the increased cost could be passed on directly to consumers; PPL could increase licence fees to users (hotels, restaurants, discos and shops as well as TV and radio). The current rate of growth in PPL's income suggests that the market could bear price increases. That would pass on the cost of performers' rights to the user in accordance with the pay-for-use principle. The eventual outcome of these changes is an empirical question that must be monitored.

8. ARE PERFORMERS LIKELY TO BENEFIT FROM THE CHANGES BROUGHT ABOUT BY THE EC DIRECTIVE?

Performers' organisations believe that increased copyright protection is necessarily beneficial. It was the stated purpose of the authors of the Rental Directive to increase the bargaining position of performers in relation to film and record companies. Economists, those perpetrators of the 'dismal science', are trained to be sceptical of such claims, however, on the grounds that markets react to changes in the organisation of property rights. Such changes may indeed cause the market to work more efficiently and therefore generate more revenues to offset payments for new and extended rights. That is clearly the belief of performers' representatives, who regard the changes proposed in the draft Statutory Instrument as 'new money'; the cake is expanding and extra slices can be taken out without reducing existing claimants' incomes. But if that is not so, 'new' money comes at the expense of 'old'.

It has been argued here that while performers in sound recordings may eventually gain access to increased earnings through reciprocal agreements, because of improved collection procedures and because the market in the performance of recordings is growing, that is not the case with video rental, where the market is declining and may not withstand new claims.

Economists are also on the look-out for transaction costs. It is obviously the case that considerable resources go into the operations of the collecting societies, which charge performers and other rights holders a hefty percentage of the monies they collect for them. Some of the costs identified here are necessary because of legal decisions (Phil Collins and the MMC report invoking the Rome Convention) and others are the result of technological developments that will in the long run improve administration of rights. However, the new rights in the UK have imposed new requirements for collecting, monitoring and distributing payments to performers, which will be costly, at least in the short run. They also may impose new costs on users depending on how the rights are administered.

Session players are likely to be better off in the short run as a result of the right in performance of sound recordings; instrumentalists because they did not benefit individually from the PPL distribution to the Musicians' Union until 1989; and non-MU members – such as actors and singers – because they received none of the PPL distribution under the previous arrangements. In the long run, it is possible that session fees could be reduced to take into account the new claim to future income. The greatest financial benefit, however, will probably come from overseas earnings. The main obstacle to this is the implementation of international Directives through national legislation which has allowed the UK to create a different balance of power between rights holders than exists in other countries. As national governments have based new legislation on existing practice, differences have remained that currently make bilateral agreements difficult. The attempt at harmonisation has succeeded in highlighting the differences in industry practice throughout Europe.

9.   CONCLUDING REMARKS

Copyright and related rights play an increasingly important role in all aspects of economic and social activity, and particularly in the cultural sector. Without statutory creation and protection of rights, creative and performing artists would be worse off. Copyright law has to be altered to accommodate changes in technology and in economic and social circumstances. That is not in dispute. What we query is the view that the changes proposed by the Statutory Instrument will automatically bring economic benefit to all performers. Some of the questions raised here should have been answered before the EC Directive was implemented.

The driving motives behind the Directives are standardisation of copyright law (harmonisation) to prevent unfair competition within the EEA and to give greater bargaining power to performers (equity). It is a standard economic proposition that the goal of equity is difficult to pursue without having effects on efficiency, that is, on incentives in markets.

Statutory protection by copyright laws is defended on economic grounds because it corrects market failure when property rights are not properly established; once they are, however, market forces take over and rights are traded for what the market will bear. The cultural industries in the UK, at least, are commercial enterprises run for profit. What the new rights are worth depends on market outcomes as new costs have to be absorbed and on performers' individual and collective bargaining power. While intervention may be intended, and indeed necessary, to correct market distortion and give incentive to performers, statutory protection cannot guarantee the outcome.

NOTES

* This article was published jointly with Millie Taylor. Millie Taylor is the researcher and Ruth Towse the principal investigator on the project 'Copyright, Performers' Rights and Incentives in Cultural Markets' funded for one year (1996) by the Economic and Social Research Council (code L126251011) under the research programme 'Media Economics and Media Culture'. We are grateful to Simon Frith, David Perrott and Andrew Burke for their comments on an earlier draft of this article and to an anonymous referee for helpful suggestions in revising it. The article was written in early 1997 and was correct at the time of writing. A number of changes have taken place since then which were noted in the pre-publication revision in 1998; however, the reader is warned that matters are moving fast in this area and details could be out of date.

1. The reader (the 'user') does not pay directly if the book is borrowed from a public library. The Public Lending Right compensates the author for that use (though not composers for music lending).

2. There are standard agreements between the Musicians' Union (MU) and the British Phonographic Industry (BPI) representing the record companies.

3. Collecting societies are more developed in music than in other cultural industries. The Monopolies and Mergers Commission Reports, *Collective Licensing* (MMC, 1988), *Performing Rights* (MMC, 1996) and *The Supply of Recorded Music* (MMC, 1994) are very informative about current music industry practice. For a historical survey of one particular collecting society, the Performing Right Society, see Ehrlich (1989).

4. There is also a smaller organisation, Video Performance Limited (VPL) which licenses and collects UK public performance and broadcasting rights for the owners of copyright in music videos.

5. On signing the Rome Convention, arrangements were made in many countries for an equal split of income from the performance of sound recordings between performers and

producers. The British Government takes the position that the terms of Article 12 of the Rome Convention are satisfied by the existing arrangements.

6. Details of how PRS allocates various types of licence income are given in MMC (1996).
7. A comparison of the administrative functions and costs of societies in nine countries is to be found in MMC (1996, Appendix 9.2). PRS and MCPS have now merged some of their activities.
8. The Dramatic and Musical Performers' Protection Act 1925 offered protection in criminal law.
9. A second society, AURA has been set up by the International Managers' Forum and other organisations as a collecting society for contracted performers. In our meetings with BASCA, RePro and PPL it was suggested that AURA would simply lobby on behalf of featured performers but that PPL would continue to distribute income to AURA's members unless they became members of PAMRA.
10. Interview at PPL during 1996.
11. US companies can copyright their sound recordings in the UK by releasing them there within 30 days of the US release; that makes them eligible for protection under UK copyright legislation. Thus, although US performers do not have a right in performance, they may be able to make a claim under UK legislation, depending on the criteria for eligibility for national treatment.
12. Such a system in Norway took about four years to become fully operational.
13. Performers are entitled to be members of collecting societies throughout Europe; however, some European societies state that if there is an appropriate reciprocal agreement, performers must be represented by it.
14. By the end of 1997 some progress had been made. However, the GVL negotiations illustrate another problem of 'harmonisation' – the German performers' right to remuneration is based (like a residual payment) on the original fee paid rather than on income from use or sale of recording. Thus PAMRA members had to convert all their hourly sessions information into earnings terms and submit the figures annually, a time-consuming exercise which deterred many of those eligible. It seems that it is only Germany, Switzerland and Austria where this applies, however.
15. PAMRA's press release (PAMRA, 1996) mentions that 24 other territories already give performers the right to a 50/50 split of income from the use of sound recordings.
16. There is rental of sound recordings elsewhere in Europe. However, GVL (the German performers' collecting society) reports that CD rental outlets are now closing in Germany as a result of the introduction of the rental right because producers who now have an exclusive right have prohibited rental (communicated to us by letter dated 19 August 1996).
17. When the new regulations finally came into existence at the end of 1999/6, authors and performers had less than two months (which included Christmas) to register their intent to claim the rental right in works created before 1 July 1994. This no doubt partly explained the absence of any arrangements. This raises the question whether legislation in this area, to be effective, must create both the right and administrative machinery. That would imply that the law is working against market forces.
18. Authors have also gained a rental right as a result of the Directive. The Authors' Licensing and Collecting Society (ALCS), which has been active in lobbying government about this particular right, have stated that such a position does not in their opinion implement the Directive and would be strongly resisted.
19. In 1996, the actors' union, Equity, substituted a royalty system of payments for the previous residual system in its standard agreements for secondary use of BBC and ITV television programmes. This is expected to increase sales of these programmes to cable and satellite companies and lead to higher earnings for actors in the long run.
20. The British Video Association provided this information in 1996. We were unable to gain access to any data, such as what amounts may be involved at various points in the distribution chain.
21. This is where companies such as Blockbuster, which has links through its parent company, Viacom, to Paramount may choose to license video rental without money changing hands.

22. RePro, which represents studio producers, believes that their members are best suited to this job and is using this as a lobbying position to support studio producers in their attempt to gain the same rights as performers and producers in the performance of sound records. RePro argue that studio producers are creative in the recording process and so should have a right equivalent to the performers' right and that they also make many of the arrangements for the recording which, they claim, gives them an entitlement to a copyright in the sound recording (like the producer's) under the Rome Convention.

23. From an interview by PPL.

24. This was the attempt by PRS and PPL to set up a joint computer database, the Performing Right On-Line Membership Services (PROMS). The system never came online. It cost PRS an estimated £8 million although 30 per cent of this has since been recovered (PRS, 1995, p. 6). This information was the position in 1997. It shows how international measures are being taken and new databases created to deal with the act, but how complicated and expensive it is. Since writing this, the MCPS/PRS Alliance has been formed to share databases.

25. MCPS representing UK and the Republic of Ireland, GEMA for northern Europe and SDRM for southern Europe have together formed BEL (Bureau for European Licensing). With the CIS (Common Information System) which is being developed in parallel by societies worldwide, there will be a database of sound recordings on which BEL can draw. SUISA is already in existence in Switzerland which contains international files for rights owners and ASCAP in the USA is expected to launch a works database next year. This central licensing will, it is hoped, will mean that only one set of administration charges will be payable and distribution will be quicker (MCPS, 1996).

26. Some code would also have to be inserted into back-catalogue recordings as the performer's right is retrospective.

27. A suggestion put to us in an interview at PPL.

28. Also from an interview at PPL. It is arguable whether this would contravene the right to equitable remuneration but given the balance of power in favour of the producer, a young performer is likely to agree to such contractual terms.

6. Copyright and economic incentives: an application to performers' rights in the music industry*

INTRODUCTION

This chapter contributes to the economic analysis of copyright in three ways: first, it draws a distinction between the general purpose of copyright law and the administration of the royalty system of payment for the use of copyrighted material; this leads to the principal–agent analysis of modes of payment. Second, this approach is applied to a specific topic, the change in copyright law in the form of the introduction of a new property right for performers in the UK that has come about as a result of the harmonisation programme of the European Union. Finally, new data were collected to assess the likely impact this change in law would have on performers' earnings using the music industry as a case study. This is novel because there has been, to my knowledge, no previous attempt to apply empirical evidence to the analysis of copyright law.

The economic literature on copyright is mostly theoretical and general; this paper concentrates on the example of a specific right in one industry in order to expose the economic issues in detail. I believe it is necessary to understand the economic problems of copyright at ground level in order to consider the loftier issues of principle of the law. The right way to evaluate policy on copyright is to undertake empirical analysis of the economic effects of changes to the law and to see how markets respond to them. It does not seem that this approach has so far even been considered in European policy-making on copyright.

In this chapter, the economic analysis of copyright is extended from its existing concern with market failure to a principal-agent approach in which payment to authors by the royalty system is seen as an incentive structure based on risk-sharing. This approach enables us to investigate the role of copyright in bargaining between authors and publishers. It throws into question the view of a synergy of interests between author and publisher that is implied by giving copyright protection to both parties, a point first raised implicitly by Plant (1934) but ignored by subsequent economists writing on copyright. At a time in which the future of copyright law is being considered in the light of technological upheaval, it is important to ask if it serves the public interest. This is an empirical question as well as a theoretical one.

In the chapter different modes of payment for copyright are explained and analysed using the principal–agent model. The results are then applied to the changes in performers' rights in the UK due to the European Union harmonisation of copyright and their effect on financial incentives to performers is estimated for the music industry, using data from the UK, Sweden and Denmark. Some concluding remarks consider the policy implications.

PRINCIPAL–AGENT MODEL OF COPYRIGHT

What is generally called copyright is a bundle of different rights in a work. A copyrighted work is distinct from an economic product, which may be made up of different works owned in the first instance by different agents. This distinction, which is always ignored, has important economic implications:

1. That transactions must take place between the different rights owners to produce and market a product comprised of the copyrighted work or works;
2. That different rights may well have different economic value. A simple example of this is the film rights of a book; an author whose book is made into a film can expect to earn more from the film rights than from royalties on book sales;
3. That the same rights often command different values in different territories, that is, geographical markets.

Authors and publishers therefore have to negotiate an agreement that takes account of these incentives and rewards.

Apart from Plant, no economist seems to have raised the question of whether the interests of author and publisher are the same or whether they conflict, though there are numerous instances (including court cases) of disputes. The general issue is important in understanding the economic rationale for publishers having copyright as well as authors.[1] Publishers are accorded copyright so as to encourage the dissemination of authors' works, presumably on the assumption that authors themselves could not or would not be able to do it to the extent that is socially optimal. If publishers had no copyright, they would act only as the author's agent and the author would be viewed unambiguously as the principal. But publishers are entrepreneurs and may hire authors to create works, in which case the publisher is the principal and the author his agent. Plant made the point that a basic conflict of interest arises even in the relatively simple case of the author of a book and her publisher: the publisher seeks a price that maximises profit, whereas the author, whose royalty depends on revenue, would set a price that maximises sales, the elementary economic point being that the optimal level of output would be different depending on the bargaining power of the author with the publisher. The outcome depends on the bargaining process between author and publisher over the terms of the contract between them. This process can be analysed using a principal–agent model of the system of payment for the use of copyright.

Contracts between author and publisher vary considerably and may be tailor-made in individual cases; however, many contracts are standardised and conform to negotiated agreements and conventions between the parties that have become accepted in different cultural industries. That allows some generalisation about methods of payment for specific rights. It is necessary first to review the different types of payments for the use of copyright, which vary somewhat as between sectors of the cultural industries.

Perhaps the most common (and certainly the best known) is a 'pure' royalty, whereby the publisher simply contracts with the author to pay a certain percentage of the sales revenue from the work (a future payment). The size of the royalty is the subject of individual negotiation, though it is fair to say that in the majority of cases, this is a standard rate (for example, 10 or 15 per cent for books). The royalty system means the author receives an uncertain payment. To reduce the author's uncertainty and to provide her with a greater incentive to create the work, the publisher may pay the author a lump sum advance on the royalties, which is recouped out of future royalty payments. The size of the advance is subject to individual negotiation and, apart from the general principle involved, is far from standard. Bargaining over the amount advanced is often the device whereby a publisher secures the author's agreement to publish with him and may, especially in the case of books or film scripts, be the subject of an auction. The larger the advance, the greater the publisher's pre-commitment and the greater his incentive to market the work; *pari passu* the lower is the author's share of the risk. The royalty system ties author and publisher into joint-entrepreneurship and ensures a shared interest in promoting the published work. It does so by forcing them to share risk.

At the other end of the spectrum of modes of payment is a 'buy-out'. A buy-out is a flat fee (spot price) for the use of a bundle of rights. On payment of the fee, the publisher has no further obligation to obtain the author's consent to use her work. This arrangement is common in situations where a hold-up problem of obtaining permission from many individuals, usually performing the same standard task, could occur. Buy-outs are to be found in the music business in standard contracts collectively negotiated between 'employers' –

record companies, advertising agencies, radio and TV companies – and musicians' unions, who represent the so-called session players (and singers), the backing artists who provide background music. Buy-outs are also used for actors in advertising and are increasingly being used in the television industry to clear rights in the original programme for subsequent use on cable TV. It may also be said that, in effect, a visual artist sells the rights of a work of art, such as a painting, with the object (though the artist retains copyright; there are finer points to this argument that require qualification (Santagata, 1995)). Buy-outs are unpopular with authors, and particularly so with their trade unions and professional associations and, though they are favoured by publishers in some branches of the cultural industries, this is not a universal preference.[2] One reason is that, despite the convenience of buy-outs and the fact that considerable transaction costs of payment by a system of royalties are avoided, publishers have to put more capital up-front and hence take a greater risk.

The question to which I now turn is which system of payment – royalty, royalty with an advance payment or buy-out – gives the greater incentive to agents (authors and publishers) to create and disseminate works.

In a perfect world with perfect foresight, symmetric information, risk-neutrality and zero transaction costs, the amount paid in as a flat-fee buy-out price that discharged the publisher from any further financial obligation to the author would be the discounted value of the author's rights over their statutory duration. Authors would be indifferent between a buy-out and a royalty regime.

As transaction costs exist in the real world, publishers would prefer a buy-out because it reduces the transaction costs of paying out royalties over a period of years. But where authors have the choice, they seem overwhelmingly to prefer to retain residual control through future payments of royalties with an advance to pre-commit the publisher. This must be explained by market imperfections and different attitudes to time preference, risk and reputation on the part of author and publisher. It is convenient to consider each point in turn.

Time preference Author and publisher are likely for several reasons to have differing rates of time preference. Whereas publishers are usually firms with a portfolio of copyright assets of differing maturity, which together yield a regular flow of revenue, authors are mostly individuals with a limited production life who need a basic income. Authors depend on a few of their own copyrighted works to produce royalties but producers control an array of different authors' works. Individual authors cannot take the longer view than firms can. Although that may suggest authors should prefer buy-outs, other reasons militate against doing so.

Risk   For similar reasons, publishers can take bigger risks than authors; they have a range of assets to cushion failure and also better access to capital markets. Authors have a restricted range of copyrights, which may have little market value without a publisher's backing and so they have little collateral to offer banks other than their human capital.

Reputation   The strongest case for a royalty system is the incentive it gives authors to maintain their reputation by creating new work that strengthens the reputation and value of their existing published work. Successive works by an author over a period of time would seem to be complements rather than substitutes and this must be the rationale of exclusive, long-term contracts between an author and a publisher, who both benefit from the enhanced reputation. Many examples come to mind from markets for works of art – paintings, craftwork, music; one example is a new recording by a pop group, the success of which would raise sales and play of its back catalogue. If the pop group had no residual rights to earlier recordings, the group could not benefit financially from the renewed interest that follows from a new recording. This reason also explains contracts between pop groups and record companies that require them to promote their recordings by going on performance tours, appearing on radio and TV shows, giving interviews and so on.

However, author and publisher may have different views about the author's chances of success. Authors are likely to overestimate their chances while publishers, who have more experience of the market, are more realistic. This is a case of asymmetric information. Another aspect of this, frequently referred to by musicians, is that publishers (music publishers and record companies) have information about potential marketing and technical change that they do not share with them. It is probably a law of life that almost every author is dissatisfied with the publisher's efforts to market her work and create her reputation! Once successful, authors often resent the less favourable terms of the original contract with the publisher, which they see after the event as exploiting their inexperience and lack of reputation at the time.

These asymmetries between author and publisher influence the terms of the contract between author and publisher and are reflected in the system of payment.

A final option that, with the Internet, is fast becoming a real possibility in all art forms, is for the author to publish her own work. This is increasingly happening in the music industry where pop groups have begun to release and completely control their music without the agency of a record company.

The range of possible methods of payment (buy-outs to royalties), the implied sharing of risk (from zero under a buy-out to 100 per cent when the author publishes herself), the transaction costs of administering royalty payments and the implied incentive to maintain the quality and reputation of the author's work are summarised in Table 6.1.

We can see from Table 6.1 that there is a trade-off between the different elements – risk-bearing, transaction costs and incentives to the parties to a contract, the author and the publisher – and different payment arrangements, in line with the earlier analysis. For example, a 'pure' royalty system gives the greatest incentive to effort to both parties but results in the highest transaction costs of administration, of contracting and possibly also of resolving disputes when co-operation breaks down. If the publisher were the dominant partner he would prefer a buy-out payment based on transaction costs alone. However, the publisher then bears all the risk with no further co-operation of the author and must put up the finance for the buy-out at the outset of the deal to secure the work and its associated rights. If the buy-out price is high, as it would be for 'star' talent, and/or large numbers of people were involved (say in making a TV drama or soap opera), the outlay and risk might simply be higher than the transaction cost savings to the publisher of the buy-out. Equally, if the costs of contracting are low, as, for example, they would be in a situation of a standard contract negotiated between authors' and publishers' representatives (say, the Musicians' Union and record companies), it would pay the publisher to push for buy-outs. The eventual payment arrangement adopted and contract struck therefore depend on a number of economic and non-economic factors, which must be traded off against each other.

Table 6.1 and the preceding analysis demonstrate that there are sound economic reasons for one or another payment regime. In concluding a contract, author and publisher (for example, performer and record company) strike a bargain that balances advantages and disadvantages, depending on the relative power of each side. It is obviously the case that changes to copyright law could disturb the operation of these markets. The change from 50 to 70 years interaction between author and publisher and duration of copyright is one that would seem to benefit large publishers more than small authors. The stated purpose of the EC Rental Directive was to alter the balance of bargaining power between performers and those who use their services, that is, it used copyright law to regulate cultural markets and the division of revenue (see Chapter 5). As firms of publishers (literary publishers, film, record and TV companies and so on) grow in size, there will be increased pressure to use the law to 'protect' authors against publishers. The economic outcome of these changes are not, however, as obvious as policy-makers suppose. Empirical evidence is needed to establish how markets react and for this we turn to the case of the music industry and evidence on payment for performers' rights.

Table 6.1 *Risk-bearing and principal–agent analysis of copyright*

Payment arrangement	Publisher buys out all rights for flat fee	Publisher pays royalties with an advance	Pure royalty system: all royalties shared between publisher and author	Author publishes, pays all costs and receives incomes
Risk-bearing	Publisher takes all risk	Shared risk: author has lower risk than publisher	Shared risk: author and publisher take equal risk	Author bears all risk
Incentive to author	Produce routine work: no promotion of own work; 'Low' reputation	Co-operate with publisher, less effort to promote own work and reputation	Co-operate with publisher to promote own work and 'high' reputation	Strong incentive to market and to promote and maintain 'high' reputation
Incentive to publisher	Maximise value of asset, use 'low' reputation authors or performers	Co-operate with author, high marketing effort to recoup advance	Co-operate with author	Not applicable
Transaction costs of payment mechanism to author and publisher	Low to both	High cost of contract and administration by publisher	High to both: author monitors publisher's accounts; High legal costs of conflict resolution	Low/zero

COPYRIGHT AND PERFORMERS' RIGHTS IN THE MUSIC INDUSTRY

In the music industry, composers (of music) and lyricists (of words set to music) have exclusive authors' rights in their works, which are licensed, usually by the music publisher (who has publication rights) to the record company (phonogram producer) wanting to record them. The record company then has the recording right in its recording. In order to make that recording, the record company hires performers, who also have rights that must be transferred to the record company. These performers may be distinguished as contracted artists, for example, a singer, a pop group or an orchestra, who by the terms of their contract with the record company are paid a royalty on sales of the record, and the non-contracted 'backing' musicians who provide the background music on the occasion of the recording session. This latter group do not get royalties on sales and sell their rights for a single fee in a 'buy-out' arrangement. We come back to performers' rights soon. The record – the final product – that is now in existence has the sound recording rights (Chapter 5) attached to it, that is, copying, broadcasting, public performance and the rest. These rights are territorial, relating to a specific territory. Thus in the process of making a sound recording of even just one work (and most recordings comprise many works), many transactions must be made; each one can vary in pecuniary worth in the different markets in which they are exploited by sales and by public performance in broadcasts, inclusion in films and so on.

The production of a sound recording requires an initial outlay, the fixed cost, for acquiring the necessary rights, advance payments on royalties to contracted artists, payments to sessions musicians and sound engineers, hire of recording studios for the production of the master tape, payments to graphic artists for the design of the packaging and promoting and marketing the record. The popular music side of the record industry (by far the greater part) is inherently risky, as consumers' tastes are fickle and, in the case of new performers, unformed, necessitating considerable investment in A&R (Artist and Repertoire, the music business equivalent of R&D) and in the production and marketing of a high ratio of 'failures' to 'successes'. Much of this outlay could be avoided by a free-rider in the absence of copyright protection. That is the standard market failure argument advanced by economists in support of copyright. Note that it relates to fixed costs, since it may be assumed that marginal costs of reproducing CDs are low and more or less the same for the record company as for legal and illegal copiers.

Evidence on costs and risk in the music industry is to be found in the report of the UK Monopolies and Mergers Commission (MMC, 1994) following its investigation into the record industry in 1994 for possible monopolistic practices in the supply of recorded music. Figures on the outlay of releasing

an album by a typical major record company show that it was in the region of
£0.25m to £1.75m, of which £125 000 to £1.4m was recoupable from artists'
royalties if sales were high enough (MMC, 1994, p.101). In aggregate, the five
major global record companies operating in the UK (BMG, EMI, PolyGram,
Sony and Warner) recouped approximately 50 per cent of their A&R
expenditure in 1993. A&R expenditure written off was 15.4 per cent of gross
sales; by way of comparison, marketing accounted for 15.9 per cent (MMC,
1994, pp. 171 and 173). Given the international nature of the recording
industry, it is likely that similar costs would be found in these same companies
in other countries. A free-rider could avoid these fixed costs *and* avoid risk
since he would know he was backing a successful recording. He would incur
only marginal costs and possibly some marketing costs of his own and thus
could undercut the initial producer. His only disadvantage is arriving later in
the market and not having the headstart of the first entrepreneur. Preventing
this competition is the incentive that copyright law offers to the publisher to
appropriate all market revenues from outlays on the creation of the work, the
sound recording in this case.

So much for the protection copyright law offers the record companies. What
about the performers?

Performers are not accorded copyright proper as are authors and publishers
but rights 'neighbouring on' copyright; in some countries called neighbouring
rights, these are called performers' property rights and non-property rights in
the UK. As explained in detail in Chapter 5, following the adoption of EC
Directives, UK performers now have individual reproduction, distribution,
rental and lending rights and the right to equitable remuneration for
exploitation of sound recording release, as do performers throughout Europe.
It is this last right that will figure largely in subsequent parts of this chapter.[3]
The right may not be assigned by the performer except to a collecting society
for enforcing the right, that is, it is unwaivable. Unlike copyright proper,
which lasts 70 years, performers' property rights and the recording right last
for 50 years.

Performers enjoyed this right in some European countries (for example,
Sweden and Denmark) prior to the Rental Directive; in the UK, however, the
adoption of the Rental Directive has necessitated changes in the administration
of royalties and remuneration. In order to predict the economic outcome of
these changes, data were collected on performers' earnings in Sweden and
Denmark and compared to the UK. The only comparable data available were
those on the remuneration to musicians for the public performance of sound
recordings. The data were obtained from the relevant collecting societies.

Throughout Europe, there are somewhat different practices concerning
collecting societies. In the UK there are some 20 collecting societies for
various rights.[4] In Sweden, SAMI is the collecting society that specialises in

performers' rights and in Denmark, GRAMEX administers rights of record companies and performers. Each collecting society has a monopoly of the administration of those right(s). In the UK, the natural monopoly (due to network costs) of the societies over these specific rights has been accepted as beneficial by the government's anti-trust body, the Monopolies and Mergers Commission (MMC); that has not stopped them, however, from investigating collecting societies, specifically the Performing Right Society (PRS) and Phonographic Performance Ltd (PPL) (reported in MMC, 1988; and MMC, 1996). Elsewhere, however, the monopoly was not tolerated: the anti-trust body in Germany ruled that GEMA, the German performing rights collecting society, was an unacceptable monopoly. In the USA, ASCAP, which administers performing rights, was forced to accept competition from BMI.

It is well known that collecting societies' administrative costs (borne by the membership) vary a lot from country to country and from society to society.[5] But there are also costs of complying with the law and changes to copyright law have transaction costs to users. These costs must also be taken into account when evaluating copyright policy.

Huge question marks hang over the future of implementing copyright because of digitalisation. Technical changes could assist in reducing the costs of collecting and distributing royalties; already SAMI in Sweden and GRAMEX in Denmark and Finland are linked by computer. We can expect to see increasing co-operation between national societies, perhaps even mergers which could reduce costs. But they would also extend the monopoly power of collecting societies and may fall foul of anti-monopoly laws which are being strengthened in the European Union through its competition policy.

DISTRIBUTION OF ROYALTIES TO INDIVIDUAL MUSICIANS

Finally, we reach the point in the chapter at which it is possible to provide empirical evidence on the value of copyright. In order to assess the extent to which copyright law provides an incentive to creative activity, and ultimately, whether changing the law can improve that, it is necessary to know how much individuals earn from their rights. Collecting society data provide a basis for this information as distributions are done on an individual basis. In the UK, each society administers a restricted range of rights, and sometimes, as in the case of Phonographic Performance Ltd (PPL), the record industry collecting society, only one right is administered, in this case that of the public performance of sound recording. New data have been obtained by the author on distributions to individual musicians in the UK for the six years 1989–95;

this was administered (in a lump) by the Musicians' Union (MU) prior to the formation of PAMRA. The sum collected by PPL and passed on to the MU for distribution to backing musicians amounted in 1994 to £3.3m.[6]

Table 6.2 shows the distribution by band of income to musicians in the UK in the left-hand column. Nearly 9000 musicians received payment. The top earner received £44 630. With these distributions so obviously skewed, the median is the measure of what the typical performer earned. The median individual payment was £450 for the six years, an average of £75 per year.[7] These figures for the UK may be compared with those for musicians in Sweden and Denmark, where performers have had these rights for over 20 years. The other two columns of Table 6.2 show figures for individual distributions obtained by the author from SAMI in Sweden, which specifically collects royalties from performers' rights, and for GRAMEX in Denmark, which collects for performers and record companies. The median Swedish performer in SAMI received less than 250 Krone in 1994 (£21) and the median Danish performer in 1995 received between 250 and 999 Danish Krone (£28–114) for performers' rights (including for the blank tape levy, which does not exist in the UK). As we can see, a few performers do very well; the majority does not. These figures do not suggest that the performers' right considerably improves performers' earnings. Nor does it significantly increase the incentive to supply. In 1990, a musician working in a West End musical in London (these musicians often do sessions work in the daytime) typically earned £22 000.[8] Clearly they could earn more from one three-hour session fee (£90), which includes a buy-out for rights from sales, than from the typical annual payment to performers for secondary use, that is, that to which performers' rights now entitle them. However, entitlement to the annual payment lasts for a period of 50 years; how much the musicians eventually receive depends on the value of public performance over the duration of the right (the present value of £75 over 50 years is £1182 at a 6 per cent discount rate).

These figures do not tell us what individual musicians earn in total from all their copyright and performers' rights. A survey of artists would be necessary to establish what they earn from different sources. What data from one collecting society show is the value to individual artists of a specific right. They show a consistent pattern and suggest that the amounts can make only a marginal impact on artists' earnings even over a 50 year period (assuming the recording was in use for so long). The incentive value of this change in the law for the majority of performers must, therefore, be doubted. On the other hand, it will increase transactions costs of collection and distribution of royalties and also the costs to users. These costs could possibly raise the price for the final product. The evidence therefore raises questions about the value of legal intervention to raise the earnings of performers, specifically whether the Rental Directive could be said to assist them; I maintain that it cannot.

Table 6.2 Distribution of remuneration from the public performance of sound recordings to individual musicians in the UK, Sweden and Denmark (various dates)

UK 1989–95		Sweden 1994		Denmark 1995	
Band of distributed income (£)	Musicians (%)	Band of distributed income Krone	Musicians (%)	Band of distributed income Krone	Musicians (%)
0–90	12	0–249	75	0–49	32
91–200	16	250–999	16	259–999	52
201–500	24	1000–4999	8	1000–2999	9
501–1000	16	5000–9999	1	3000–4999	2
1000–2000	14	10000–49999	1	5000–9999	2
2001–5000	12	50000–99999	>1	10000–19999	>1
5001–10000	5	100000+	>1	20000–29999	>1
>10000	1			30000+	>1
Total	100	Total	100	Total	100

Note: These figures should be divided by six to obtain an annual amount.

Source: Data provided by Musicians' Union to the author.

Note: In 1994, there were 7.7 Swedish Krone to the US dollar, 9.2 to the ECU and 11.8 to the £ sterling.

Source: Data provided by SAMI to the author.

Note: In 1995, there were 5.6 Danish Krone to the US dollar, 7.3 to the ECU and 8.8 to the £ sterling.

Source: Data provided by GRAMEX to the author.

CONCLUSION

Just as earlier economists analysed the underlying economic rationale for copyright law, I have shown there is an economic logic to the royalty system of payment for the use of copyright.

Following Plant (1934), I have questioned the view implicit in all other economic literature on copyright of a harmony of interest or synergy between author and publisher and shown that the bargaining over risk-sharing is played out in the method of payments – royalties or flat fee buy-outs. By adopting a principal–agent model of incentives to author and publisher, the trade-off is exposed between risk-bearing over the life of the copyrighted work, the amount of effort at marketing and maintaining the reputation of the work and the transaction costs inherent in the different payment methods. The drafters of the Rental Directive attempted to counteract market forces by making some performers' rights unwaivable. It seems unlikely that they took account of the economic arguments for and against buy-outs in so doing.

The analysis naturally leads to the question of policy implications. Would strengthening or extending copyright law result in higher earnings to artists that could increase the incentive to creative activity? Can the bargaining position of artists be improved by regulation? Even if such measures were applied, how would they affect the costs of collection and monitoring use? The approach of economists is to ask if the marginal improvement in benefits would outweigh the extra costs over time. At present we do not have sufficient data to answer these questions fully. The empirical data in this chapter, however limited, are the first attempt to estimate the individual value of specific rights under copyright law. What they show is that, despite high aggregate earnings from copyright in the music industry, the vast majority of musicians earn relatively little from specific copyright and performers' rights. The large sums of royalty income that copyright law enables to be collected goes mainly to the publishers (music publishers and record companies) and to a small minority of high earning performers and writers. These are persons who can defend their own interests in the market place by virtue of their bargaining power and ability to hire advisers (managers, lawyers and accountants) to control their own affairs by contractual arrangements.

This does not imply that there is no case for copyright. Property rights must clearly be defined and enforceable for markets to work. Copyright law provides the framework for transactions in the cultural industries and enables artists (authors and performers) and firms to appropriate returns to their investment, thereby increasing the incentive to supply.

How much is earned is, however, a market outcome and the division of revenues is governed by complex interactions between economic incentives and administrative arrangements. Any attempt to regulate these outcomes must take account of the underlying economic logic of the organisation of the industries concerned and recognise that regulation may impose costs, not only on those directly involved, but also on society at large.

NOTES

* The author is grateful to Professor Francesco Silva and Dr Giovanni Ramello and to two anonymous referees of *Kyklos* for their helpful comments on earlier drafts of the chapter. The research reported here was financed by a grant L126251011 from the UK Economic and Social Research Council Media Economics and Media Culture Programme and conducted with the research assistance of Millie Taylor at the University of Exeter. The opinions expressed in this chapter are the author's and should not be taken to reflect those of any of the people or organisations involved. Any errors or omissions are the author's.

1. This issue is increasingly being questioned in the literature of cultural studies. See, for example, Woodmansee (1994, pp. 35–55). For an economist's view, see Frank (1996).
2. See Caves (2000) for a comprehensive treatment of optimal contract theory to the creative industries.
3. The choice of this particular right from the bundle is somewhat arbitrary and is due to the fact that empirical data relating to it were obtainable. It does not really matter which right is analysed as the economic arguments would be the same for each. However, until further empirical research is done on the value of each right in turn, it is not possible to say how 'representative' the earnings from equitable remuneration for sound recording are of other individual rights.
4. The income of the collecting societies in the UK music industry in 1994 was:

Performing Right Society (PRS)	£167.6m
Mechanical Copyright Protection Society (MCPS)	£130.1m
Phonographic Performance Ltd. (PPL)	£ 39.8m
Video Performance Ltd. (VPL)	£8.6m
Total	£346.1m

Source: Societies' Annual Reports and Dane et al. (1996). The total value-added of the UK music industry was estimated to be £2.5bn.

5. See Chapter 5.
6. See Chapter 5 for full details and discussion.
7. It should be noted that averaging the figures over the six-year period disguises the fact that PPL revenues are growing; they rose by 34 per cent from 1992/93-1993/94 and 11 per cent the next year.
8. Figure communicated to the author by the Musicians' Union.

PART IV

Copyright and cultural policy for the
information age

7. Copyright, risk and the artist: an economic approach to policy for artists*

INTRODUCTION

While most countries have an arts policy, few have a specific policy on artists. Training and higher education for creative and performing artists is often subsidised or directly provided by the state but support stops at the point of entry to the labour market. In some countries, particularly the Nordic countries, there is a systematic policy of supporting artists by providing them with a regular income.[1] In the USA and the UK, however, little direct financial aid is given to artists and it would not be an easy task to explain exactly what policy towards artists is.

Two developments in the UK have provided the motivation for this chapter; one is the increasing emphasis on copyright law as a means of supporting artists through the establishment and protection of their property rights in preference to direct grants; this was first stated as a clear policy in the UK in *A Creative Future* (Arts Council, 1993a) but the emphasis on copyright has pervaded many subsequent policy statements. The second is the introduction in the UK of NESTA, the National Endowment for the Sciences, Technology and the Arts, financed from the National Lottery with a specific purpose of sustaining new talent.[2] These two developments represent the opposite ends of a spectrum of doing nothing to support artists beyond according them property rights to arm them in the market place and the novel possibility of offering individual artists substantial financial support to develop their talent entrepreneurially. This juxtaposition was intriguing because my work on copyright has emphasised risk as its economic rationale. The enormous success of the National Lottery, due, of course, to the public's willingness to gamble, has led to a considerable increase in funds for the arts since a share of the proceeds is dedicated to them, a feature that was built into the lottery from the start.[3] Yet the public barely supports *artistic* risk-taking by creative individuals who gamble heavily on a small chance of making a successful career. NESTA allows these two activities to be co-ordinated.

The notion of a lottery can also be used metaphorically because art as a profession, like the legal profession to which Adam Smith memorably referred in 1776 in *The Wealth of Nations*, is a lottery.[4] This seems an appropriate characterisation of artistic behaviour in markets, which are increasingly dominated by superstardom.[5] Thus several strands of work in cultural economics are drawn together to assess a policy of supporting artists through NESTA. Starting with the general arguments about market failure and state intervention, I go on to discuss copyright law as a response to market failure caused by risk in cultural markets. The next topic to be surveyed is artists' labour markets and the role of royalties in artists' earnings. I then discuss incentives to artists and the possible role of NESTA.

THE ECONOMIC APPROACH TO POLICY ON ARTISTS

The standard economic justification of state intervention, whether by economic, political or legal measures, is market failure – the failure of the market system to allocate resources efficiently through prices. Equity or social justice also justifies intervention but most economists would regard efficiency arguments as making the stronger case. Market failure may be 'corrected' by economic incentives (taxes and/or subsidies), direct provision, as with state provided education and health, or by the creation or adjustment of property rights, that is, regulation. This economic approach is applied to a wide range of social and economic problems, including arts provision. Policy on artists can be approached in the same way, that is, we may discuss grants (subsidy) to artists and copyright laws as alternative means of overcoming market failure in the labour market for artists. Seeing these as alternative policy options is not only the approach taken by economists; I believe that this has been the stance of arts policy-makers in the UK until NESTA. But to pursue the economic agenda, first the case must be made that there is market failure which calls for some intervention to assist artists.

One of the difficulties of making a case for assisting artists is that there is generally a plenteous supply of them, even an over-supply: more artists offer themselves and their work to the market than there is demand for their services and products, even at very low prices, with the result that artists' earnings are on average lower than those of other workers of equivalent educational achievement. Of course, this statement depends to some extent on how an artist is defined but by now there has been a lot of work on this question, which shows evidence of over-supply whatever definition is adopted.[6] Over-supply is undoubtedly in part linked to generous state subsidies or, in some countries, free provision for training artists (which in the UK took the form of free tuition plus maintenance grants until 1998). This is public policy failure rather than market failure, since the policy is what causes the undesired labour market outcome. However, it is important to distinguish between established artists and new entrants or trainees; this paper is concerned with artists already practising, who so far in the UK have received little financial support (by contrast to arts students). I hope to provide a persuasive case that established artists merit financial support even though it has to be recognised that this could act as a further incentive to supply an already crowded labour market.

Why might the labour market for artists fail? Some economists hold that it does not, that markets can work efficiently in the arts as they do elsewhere; for example, Cowen (1998) argues vehemently that markets do work in the arts. Others, such as cultural studies and literary specialists, but also some economists, notably Klamer (1996), argue the complete opposite: they believe that the equation of value with price is wrong; price cannot measure aesthetic value.[7] An intermediate position is taken by those such as Waits and McNertney (1980) and Santos (1976) who argue that markets fail because artists face higher risk and uncertainty than do other workers; mean earnings are lower and their variance higher than in other professional occupations. Labour markets, along with other markets in the arts, might also fail because of information problems, particularly with respect to quality; one that artists share with scientists, is their inability to appropriate in full the benefits of their work because of strong externalities (such as style, creativity, trend-setting and so on); this idea is put forward by Wijnberg (1994).

Just as the case for state support for R&D for science and technology can be made on the grounds of market failure, so it can be made for supporting creativity in the arts. The question is how should this be done – by subsidy to institutions or to artists or by regulation through intellectual property law that creates property rights but leaves the market to determine the reward to economic agents. Arts policy in the UK emphasises the latter approach and we therefore hear a great deal about copyright (or rather about piracy, the failure of copyright to be implemented). The role of copyright for artists is increasingly emphasised in other countries too.

MARKET POWER AND ITS INFLUENCE ON THE EARNING POWER OF ARTISTS

Much is made of the size of the cultural sector and the economic importance of the 'copyright-based' industries but there has been little research on the distribution of revenues within the industries and on how much individual artists earn from copyright. Although we do not have comprehensive data on the distribution of royalties, there is enough partial data to indicate trends; these confirm what is anyway already well known about artists' total earnings, namely that a few superstars make very high incomes but most artists earn less than the national average. Artists' earnings and other aspects of artists' labour markets were discussed in detail in Chapter 3. In this section, I argue that an unintended consequence of copyright is that it has facilitated the development of large multinational corporations in parts of the cultural sector of most countries by the creation and protection for 50 or 70 years of valuable, tradable assets. This has lead to artists' bargaining power being increasingly weakened with the growth of large firms that are strengthened by copyright law.

Though there is mutual interest between author and publisher to produce successful works that earn them the greatest return, there is huge scope for friction between them within that general proviso. The royalty system of payment goes some way to secure a mutual interest because it ties author and publisher in to joint entrepreneurship and risk-sharing.[8] However, the share of revenue and of outlay is almost certain to be unequal and the contribution of one party rather than the other to the eventual success or failure of the product difficult to gauge.

The mirror image of the weaker bargaining power of authors is the stronger bargaining power of publishers. The industries that make up the cultural sector have a typical oligopolistic structure, that is, a few large firms dominate, there is little price competition and many small firms are tolerated as long as they only occupy niches in the market and do not contest the position of the dominant firms. The firms in these industries are multinational and multi-product. Their growth has been assisted by the amalgamation of assets that are copyrights (playing much the same role as patents in manufacturing industries). It is worthwhile explaining the origin of these assets, as it makes them unlike other capital assets.

We are all familiar with the idea that paintings and other works of art in the form of objects may be bought as assets and wealth stored in art. Less familiar is the idea that a performance that is recorded in some medium has value as a source of future income. Its value would probably not be great as a collectible but since it can be used to produce copies, it is a business investment. Without performances being recorded, performers have to be hired and paid for each appearance and that was, indeed, the situation before the production of sound recordings, films and the rest. The recording therefore translates the human skill of the performer, which performed live must perforce require the physical presence of the person, into a master tape (or whatever) that can be reproduced without the labour of the performer. The performance is thus transformed from labour to capital and as such may be purchased and exchanged on the market without the intervention of the artist, unless some restraint is placed on this trade. Copyright, and in particular the moral right, places some restraint on it by giving the performer the right to authorise the use of their recorded performance. However, that right is limited and is exhausted once it has been exercised so that, for example, once a singer has contracted with a record company to make a sound recording, the performance becomes the property of the record company. Of course, the record company must pay the singer a fee or royalty but this is a small percentage and anyway the singer cannot stop the record company from marketing the record (in agreed territories); nor can she force it to promote the work. What is important for the argument being made here is that the record company with which the singer made the original contract can sell the master tape and the rights to its use to another firm without the singer's consent. Thus firms may take over copyright assets as part of their growth process.[9]

So far, all that has been said is that the establishment of property rights by copyright law enables trade to take place. But copyright law does something else too; it determines the life of the asset by the duration of copyright protection, 50 or 70 years, depending on the work. Clearly the longer the duration, the greater the value of the copyright asset. The intention of protecting the economic interest of the author or performer by a longer-lasting copyright is precisely what has enabled the formation of large corporations with considerable market power. Ironically, the unintended consequence is that authors have to bargain with more powerful firms than they would have to were copyrights weaker and of shorter duration. Only superstar artists and their heirs have sufficient market power to strike a bargain on equal terms.

There is a further aspect to the economic effect of the duration of copyright: the longer it lasts, the greater the chance that the market for the work will change in ways that could not be predicted at the time of the original contract. We have seen this with back catalogues of films, TV programmes and sound recordings, for which new broadcasting techniques and markets worldwide have provided a large demand. Economists usually argue that such unpredictable events lead to losers as well as winners. The point is that winners are assisted by copyright law in their gains. These are not assets traded in a free market but ones that get pure economic rent from statutorily created property rights.

The problem of unequal power and the need to counteract it is recognised by law-makers, specifically by the EC Rental Directive and generally by the creation of statutory tribunals to mediate copyright disputes; this is done in the UK by the Copyright Tribunal.[10] Most countries have a similar body performing the same role of regulating and/or mediating between parties for the use of copyright material.

The question is what is the effect on artists' earnings and incentives? Without protection of their property rights by copyright law, artists would not be able to appropriate the value of their output. On the other hand, I have argued that copyrights are a double-edged sword that are instrumental in the growth of large corporations with huge market power and bargaining power over the division of revenues that only really successful artists (or really strong artists' unions) can assail. A balance must be maintained between the need to provide artists with protection of their incomes – and thus an economic incentive to supply their work – and monopoly power generated by copyright (or other intellectual property law). I believe, that in practice, this balance tips in favour of firms in the cultural industries rather than artists (the authors and performers). Regulation by copyright law is not an alternative to subsidies and there is an economic case for some form of financial assistance to artists.

INCENTIVES TO ARTISTS

Surveys of artists have shown that what artists most want from arts policy is a means of buying time to devote to art work.[11] The research on determinants of artistic supply, reported in Chapter 3, has shown that artists respond to an increase in payment for the time they devote to the production of art, while an increase in non-arts pay causes them to switch to more hours of art work; thus artists are responsive to pecuniary incentives and we could expect greater artistic output to result from a programme of financial assistance to artists. This is an important finding for the argument of this chapter because it shows that the supply of art can be increased by policy measures. The question is whether this is achieved better by direct subsidy or indirectly through the market by copyright regulations.

Market failure in the arts could lead to under-production of risky new art and threaten artistic quality. Artists, many of whom should be viewed as entrepreneurs, inevitably take risks in untried markets with new products. The economic rationale for copyright as a means of overcoming market failure because of risk has already been explained. Both authors and publishers take risks; the risk to the latter, that is, to firms in the cultural industries, is accepted as meriting special consideration; in the UK, the Monopolies and Mergers Commission viewed copyright as a necessity in an industry as risky as sound recording (MMC, 1996).

My argument is that artists have an even stronger case for special measures on these same grounds; risk is not symmetric between firms and artists because firms have far greater advantages in the market place. Artists cannot spread risks as firms can because they have a limited portfolio of their own copyright assets whereas a firm can spread risk over many artists' works. Artists' assets are often concentrated in human capital, which means they have little collateral to offer the capital market, by contrast to firms, which have capital assets as collateral. Artists make a considerable outlay of training, time and forgone income in developing unique works; they bear the burden of research and development in the arts. Firms (think of art dealers, record companies, shops buying craftwork, literary and music publishers) can pick the lines they think will be successful without financing the R&D. If markets were competitive, artists would be compensated in the price paid for their work (whether royalty rate or spot price). One reason why markets are uncompetitive is because copyright law makes them so, strengthening, as I have argued, the position of firms (publishers) *vis-à-vis* artists (authors).

In economic language this is a classic case of second best. When distortion occurs (or is created) in a market, destroying the possibility of a first best Pareto optimal allocation of resources, some compensating intervention is justified on the grounds of economic efficiency. This argument supports some form of assistance to artists, such as grants, loans or prizes to encourage creative risk-taking.[12] I concentrate here on grants, which, however, could be converted into loans with a scheme that had provision for repayment by successful artists, say, out of royalty earnings.

GRANTS TO ARTISTS: NESTA

There is an inbuilt reluctance to give direct financial grants to individual artists. This is odd in a country like the UK which has extensive means-tested and universal state welfare payments, grants to small businesses and, at one time, an Enterprise Allowance Scheme designed to enable unemployed individuals to get started as self-employed enterprises, unintentionally benefiting artists. There are, of course, particular problems associated with grants to artists because of the difficulty of assessing output and even of who can be said to be an artist. There are also moral hazard problems of providing incentives to artists, on the one hand to do work that could not meet market criteria, and on the other, to put their feet up and do nothing! Also, any extra support to artists might be interpreted as encouragement to even greater supply of trainee artists. These are standard public finance problems for expenditures from tax revenues.

The National Lottery in the UK and especially the introduction of NESTA (National Endowment for Science, Technology and the Arts) have created the opportunity for a new approach to arts policy as well as new money which is earmarked specifically for the purposes of fostering talent and enterprise in the arts. There seems to be poetic justice in the transformation of the expenditure of gamblers who gain pleasure from taking risks into the provision of insurance for those who are forced to take risks as part of creative activity! The National Lottery already has in place administrative arrangements for the processing and assessment of grants to small-scale arts projects, particularly those of the Arts for Everyone scheme (A4E Express) which distributed over £20m in 1997/98 to many organisations that had not previously had arts subsidy.[13] Artists applying to NESTA for development of their work should similarly be asked to submit a business plan and evidence of past output, sales and income as would any other applicant. The grants should be targeted at risky creative work or performances that would not normally attract tax-based grants from tax-based arts subsidy. It must be accepted that offering the chance to succeed inevitably means that many recipients will produce work that does not succeed in the market place. Art itself is a lottery.

CONCLUSION

At the heart of discussions on subsidy to the arts is a fundamental confusion: do we give subsidies to popular work that attracts large audiences so that taxpayers 'get their money back' or do we give subsidies to new, difficult, not yet (or maybe never) popular work that could not succeed in the market place? This discussion is often couched in terms of access and quality or equity and efficiency in economic language. Fostering creativity, a phrase much used by arts policy-makers and by none more than the present (2000) UK government, is an objective of cultural policy in most countries and there is economic justification for subsidy for it. Yet the pattern of state subsidy to the arts rarely bears out that objective (see Towse, 1994). Subsidy mainly goes to large established arts organisations rather than to small new ones, even though it is widely acknowledged that creativity and innovation stem from small-scale or even one-person enterprises.

Cultural economics tells us that there is market failure in arts markets but it cannot tell us how much subsidy would overcome it. This is a problem of economics in general and may be found in the economics of education, health or any area of life in which social benefits exceed what people pay in user charges. Cultural economists have also tried to tackle the problem of measuring both the quantity and quality of cultural production. Those who argue that the market is capable of producing the socially desirable quantity and quality of art reject the notion of absolute standards of quality. But even free marketeers recognise that cultural production requires copyright and other property rights to be established for the market to work.

This chapter argues that copyright inevitably distorts markets by strengthening publishers (firms) more than it protects authors (artists). This distortion requires correction by some means of countervailing power to assist artists. NESTA in the UK would seem to be a serendipitous opportunity to offer small-scale grants or loans to artists to encourage risky creative activity financed by the voluntary tax of the National Lottery. The same economic argument can also be applied to other schemes for supporting artists and entrepreneurship in the cultural industries out of taxation. It is just that the lottery of art and art from the Lottery seem so well-matched.

NOTES

*An earlier version of this chapter was presented at the 10th International Conference of the Association for Cultural Economics International in Barcelona in 1998 and also at the universities of Groningen and Erasmus, Rotterdam in the Netherlands. I am grateful to several people attending these presentations, to Andrew Burke, David Throsby and Mark Schuster for comments. The chapter has been abridged to avoid repetition with material in previous chapters of this book.

1. Finland is an example of this and considerable research on the economic side of policy towards artists has been done by the Arts Council of Finland over a number of years. See Heikkinen and Koskinen (1998) for a recent publication on this topic that draws together international experience.

2. NESTA was first proposed in the government White Paper *The People's Lottery*, Cm. 3709; it is administered by the Arts Council of England. See Arts Council of England (1998).

3. The Arts Councils of England, Scotland, Wales and Northern Ireland received 5.6 per cent, amounting to £822m, from the start of the National Lottery in late 1994 to mid 1997. See Creigh-Tyte and Ling in Heikkinen and Koskinen *op. cit.*

4. 'In a perfectly fair lottery, those who draw the prizes ought to gain all that is lost by those who draw the blanks. ... The lottery of the law ... is very far from being a perfectly fair lottery; and that, as well as many liberal and honourable professions, are, in point of pecuniary gain, evidently under-recompensed.' (Adam Smith, 1776[1976], pp. 122–3).

5. See Chapter 4 of this book.

6. See Chapter 2 of this book and O'Brien in Heikkinen and Koskinen *op. cit.* See also in that volume chapters by Alper and Wassall, Solhjell, Karttunen and Karhunen relating to the US, Norway and Finland.

7. Klamer's inaugural lecture as Professor of Cultural Economics resulted in a whole publication, Klamer (1996), devoted to the topic.

8. This is explained in detail in Chapter 6.

9. This trade was the basis of the George Michael case (Panayiotou v. Sony Music Entertainment (UK) Ltd.) (1994) EMLR 229.

10. For details, see Chapter 5.

11. See Chapter 3.

12. See Chapter 1.

13. See *The Arts Council of England Annual Report 1998*.

8. Incentives and access to information: economic aspects of limitations and exceptions to copyright in the digital world*

1 THE ECONOMIC LITERATURE

Introduction

Nearly all policy-making in practice involves making choices that benefit some group at the expense of others. That is also the case in the topic studied here, access to information provided digitally over the Internet. One current policy concern is this: digitalisation makes it technically possible to keep tabs on a number of things that in an analogue world were difficult and expensive to identify – the authorship of every piece of information; the owner of the copyright of every piece of information; the user gaining access to that information; and a means of charging users for or preventing them from using information that they do not pay for. The 'information' in question potentially includes a lot of what we now think of as cultural provision – music, literature, films, television programmes, visual art; I do not wish to suggest (as some people do who are overly excited by the digital revolution) that this will happen overnight; it will not. However, important questions, including the appropriate legal framework of copyright law, are being considered now which could influence the quality and nature of the supply of information goods and consumers' access to them. This has clear implications for cultural policy.

These implications are being debated in Europe, in the USA and worldwide by the World Intellectual Property Organisation. There is an increasing literature in law and economics on the subject. The change that this technical development could bring about is that material that users previously had free can now be charged for. However, this is not just a simple piece of economic arithmetic: copyright law embodies within its doctrines the trade-off between the protection of authors and publishers and the rights of citizens to freedom of information and freedom of expression. Copyright is a statutory monopoly and to counteract the reduction in access that this makes possible by enabling authors and publishers to charge higher prices, some unauthorised use (that means the author does not have to be asked for permission) without payment is allowed by law as an exception to copyright. There are other exceptions and limitations to copyright, such as the freedom to quote, parody and cite for criticism. They are collectively known as fair dealing in the UK and fair use in the USA. These freedoms may now be lost as authors could charge for each use and also block use. Thus the issue is one of balancing incentives to authors and publishers to create and supply information with access to information.[1]

The purpose of this chapter is to review the economic literature on limitations and exceptions to copyright and to try to provide some estimates of their value. The empirical analysis concentrates on fair dealing in the UK. That may be thought of either as the income lost by copyright owners due to fair use or as the amount users would have to pay if fair use were no longer to be free. The figures could only be produced by extremely rough-and-ready calculations; they should be treated with great caution! Still, the problem is an interesting one and the substantive issues are obviously of considerable importance to cultural economists and policy-makers.

Economics of Fair Use and Fair Dealing

There is a considerable literature on fair use/fair dealing but even on a broad definition, there is little that could be called 'economic'. None is empirical. Landes and Posner (1989) make an interesting distinction between the economics of copyright and the economics of copying. I have surveyed both literatures and condensed them here.[2]

The economic view of fair dealing is concerned with efficiency questions in contrast to the justice approach taken by lawyers.[3] Economists have two notions of efficiency: private efficiency is the optimal use of resources where all costs and benefits are paid through the market; social efficiency encompasses private efficiency but recognises that all of society's aspirations cannot be met through unregulated market exchange and, in addition, markets cannot always price costs and benefits. State intervention seeks to achieve social efficiency where markets do not do so. Intervention, however, alters relative prices and therefore incentives to producers and consumers and these distortions must be minimised. Thus this type of welfare economic analysis by economists has a counterpart in the legal doctrine of balancing different interests. The statutory benefits to authors and publishers conferred by copyright have costs to users (consumers) that can be counterbalanced by exceptions and limitations. Fair dealing and fair use may be viewed as a means of compensating consumers for higher prices.

Following the forgoing analysis, several issues may be identified as the economic aspects of fair dealing:

- Substitutability: depending upon the extent of substitutability between a copy and the 'original' – say a photocopy of part of a book and the book itself – there would be loss of potential revenue and consequent diminution of the incentive to supply.
- Relative prices of copies and 'original': if copying is very expensive and the original cheap, consumers will prefer the original and *mutatis mutandis*.
- Transaction costs of copying in relation to its value to the user.

These general points are discussed with application to the two specific areas of empirical investigation reported below: photocopying for educational purposes and off-air recording of broadcasts in the UK.

Substitutability
Substitution is governed by a combination of 'technical' factors, such as the similarity between two or more goods, and their relative prices. People make their choices between the 'original' and a copy by weighing up their preference for each, bearing in mind the difference in price between them. The theory assumes there is an effective choice between the original and a copy; this is often not so. In the case of broadcasts used for education purposes, it is very unlikely that a school or college would create its own programme; without copying, the experience would not be available.[4] The photocopying of books and journals has other exceptional features. The choice is not effective where books are out of print, as many of those still in copyright are.[5] Second-hand markets do exist (and are serviced by agents who match buyers and sellers) but they are a cumbersome means of access to out-of-print material. Scientific journals are a different question; they serve highly specialised professional markets (and are priced accordingly). Very few students are likely subscribers to any journal and their primary means of access to information in journals is study in the library or through photocopies. A further point is that there is unlikely to be a close substitute for specific articles, because one author is hardly a substitute for another and also because teachers direct students to specific material. The notion of substitutability carries quality as well as quantity implications and, although this is a market for information, information about that information is particularly difficult and time-consuming to acquire without guidance. The increasing use by teachers of coursepacks of photocopied materials reflects one or more of the above problems.

The role of relative prices
The relative prices of copies and the original only come into play where there *is* effective choice between the two, that is, where substitution can take place. In general, consumers' willingness to pay for an item depends on the strength

of their desire for it, their incomes, the proportion of their budget spent on this item and prices of alternatives. Fair dealing allows copies to be made by individuals for their own use and therefore reduces the market for paid-for copies and the 'potential' revenue of authors and publishers. Beyond the limits of fair dealing, there is a market for copies – let us say photocopies for teaching purposes – and we can see that major purchasers of photocopying, such as local educational authorities and universities, may well scrutinise this use of their budgets and decide between the number of copies of a book they purchase and how much photocopying of it they are prepared to pay for. Relative prices influence this decision. Their ability to pass the cost of photocopying on to students by charging for use of photocopy machines and so on will also influence the decision. Clearly, government policy on student numbers, student loans, funding per place and suchlike has an effect on choice between primary and secondary markets (where purchase of material is primary use and photocopying is secondary use of the material).[6] In schools, educational policy on modes of learning and so on may also influence choice of textbooks versus copies of a wider range of publications.

Transaction and compliance costs

Gordon (1982) gives the size of transaction costs in relation to the value of copying to the user as the main economic rationale for fair use; the same reasoning is used to justify blanket and compulsory licensing. If users had to contact authors/publishers individually for authorisation to legally copy each work, for example, by photocopying, the value of the copy would be greatly exceeded by the costs of compliance and transacting and no market would exist. In such circumstances, legal provision such as fair dealing and compulsory licensing can 'artificially' create a market (which, however, will not work according to market principles, because the price is set by the legal process).[7] Fair dealing is mostly permitted when the value of the use is small to individual consumers. The problem is that the sum of all individual small uses may add up to deprive authors and publishers of considerable revenue – hence their membership of copyright collectives and blanket licensing. The costs to users partly depend upon how well markets are organised and on the technology available for record-keeping. ISBN and ISSN coding has already made tracing of authors vastly easier and digital delivery is likely to reduce costs of obtaining permissions (compliance), tracing users and of collecting remuneration.

In Chapter 1, the economic analysis by Meurer (1997) and Bell (1998) of the impact of digitalisation on fair use was discussed.

Meurer and Bell believe that the ability to charge will increase with digitalisation but that charges will become more fine-tuned with greater price discrimination and that price discrimination will in turn increase as markets become more separated. Both anticipate that individual contracting between user and supplier of copyright material will become prevalent. Hence, fears of wholesale rights evasion becomes just another in a long series of industry 'panics' (Litman, 1994). Litman lists a series of technical changes, starting with piano rolls and continuing through photocopying, home taping and videoing, which representatives of established industries attempted to stifle because they feared loss of income; these changes, however, came eventually not only to be accommodated by markets, but even to increase the market size overall. She sees the move to digital technology as merely another such change. Governments should therefore adopt a policy of wait-and-see before leaping in with new legislation.

Summary
The demand for material in the form of copies or originals may be thought of as a demand for particular pieces of information, and the means of delivery (as opposed to content) may well not matter to the consumer in some cases, such as scholarly articles. As the quality of the copy increasingly approaches the quality of the original, we may expect the demand for copies to grow at the expense of originals unless the price of copies increases or that of originals falls. This is discussed again later. On the cost side, costs of production and royalties are only one aspect; costs also include costs of transacting and complying. Even if these costs are not borne by users directly, someone must pay for them – the local education authority or university in the case of off-air recording and photocopying. The forgone royalty of the author or publisher is the private cost of fair dealing. It is also the cost to users if they did not have benefit of the fair dealing exception. There are in addition external benefits and costs of having copyright protection. The balance of social benefits and costs in considering the welfare effects of copyright (the incentive effect to authors and publishers as against the disincentive to users of higher-than-competitive prices and the costs of complying with copyright law) is the economist's mirror image in efficiency terms of the lawyer's concerns over access versus the author's 'just deserts' in receiving financial reward for her creative effort and the publisher's for her entrepreneurship. In economic terms, fair dealing is a way of redistributing some of the cost of the monopoly of copyright from author to user.

Collecting Societies, Blanket Licensing and Compulsory Licensing

Collecting societies are market solutions to the problem of the high transaction costs of collecting revenue from and monitoring secondary use. They are typically non-profit collectives (co-operatives) and may be analysed as clubs (Besen and Kirkby, 1989a; 1989b).

Membership consists of persons with financial interests in collecting revenue for the use of copyright material; membership may be closed, though open entry is sometimes a statutory requirement; some collecting societies charge a registration fee, while others do not, instead adding the cost of registration to the charge they make for collecting and distributing revenues that they deduct as commission.

Many of the goods and services which incorporate copyright are both sold and licensed. They are sold in primary markets and secondary use is licensed by collecting societies. This is rather difficult to grasp for economists used to thinking about markets in which tangible products are 'taken home' after being sold on the market. Copyright confers several different rights upon authors and publishers of works, which they can sell on to others. Therefore the author of a book may well own the copyright while the publisher owns the reproduction and distribution rights. The idea of setting a price for the sale of objects is familiar but the economics of licence fees is less so, yet a huge amount of trade takes place under licences and this can be expected to increase in the information age.

In general, the owner of a copyright (or other IP) asset, who has a right to future income from secondary use, such as photocopying or public performance, will seek to set a charge for that use (licence fee) that reflects the spot price the asset would fetch if sold outright. This present value reflects the cost of its production, the costs of transacting and maintaining it, the life of the asset or, in the case of IPs, the statutory duration, and the discount rate or interest rate which reflects the returns to their capital owners could get from alternative investments. In practice, though, many copyrights are administered by collective or blanket licensing, which necessarily only approximates the price which the individual owner would set. In some markets for information goods, secondary use generates considerable income, which could easily dominate that from 'first use' – sales of a book or journal article. Copyright owners take account of this in pricing their product for sale.

Collecting societies are mostly, and for good economic reasons, monopoly providers of a specific service, usually the administration of one right or a tight bundle of rights in a particular medium. Because of their monopoly, collecting societies are able to price discriminate, that is, charge some users more than others; this is possible when markets are discrete and no arbitrage can take place. They usually contract by collective agreement with trade associations, charging what the market will bear and in rough accord with the size of the market (number of users). With blanket licensing, the collecting society charges a flat fee to all of one type of user (the fee is discriminatory between different types of users) for the use of the whole repertoire of copyright works which are assigned to the society or the society is licensed to administer. The economic significance of this is that 'high cost/quality' works are charged for alongside 'low cost/quality' works at the same flat rate. Thus incentives and market signals are weakened by blanket licence fees since the distribution of fee income only crudely, if at all, reflects the amount of secondary use made of an individual author's works. That is estimated through surveys and other monitoring devices. So, to take the example of licensing of photocopies in the UK by the Copyright Licensing Agency (CLA), the organisation set up jointly by the Authors' Licensing Collecting Society (ALCS) and the Publishers' Licensing Society (PLS); the CLA sells a blanket licence to users, say, all institutions of higher education, at a standard rate regardless of the sale price of the book.[8] In the USA, the Copyright Clearing Center was set up to provide a similar service.

Does Fair Dealing Necessarily Mean Loss of Income?

It was assumed in the discussion above that fair dealing, as an instance of exceptions to and the limitations of copyright, is not charged for because royalties are not paid to authors for this use of their works and they therefore lose potential income. This is not always the case, however. Academic authors may be *indirectly* compensated by promotion to a higher paid job; academic promotion depends on publication record and even on frequency of citation, that is, on objective bibliometric measures of 'success'. Copyright-owners have other means of gaining economic benefit for copying even with fair dealing; publishers price-discriminate between hardback copies, mostly purchased by libraries, and paperbacks, the extra revenue (which is also passed on in royalties to authors) being some compensation for repeated lending and photocopying of library stock. Scientific journals have two-tier pricing for institutional and individual subscriptions. The ability thus to obtain compensation has led some economists to the view that fair dealing is compensated for and no further remuneration is needed (Liebowitz, 1985).[9]

In some countries the problem of charging for personal copying is dealt with through levies on blank tapes and/or the hardware used for it, for example, by photocopying machines. The UK government has always resisted this approach – for example, unlike many EU countries, the UK has no blank tape levy.

2   EMPIRICAL FINDINGS

Licensing for Secondary Use of Copyright Material in the Education Sector

In this section, we report data on licence income for two forms of secondary use – photocopying and off-air recording in the UK educational sector. The data allow us to approximate income forgone under fair dealing in these areas. There are four agencies involved: the Copyright Licensing Agency (CLA), the Educational Recording Agency (ERA), the Design and Artists' Copyright Society (DACS) and the Newspaper Licensing Agency (NLA). The Copyright Licensing Agency, which was set up by ALCS and PLS (respectively, the Authors' Licensing and Collection Society and the Publishers' Licensing Society), represents the interests of authors and publishers in respect of copying extracts from books, journals and periodicals. The ERA licenses recording and retention of off-air broadcasts (TV and radio) and cable material; members include the BBC, ITV, Channel 4 and so on. The licence is akin to a true blanket licence in that it permits recording for educational purposes of virtually all TV and radio programmes.[10] The Design and Artists' Copyright Society and the Newspaper Licensing Agency are significantly smaller than the CLA or the ERA. DACS deals with copyright clearance for the use of slides of artistic works. The NLA licenses copying of articles from the national daily and Sunday newspapers.

Licences are negotiated with user organisations, local education authorities for schools and Further Education (FE) and the Committee of Vice Chancellors and Principals (CVCP) for Higher Education (HE), the universities and colleges of HE. Tariffs are based on formulas reflecting pupil/student full-time equivalent numbers and a price per item (Table 8.1).

Table 8.1 Summary of the tariffs of the copyright licensing agencies in higher education, 1999

Licensing agency	Tariff formula 1999/2000 prices
The Copyright Licensing Agency	A 'two part' payment system: Part 1: blanket licence fee of £3.09 +VAT per student per year for limited rights[a] Part 2: the CLARCS licence: 5p per A4 sheet in course packs
The Educational Recording Agency	£1.28 per student per year for blanket licence
The Newspaper Licensing Agency	£20 per title per year for blanket licence to reproduce any article within a newspaper
The Design and Artists Copyright Society	Payment on a per slide basis

Note: a. 'Limited rights' is interpreted as: making a single copy of up to one chapter or 5 per cent of a book; one article from an issue of a journal; a report of a case from a set of judicial proceedings. The CLARCS licence permits copying over and above this, for example in the production of course packs, and is negotiated for a bundle of works. This figure rises to £3.25 + VAT for 2000/01.

In 1998, total revenue of the CLA was £19 231 121, up 13 per cent on 1997. Of this, £16 632 232 was generated within the UK, the remainder being payments from foreign licensing agencies for the use of UK copyrighted material (Table 8.2).

Table 8.2   Sources of Copyright Licensing Agency revenue, 1998

Institution	Type	Revenue	Percentage
Education	Schools	£6m	31
	Further education	£3.2m	16
	Higher education	£3.6m	19
Other	Business and government	£3.8m	20
Total UK		£16.63m	86
Total		£19.23m	100

Source: Copyright Licensing Agency *Financial Report*, 1999.

The Education Recording Agency charges a per capita tariff according to the level of educational establishment. Based on 1998 tariffs, we calculated revenues from each level by multiplying pupil/student numbers by the rate charged (Table 8.3).

Table 8.3   Educational Recording Agency licensing income, 1998

Level of education	Tariff	Revenue[a]
Schools: Primary	21p	£3.02m
Secondary	42p	
Further education	78p	£1.29m
Higher education	128p	£1.98m
Estimated total		£6.29m

Note: a. Estimated from ERA tariff and pupil/student numbers (see text).
Source: Educational Recording Agency, 1999.

It is clear from the tariff structure that total pupil/student numbers in UK education, as well as the number in each level, are a crucial factor in explaining the amount of revenues from licensing for educational purposes. The pedagogic requirements of each level are likely to be different with regard to copying copyright material and this partly explains the differential tariff. According to data in the *Annual Abstract of Statistics* (Office of National

Statistics, 1999), there were 9.9 million pupils in primary and secondary education in 1997. Given that education from 5 to 16 years is compulsory, and the population size is reasonably static at the present, this figure is unlikely to change in the near future. In 1987 there were 9.4 million pupils, an increase of 5.3 per cent over the previous 10 year period.

By contrast, the further education (FE) and higher education (HE) sectors, where enrolment is voluntary, have seen big increases in student numbers over the past 20 years. There were 859 600 full-time and 1 575 700 part-time students in FE in the academic year 1996/7. Full-time students had increased by 35 per cent over 10 years. In HE, there were 1 194 600 full-time and 696 900 part-time students. It is difficult to describe growth rates in HE student numbers due to the increased number of degree awarding institutions. Nonetheless, we find a growth rate of 52 per cent within the 'old' universities over the period 1985–93, with student numbers in these institutions increased from 310 145 to 470 565. Student numbers in the HE sector have possibly been growing even faster since then.

Average Rate of Photocopying per Student

We now look at the second factor that influences licence fee income from secondary use and concentrate on photocopying in universities.

The tariff that the CLA sets for the respective education levels is based on *estimated* usage. The CLA engages in a 30-day survey of representative universities and, having established usage, extrapolates an aggregate licence fee on negotiation with university representatives. At present the full tariff is composed of two parts. The latest accord entails an annual blanket licence, and a further CLARCS licence for course-pack productions (see Table 8.1 above). The blanket licence is based for the next year (2000/01) on an estimated photocopying per FTE student in higher education of 65 pages.[11]

Using data from the Standing Conference of National and University Libraries (SCONUL) for the whole HE sector, we calculate the average number of photocopies made per student overall in the UK. This was 200 in 1996/97. We also find that there has been a 2.3 per cent increase in photocopies made over the period 1991/2–1996/7. This is presented in Figure 8.1. It should also be added that aggregate photocopying itself increased by 58.3 per cent (Figure 8.2) but this was almost matched by increases in student numbers over the same period.

Other Factors Influencing Photocopying

Use of university libraries has changed dramatically in recent years in response to changes in technology and the changes in the student constituency.

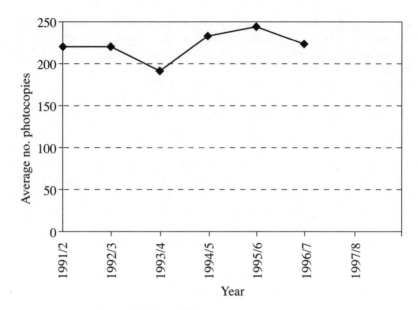

Source: Calculated from SCONUL (1999).

Figure 8.1   Average number of photocopies per HE student in the UK

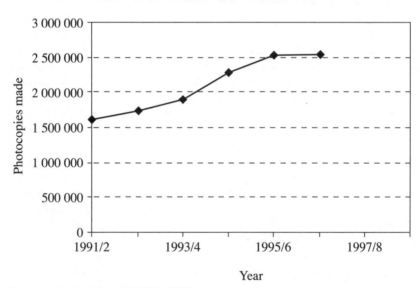

Source: Calculated from SCONUL (1999).

Figure 8.2   Total number of photocopies made by HE students in the UK

Student use of libraries has increased and students purchase fewer books. Two services provided by university libraries are relevant to analysing use of copied material. The first of these is inter-library loans (ILL), an arrangement for borrowing works from other libraries when they are not available *in situ*. Often this entails a request to the British Library, which supplies works to libraries for a fixed fee; in 1999 this was set at £6.40 per work. It is of relevance for the study of copied work use because whenever an article from an academic journal is requested, a photocopy is supplied. The British Library is the biggest single CLA licensee. When full texts are requested, they are supplied in their original form. The total number of inter-library loans in the UK rose dramatically from 17 056 to 209 283 over the period 1991/2 to 1996/7 (SCONUL *Annual Library Statistics*) and this must have entailed an increase in use of photocopies. The second facility of interest to us is material held in libraries for very short-term borrowing – often known as the temporary reserve collection. As student (and library) incomes fall and numbers increase, there is likely to be increased use of material in these collections. We have no information, however, on the breakdown of the type of work copied and whether it is in copyright. Further research is clearly required to establish details of the works being copied in all media and by different users.

3   ESTIMATING THE VALUE OF FAIR DEALING

There are no data on the value of copyright material copied by users in fair dealing. As no authorisation is obtained and no payment made, no record exists of the amounts involved. Therefore, the value of fair dealing can only be estimated from the information that is available for licensed and paid-for copying. We do this from the data presented above, concentrating on one category only, photocopying in higher education. The method adopted is, however, a general one and may be used for all users when the necessary basic information is known.

In order to proceed, we need to make assumptions about how much photocopying students in HE do under fair dealing. In the absence of other guidelines, we made the heroic assumption that they copy for themselves the same number of A4 pages as is covered by the CLA licence. The average figure for HE was calculated to be 220 in 1999 (see Figure 8.3). With approximately 1.5 million FTE students, the quantity for the estimate is therefore 330 million pages.

Choosing a price for the calculation is also an arbitrary decision: the two prices suggested by the CLA data are the 5p a page for the CLARCS licence and 1.1p for the blanket licence. However, it must be stressed that these prices may well not be ones that would apply if all photocopying had to be paid for.

The market would not bear the same price for double the quantity. If students have to pay for what they now get free, they would reduce the amount they photocopy. Using the higher price yields a figure of income 'lost' to authors and publishers due to the fair dealing exception to copyright of £16.5 million and using the second figure produces a much lower estimate of £3.6 million.

These simple calculations clearly demonstrate the factors which determine the total value. A rise in student numbers and/or an increase in the average number of pages photocopied will raise the total; a 10 per cent increase in either – both likely – using the lower of the two figures above would increase the total by £363 000. It must be emphasised, however, that these figures are estimates based on arbitrary assumptions about consumer behaviour, which would change if the underlying factors affecting that behaviour changed. They are crude ballpark figures.

We do not yet have the information needed to undertake the same kind of calculation for photocopying at other educational levels. However, it seems likely that student numbers in FE will rise and, as more schoolchildren are taking Advanced Level examinations, the value of photocopying may be expected to rise here too. And, since the formula for the ERA licence is also based on pupil/student numbers, the same would be true for off-air recording.

4   CONCLUSIONS

Fair dealing is one of the tolerated exceptions and limitations to copyright. It is a concept not defined in the statutes, which provide for it in the UK and the USA (there called fair use), where it is subject to judicial interpretation. This is not the case in some other European countries, where fair dealing is explicitly itemised. An economic analysis of fair dealing based on private efficiency predicts that fair dealing is tolerated in any area covered by copyright where the value to the individual of copying part of a work for her own use is less than the cost of transacting a deal (clearing rights, making payments and so on). To this can also be added the cost of detecting copying, prosecution and so on, that is, of preventing copying from taking place. This applies to photocopying, home taping of audio and audio-visual material and downloading from the Internet. But although the value to the individual user may be small, the aggregated overall effect can be considerable.

To say there is loss of potential income to copyright-holders from fair dealing depends first of all on whether or not a market can be created. Blanket licensing combined with regulation and effective sanctions can 'create a market', in the sense that users can be forced to pay and suppliers to supply to all users; however, that is not a market in the usual economic sense, as prices are administered rather than determined by competition between buyers and sellers. Prices are determined instead by bargaining between bilateral monopolies, such as CLA and ERA transacting with SCONUL representing all university libraries, with the libraries being held responsible for enforcing the agreement and statutory requirements. This model is typical of most markets for secondary use of copyright.

But to say that these are not standard markets is not to say that economic forces do not come into play – they do: demand for copies responds to changes in the price of copies and the price of the original, as well as to users' incomes; moreover, as the cost of the use of copying machinery is low and it is easily available, cheating is extremely easy. The higher the price charged for the copyright element (the royalty or remuneration) in copies, the greater the amount of illegal copying that may be expected to take place. Another aspect specific to HE photocopying is that student use may be charged for by the institution and/or amounts controlled by quota. That happened with inter-library loans when the charge for them increased; in many universities, graduate students were required to pay for them, whereas they had been free to them previously. As university expenditure per student in the UK continues to fall, all library services will be reduced or charged for and this will, on the one hand, exacerbate illegal copying and, on the other, increase the demand for photocopies, as argued earlier. Library, and particularly journal, acquisitions are often controlled by quotas as well as by the budget.

Fair dealing applies outside these negotiated arrangements. There are no figures on the quantity of material copied nor is there a price because there is no market. Therefore approximations have to be made from a 'simulated' market with existing patterns of use and prices. That is what we did in Section 3 above. One caveat to this approach (apart from the inevitably approximate nature of the exercise) is this; fair dealing is free to the user and we would therefore expect figures obtained from such a calculation to underestimate the value of fair dealing, since people would demand more copies at zero price.

These figures could be refined and improved in several ways:

- Surveys can establish what material is being copied, in what quantities and for what reason, for example recommended or required reading.
- Data on library and school book buying patterns per capita can be obtained.
- Student expenditures on study material can be studied.
- Trends in prices of originals (particularly books) and in charges for copies can be charted.
- All the above can be analysed by type of study (sector, level, course).
- A statistical analysis of the determinants of these factors can be undertaken.

It should also be said that the economic stance on fair dealing is entirely pragmatic. From the economic point of view, there is a line in the sand: on one side of it one set of people benefit and on the other side, another set of people does. The same is true of loss, whether of actual or potential income. However, fair dealing may also be viewed as a way of redistributing some of the cost of monopoly of copyright from author to user.

Fair dealing is tolerated because it would be too costly to act otherwise. If new technology introduces new means of delivery, detection of use, prevention of unauthorised use, clearance of rights and charging for the use of copyright material, a 'free' market can develop that will replace fair dealing. This may well be possible with digital technology.

To conclude, some comments may be made about the general economic effects of technological developments which are relevant to policy issues now being considered about the Internet. First, things do not change overnight: technical change is adopted in stages not in one fell swoop. Even if all new material now being created and published were immediately made available on the Internet, there is a huge body of existing publications that are unlikely to be digitalised; students will need photocopies and off-air recordings of analogue material for some years to come. Second, economic progress creates 'losers', be they handloom weavers, printers or miners, who bear the costs of technological and product innovation; governments may alleviate the distributional effects of change for equity reasons but they do not do so for efficiency reasons as they seek to promote economic growth and progress. Potential losers are prone to lobby governments to intervene through subsidies or changes in the law in order to maintain their status quo. Third, when competing firms collude to lobby governments, it is because they expect to gain higher returns than they can obtain through the market. Copyright law is increasingly seen as a source of rents, or rather, the size of potential rents is increasing with the growth of the production of material covered by copyright. Governments have other means than copyright law for regulating information industries: competition rules on ownership and market shares may be more effective and direct instruments of control. Property rights are necessary for trade to take place but their value is established by market forces. The market is the chief arbiter of private costs and benefits.

Copyright laws and markets have adapted to huge technical changes, which have taken place over three centuries, with the same principles more or less intact; however, technical change frequently redistributes benefits, pecuniary and non-pecuniary (freedom of expression, access to information and so on) between market players – producers of 'old technology' goods and services, producers of 'new technology' goods and services and consumers. The questions asked with every new technological revolution are the extent to which it could radically change markets, trigger off social change and require a different paradigm of laws and legal and economic institutions. Policy-makers have to make decisions under conditions of asymmetric information: they know more about the present than the future and their information on the effects of new changes to markets, as is well known from the economics of regulation, is provided by interested parties, those with the most at stake – potential winners and losers. Economic costs and benefits, however, may be greatest in total to large numbers of 'small' gainers/losers, such as consumers, who do not organise and lobby.

Two other observations may be made from the corpus of economic theory: throughout the long history of research by economists on the role of patents in stimulating innovation, no firm conclusions have been reached about the need for IP law to support new industries. Second, changes to law inevitably lag behind technical changes, though markets are able to adapt quickly. Both these points argue for a less interventionist approach by law-makers to new technologies.

NOTES

*This is a revised version of a paper commissioned by the Intellectual Property Institute, London. I was asked to prepare a report on the economic literature on fair dealing and to estimate the economic effects of a possible reduction in fair dealing due to digitalisation. The research for this paper was undertaken at the University of Exeter, UK. I am indebted to Andrew Pickering for research assistance in preparing Section 2 and to Alasdair Paterson, the University Librarian at the University of Exeter for his valuable advice and for providing data. Helpful comments and corrections were made to earlier drafts by John Adams, John Reid, Jonathan Startup and Jack Black. The views expressed here are mine alone and do not represent those of the IP Institute or any of the above.

1. For a spirited discussion in the legal profession of the tension in copyright law between authors and users in a cultural context, see Ginsburg (1998).
2. A more detailed treatment was provided in Chapter 1.
3. Landes and Posner (1989) themselves discuss fair use but base their analysis on Gordon (1982). Posner (1992) has only a short reference to it based on Landes and Posner (1989).
4. It is anyway in the nature of radio and TV programmes and of films that it is copies not the originals that are distributed.
5. Breyer (1970) was the first to establish the fact that the vast majority of books still in copyright are out of print and draw implications from it (see Chapter 1). It is an important area of investigation for understanding the motives for photocopying.
6. University librarians observe greater use of libraries and of photocopies and less purchase of books by students. One explanation is that students are poorer and textbooks are rising in price.
7. This is also the case in the UK when the Copyright Tribunal intervenes in the event of dispute between parties to set a price.
8. According to the CLA web site (www.cla.co.uk visited 23 November 1999) there is a default price (5p per page) though some publishers may charge 6–12p per page. This is, of course, likely to have changed.
9. Liebowitz (1985) points out, however, that there is still the problem of compensating popular authors, since publishers rarely price discriminate by author and libraries do not always buy more copies of popular books; they either just lend them out more or they are more frequently photocopied. Incidentally, this is an efficiency issue not an equity one, as often suggested, as markets should signal to successful authors to supply more works.

10. Programmes which are not covered by the licence are relatively few but include the broadcasts of the Open University and commercially purchased videos.
11. Taken from the SCONUL web site sconul@mailbox.ucc.ac.uk visited 23 November 1999; several important changes have taken place since this date. In 2000, the CLA was referred to the Copyright Tribunal by the CVCP.

9. Conclusions and implications for cultural policy

Several strands run through this book: an empirical, institutional approach to cultural economics and to the economics of copyright; a belief that cultural economics should be at the forefront of understanding the importance of the creative industries in the information age; the primacy of creativity in the cultural sector and therefore of the importance of analysing artists' supply behaviour and their response to incentives and rewards; the inherent riskiness, even radical uncertainty, of producers and products in the creative industries, which often results in over-supply even in private enterprise; copyright as an incentive to creative activity through the internalisation of rewards; the unintended consequences of some copyright legislation. I have tried to integrate these strands and to draw conclusions for cultural policy from them. In this chapter, I justify this approach and move the debate on by arguing that the information age calls for a unification of cultural policy with that on copyright and the cultural industries.

AN EMPIRICAL APPROACH

Like many economists of my generation, my first experience of economics was a combination of what used to be called 'pure' and 'applied' economics, that is, we learned economic theory and we studied industrial organisation, much as management students do today, by looking at what firms in a selected industry actually did. Curiosity about the 'real world' was an important motivation for studying economics. I have retained that interest, despite the changes in economics as a discipline that have taken place. That interest is nurtured by theory, however, and I have tried in my work to look for theoretical explanations of empirical observations. That is my approach to cultural economics, which is an area of applied economics where the combination of theory and practice sits comfortably; it has also been my approach to the economic analysis of copyright where empirical testing proved to be novel.

In order to be able to do empirical analysis, though, it is necessary to have data to work with. The collection of data on the cultural sector has slowly improved over the last 20 years but it is far from complete. Labour markets have been a notoriously difficult area, as the appendix to Chapter 2 demonstrates. In Chapter 2, I traced the history of data collection for the arts in the UK and the Netherlands, showing how this is now being repeated in the information age with copyright as the unifying idea. The collection of data on the creative industries – defined as the subsidised arts together with a range of private enterprise industries whose output is information-based copyrighted material – is a prelude to an integrated government policy for the traditional arts and heritage, the cultural industries and copyright.

But facts do not speak for themselves and anyway are rarely collected without some underlying hypothesis about what they explain. Indeed, data are often used persuasively – what I call 'data for advocacy' – to demonstrate the avowed 'importance' of a sector or industry in the economy, such as the arts or the copyright industries, and so to make the case for some preferential treatment of it by the government. The worldwide anti-piracy campaign is a current example of this type of rent-seeking; it relies heavily on citing figures for theft of copyrighted material, which are probably fictitious and anyway are provided by those with the most to gain, the industry lead bodies representing the music, film and computer software industries. It is really only governments who have the facilities for collecting objective data on these industries from national income accounts and census sources. This is a task still to be completed for the cultural sector in many countries.

CULTURAL ECONOMICS AND INSTITUTIONALISM

Cultural economics is now· a well-established subject with a developed literature centred around the arts, heritage and cultural industries and with a tradition of policy-oriented analysis. The field is catholic in approach and accommodates economists from different intellectual traditions. An institutional approach therefore fits in easily. That can be interpreted in several ways; I would loosely use it in the sense of being the economic analysis of specific institutions and describe my work on artists' labour markets and on copyright law as adopting this approach. My starting point is to ask why do things work as they do; is there an economic logic? What are the incentives? How do people respond to them? What institutions formalise incentives and rewards? What economic features do these institutions have? We may not, for example, understand exactly what artistic talent is but we can try to understand whether offering talented people higher pay or longer contracts or protecting their legal rights influences their work practices (how much and what work they do and so on). We also want to know how talent is recognised and nurtured by other artists, by audiences and by organisations, such as arts councils, who seek to encourage talent and its appreciation.

What all policy-makers, whether in the arts or in a wider context of social and economic policy, have to recognise is that if people – artists, promoters or audiences – do not respond to economic incentives in some way, there is no point to subsidies. For the purposes of cultural policy, it has to be judged how much, if at all, supply of good quality art (performing and creative arts) can be stimulated by the incentive of subsidy. The answers to these questions should determine the amount and type of subsidy (Towse, 1994). The same question has to be decided in relation to the training of artists; can artists be 'created' and art improved by the expenditure of public (or private) money? This is the rationale for studying artists' earnings and supply and the organisation of labour markets in the arts and cultural industries.

REWARDS, CREATIVITY AND TRAINING FOR ARTISTS

In my book on the labour market for classically-trained singers, I linked the economic analysis of training to the labour market outcome (Towse, 1993). I asked the standard economics of education question: if a singer had to borrow the money to pay for her training and pay a commercial rate of interest on the loan, would it conceivably 'pay'? That is, could she expect to earn over her career sufficient to pay back the loan? In the UK before 1998, students did not have to pay for their higher education if it was at degree level and they received maintenance grants based on parental income; thus many singers trained for four years financed by taxpayers' money. There had been concern on the part of the government about the considerably higher cost of training singers and the fact that many of them could not get sufficient work after graduation to make a viable career. Public finance of arts training effectively changes it from a matter of private decision-making to one of social policy. These points set the scene for the study. However, applying economic analysis to arts training was anathema at the time to the arts lobby. The book was nevertheless surprisingly well received.

I managed to scrape together quite a lot of new empirical data, including on the earnings of singers, that previous researchers had not tried to obtain. I did this by interviewing many singers, singing teachers, singers' agents and people on the hiring side of the market (opera company managers and suchlike). My research also yielded figures on the total number of singers receiving training at public expense; while earlier enquiries had focused on the specialist music colleges, I found that many singers who were seeking work on the job market had had training outside the music colleges, in other subsidised institutions of further and higher education or with private teachers. This finding justified my economist's instinct to look at supply on the labour market rather than count the output of trained singers from music colleges, which had been the line previously taken by educationalists and arts administrators. That approach overemphasised the importance of specialist training and ignored the economic reality of hiring and employment practices in the market for singers. These issues are relevant to policy on training artists in other countries in which generous subsidy is available.

As may be seen from Chapter 3, artists and craftspeople get their training in many ways. They typically have higher levels of educational achievement than the workforce in general but earn less. Research on artists' labour markets has, on the one hand, confirmed standard theories of labour economics and, on the other, found them wanting. One feature of artists' labour markets that makes them very different from other labour markets is the undefinable element of talent and creativity. Whereas other outstanding features of individuals, such as high intelligence or educational attainment, have been measured and ranked, however imperfectly, there is no recognised way of defining creativity. Yet markets reward it very highly and it is much sought-after by both suppliers of cultural products and by audiences, who are prepared to pay high prices for the services of talented artists. Because it is not clear what it is, we do not know how to produce or reproduce creativity and this has implications for policy on artists. One of these implications is that we may well have to train more artists than the market can absorb in order to maximise supply of creativity. Thus over-supply of artists may have efficiency benefits as part of the search for new talent and creativity.

But who bears the costs of this policy? Obviously, all who aspire to becoming successful artists will not succeed. If their training is paid for by state subsidy, the state bears some of the risk and costs but not all: trainees have opportunity costs arising from forgone income or alternative training possibilities. State grants to support practising artists also mitigate some risk. Even so, the fact that artists are not well rewarded by markets means they bear most of the risk over a lifetime by earning less money than workers with equivalent human capital and similar age in professional occupations. Artists pay the price of their intrinsic motivation of wanting to be creative. The risk factor is very high; record companies, for example, calculate that only one or two of every ten records will be successful (MMC, 1996). Think of how many wannabee pop singers there are for every recorded artist! In fact, we do not have data of this kind. I tried very roughly to calculate how many trained singers there were in the 1980s for each of the estimated number of regularly working 'classical' singers in the UK; I guessed that to be about 500 to one. The ratios in pop music, musical composition, visual arts, dance and theatre are probably much higher. Without longitudinal studies of artists' training and labour market experience it is impossible to trace career development. However, we can infer from the predominance of younger people working or trying to find work in the cultural sector that many eventually drop out and move into other careers (see appendix to Chapter 2 and Chapter 3). Their 'lost' output is the opportunity cost they and society bear for taking the risk of trying to become artists. These are all efficiency aspects of artists' supply, which are relevant to cultural policy. Questions of equity or fairness also come into play, however, which are less amenable to economic analysis (see Chapter 3).

RISK AND OVER-SUPPLY IN THE CREATIVE INDUSTRIES

Uncertainty about consumers' tastes, the shifting of taste due to changes in fashion, social change, technological change leading to new products and production processes, globalisation of culture and the effects of economic growth and development all make for risk on the part of entrepreneurs in the creative industries as well as for the artists who supply novelty. Analysis by cultural economists has shown that success of film and record titles, pop groups, works by writers, visual artists and composers and the rest, that is, of the output of the creative industries, is unpredictable. This leads to over-supply because everything that is created cannot be sold. Information goods are frequently characterised by having high fixed costs of producing the 'master copy' and with very low marginal costs of supplying copies to the market. This makes for considerable risk on the part of firms in these industries. Their oligopolistic structure enables them to charge prices that reward risk-taking and to spread the cost of failure across a portfolio of products. As we saw in Chapter 1, reducing the disincentive to creative activity from free-riding by copiers was one of the justifications for copyright law; however, that is 'paid for' by consumers who have to pay higher monopolistic prices for copyright material. In Chapter 7, I put together these observations about risk-taking by firms with those taken by individual artists and argued that artists are being made to bear disproportionate risk in the production of creative output by the asymmetry of market structure in the creative industries. The bargaining power of any but the superstar artists with multinational conglomerates in the cultural industries is weak. If there were no over-supply of artists that exploitation could not occur but as I argue in Chapter 4, the chance of becoming a superstar, however small, and the very high intrinsic and extrinsic rewards that offers is the incentive for excess supply of artists to the creative industries.

COPYRIGHT AND RISK

The language conventions of the copyright literature being what they are, I shall now switch from the term artists as used above to a focus on authors as the originators or creators of artistic work. Just as 'artists' was a convenient inclusive word for a range of creators and performers, so 'authors' means any person who creates a copyrightable work; 'publishers' are those who disseminate the works of authors, that is, literary and musical publishers, record companies, broadcasters and the like, who own copyrights of their contribution to the creation of information goods. Authors and publishers are protected by copyright law because they need property rights in order to trade their works by sale or licence to the public. The literature on the economics of copyright as applicable to the cultural sector was surveyed in Chapter 1 and my own contribution to that literature is in Chapters 5 and 6.

Copyright law has expanded its scope from authors – creative artists – to performers and from artistic work to a broader swathe of work, such as databases and computer software with no artistic input but sufficient originality to comply with copyright requirements. The spread of copyright has had two effects on artists; it has offered them a conduit for societal recognition of their professional status; and, by raising expectations that copyright can increase earnings through statutory means rather than contracts, it causes more and more groups of cultural industry workers to seek inclusion. Thus, performers' rights have been extended in Europe and *droit de suite* has been recently (in 1999) the subject of a European Union Directive. The spread of copyright has also been coterminous with the development and growth of the cultural industries. Indeed, as was argued at length in Chapter 2, copyright coverage has become the basis on which cultural industries are defined and measured.

These tendencies are an unintended aspect of copyright law and they threaten to dilute the incentives to artistic creativity. Another unintended consequence of copyright law is that it allows firms in the cultural industries to capitalise on an author's work through the creation and protection of tradable assets and this has a detrimental effect on the author's bargaining position. Consider the changes in the labour market for musicians during the twentieth century. Before the First World War, all music was live; every theatre and music hall had a band, as did hotels, restaurants and tea shops; pianists were ubiquitous in shops, pubs and elsewhere. The advent of sound recording gradually reduced the demand for live performance in those venues but the new cultural industries of radio and cinemas also increased it. After the Second World War, subsidies to the arts assisted 'classical' orchestras and sometimes jazz bands and, until the 1980s in the UK, the Musicians' Union secured various agreements to protect live performance by restricting the use of recorded music, especially on the radio. Two sets of laws reduced the market strength of musicians; the 'closed shop' was outlawed by labour law legislation in the UK under Mrs Thatcher and, before that, the Performing Right Tribunal, the legal regulator of composers' performing rights, reduced the rates being claimed for radio play by the BBC (the British Broadcasting Corporation, which had the monopoly of radio at the time) by the Performing Right Society.

That is the story in brief. But now consider the economic implications. Sound recording displaced work for musicians in two ways: by allowing users to substitute mechanical for live performance at any one point in time and by creating a durable replica of a live performance by a musician that would compete over its lifetime with that musician's live performance possibilities. The duration of the copyright on a sound recording was at first 25 then 50 years. Thus the labour of the musician was replaced by the capital good – the recording – that his performance had created. To the record company, this capital good is an asset that it can exploit in the most profitable way. That company gradually came to be part of a huge multinational corporation through stockmarket transactions of assets, including our musician's back catalogue, over which she has no retroactive control.

Globalisation of the cultural industries has been assisted by copyright law's creation and defence of property rights worldwide, which have resulted, for example, in a global music business with five major firms sharing about three-quarters of a world market of US$40 billion. These firms are horizontally integrated across the whole range of arts and entertainments and vertically integrated so that in the music business the same conglomerate owns music publishing, record labels, record shops and radio stations. As a result, artists have to bargain with ever larger and more powerful enterprises from an ever weaker position. The conglomerate joins others to advance the case for strengthening copyright and extending its imposition worldwide, adopting the rhetoric of upholding the law by opposing theft and illegal behaviour; governments respond by assisting the process nationally and through international conventions, strengthening the protection of copyright assets. Thus copyright law has, intentionally, enabled musicians to earn a royalty from recording, but in so doing it has unintentionally created economic conditions which keep the amount they can obtain from it low by fostering the growth of firms and thereby reducing performers' bargaining power.

Perhaps these developments are no different in kind from those that have taken place in many industries as labour is replaced by capital. After all, scribes were made redundant by the advent of printing and craftwork has been supplanted by factory production in most areas of the economy, ultimately making goods cheaper and enabling more people to purchase them. Perhaps this is a Luddite view. I think, however, there is a difference because the process I described is not just due to market response to technical and economic change; it has also been assisted by legal intervention. Changes in other industries have been made possible by technical inventions protected by patents in more or less the same way as copyrights have assisted artistic creativity. Patent licences are traded and form assets in knowledge-based industries, such as pharmaceuticals, in the same way as copyrights do in the creative industries. The difference is, though, that patents must be applied for and the case made for each and they are of considerably shorter duration. Pharmaceutical companies have massive outlays on research and development and must satisfy a vast regulatory regime of the case for a patent. A film company may have a similar outlay but its copyright lasts far longer than the pharmaceutical patent and it need do nothing at all, apart from complying with decency laws to obtain its copyright. Yet one enterprise is hardly more risky than the other nor more socially beneficial.

To return to the case of the musician. Performers' rights were created that give the musician a right to residual income from sound recording. In economic terms, the performer therefore shares the risk of the success or failure of sound recording titles with the record company. The purpose of including performer's property rights in copyright law was undoubtedly to provide a counterbalance to the increased power of the record companies. Indeed, some of the new performers' rights in European Union countries have been made unwaivable in an attempt to protect the bargaining power of 'small' artists in their dealings with 'big' companies. *Droit de suite* for visual artists is also an unwaivable right. These measures, however, prevent authors from trading their rights freely as they wish. This clumsy paternalistic move to redress the undesirable effects of copyright law is naive because it ignores the underlying economic incentives of royalties as an economic institution.

The economists' approach is to ask what are the benefits to artists (authors) of a royalty system and what is its economic function. I have begun to explore this topic in Chapter 6, where I outline the incentive structure it provides. One problem with a royalty system is that it requires an edifice of collecting societies to enable individual artists (or at least all but the superstars) to collect royalties and remuneration from licence fees. Indeed, without collecting societies' blanket licensing, copyright law would be impossibly expensive to administer. The transaction costs of most of this, however, are charged to artists and these costs can be considerable (anything from 10 to 40 per cent). Users – restaurants, radio stations, shops and so on – benefit from blanket licensing as it reduces their transaction costs. Even so, in several countries anti-trust authorities have curtailed and regulated collecting societies and even enforced new entrants. In some cases, the government acts in lieu of a collecting society to administer copyrights and related rights; in the UK, the Public Lending Right is administered by the government with disproportionate transaction costs. In Chapter 8, a detailed account was given of how photocopying is licensed in the UK; this illustrates some of the complexity of copyright administration even in a simple case.

Despite all this, however, tentative data that I have assembled on artists' earnings from copyright suggest that it has not led to artists (musicians in my study) earning very much (Chapter 6). Indeed, analysis of the introduction of performers' rights suggests that if performers do earn more, it must be at the expense of other rights holders or the public paying higher licence fees (Chapter 5). Given this information, I have tried to formulate an economic rationale for this seemingly unrewarding adherence to royalties and risk-sharing on the part of artists and firms in the cultural industries. In keeping with an institutional approach, there has to be a good economic explanation for a system that is so persistent and prevalent. After all, payment could (unless prevented by law) take the form of a one-off spot fee that would buy out residual rights to future payments, thereby reducing transaction costs for all parties. But the royalty system is clearly preferred by authors and publishers. One reason seems to be that by retaining a financial interest in their past work, artists have the incentive to maintain their reputation and the quality of their present work, which is beneficial to both parties – authors and publisher – as well as being of benefit to consumers. Moreover, the royalty system also performs a signalling function on the supply side by allowing authors to track the success (or lack of it) of their creations; this provides information about what to produce in the future.

Another reason is that given the speed of technical change in the cultural industries and changing fashions and tastes (including revivals of old stars – Elvis Presley earned more 20 years after his death than at that time), there are too many uncertainties and unanticipated rewards to make it a preferable strategy for artists to sell rights outright (in a buy-out) than to retain residual rights and thereby accept a share of risk. Why do publishers prefer a royalty system, though? An obvious answer is that entrepreneurs do not have to bear all the risk; nor do they have to put up the capital outlay to buy up rights that in some industries could be prohibitively high (an example is the cost of all participants' rights in making a TV series). Clearly, artists' willingness to accept a share of risk eases the way for firms in the cultural industries.

This again brings us back to artists' attitude to risk. Not only is a career in the arts inevitably risky, artists also overestimate their chances of success. They prefer a royalty to an actuarially equivalent flat fee because they have a chance to 'win the lottery'. Artists appear to be risk-takers in the textbook sense of preferring a gamble to a fair payment based on known probabilities. What we do not know is whether they like risk or whether it is forced upon them by habit and custom in the arts and cultural industries. If they do not like risk, cultural policy-makers should place less emphasis on copyright as a means of supporting artists' incomes and certainly should not make rights to royalties unwaivable because that forces artists to take risks. In this context, I have reconsidered the view that grants and prizes are a preferable alternative means of offering artists rewards and incentives to create as considered by

Plant (1934) and other early writers on the economics of copyright (see Chapter 1). As argued in Chapter 7, I have come to the view, based on the empirical evidence and my understanding of the unintended consequences of copyright law for the growth of multinationals in the creative industries, that grants to artists are a necessary part of cultural policy.

CULTURAL POLICY AND INCENTIVES AND REWARDS TO ARTISTS

The central element of cultural supply is the creativity and talent of artists. Cultural policy must rest on an understanding of artists' motivation and response to incentives, among which are payment for their work and copyright protection. Thus this book links up my work in cultural economics on artists' labour markets and the economics of copyright in the cultural industries. I now turn to the policy implications of my analysis and argue the case for an integrated cultural policy that covers all these areas. In the UK, policy for the creative industries includes both subsidised non-profit cultural organisations and the unsubsidised, profit-making cultural industries. I welcome this approach, which overcomes an out-dated and increasingly irrelevant divide that seems to persist elsewhere. I also argue that is now time for cultural economics, which has concerned itself over the years with cultural policy for the subsidised sector, to provide an analytical background for policies for the market-orientated unsubsidised sector.

Policy on copyright in the UK, however, is still divorced administratively from cultural policy, despite its manifest importance for incentives and rewards to creativity, particularly as the requirements of policy for the information age emerge.[1] Copyright policy, by which is meant governmental policy on changing copyright law, should be considered part of cultural policy because copyright law influences the supply of creative work by artists and by the cultural industries which use their services. We have seen that the EU has sought to influence the shares of income that go to artists and to the firms in the cultural sector through copyright law in the case of performers' rights, *droit de suite* and, in a digital world, is considering doing so through fair use. Elsewhere, different interest groups have achieved different policy outcomes: in the USA, performers do not have rights equivalent to their European counterparts, nor do they in Australia; in Japan, by contrast, performers have had a well-established range of rights since the 1970s. However, an important message the empirical approach has demonstrated is that, despite the rhetoric of copyright lawyers, the mere fact of having rights does not mean that artists will earn much from them; the financial value of different items in the bundle of rights we call copyrights depends upon global market revenues in the cultural industries and the share of them that artists are able to negotiate for themselves. This is a hard lesson that artists' interest groups are having to learn.

Where rewards to artists can be more directly controlled is in the subsidised arts sector. In most countries, a condition of the grant of subsidy to an arts organisation is that artists are paid according to an agreed minimum pay scale. What differs considerably between countries, though, is the extent to which arts organisations are subsidised. A considerable effort of cultural accounting has gone into trying to make good inter-country comparisons of cultural subsidies but they remain difficult and unreliable; one measure that has proved useful, however, is the proportion of subsidy in total revenue of individual organisations or of a specific sector. So, for example, theatre in the UK receives about one-third of its revenue from subsidies while in the Netherlands that figure is more than double. The subsidised cultural sector in the UK veers towards a market economy, whereas that of the Netherlands is more like a planned economy. This has implications for artists' labour market behaviour and for their earnings. In the UK, as in the USA, there is considerable interaction between the subsidised and unsubsidised sectors. Creative artists – composers, authors, visual artists, film-makers – typically work in both. In countries with relatively high subsidies to the arts, like the Netherlands and Germany, artists can rely far more on regular employment with good conditions of work in the subsidised arts and therefore have less incentive to work on the 'open market'. An example is opera singers and orchestral players in Germany, who are civil servants with paid holidays, regulated rest periods, job security for life after an initial period of employment, and the other perquisites of state employees. Their salaries are negotiated nationally between the representatives of the performers and theatre managements (Towse, 1993). This is all a very far cry from the 'free' labour markets for artists in the UK and other countries where the arts receive relatively little subsidy. Artists in the former soviet-type economies of Eastern Europe, previously generously supported, now face enormous changes in their labour markets, which have an impact on those in other countries.[2] And, as culture is increasingly globalised, there is growing circulation of artists. Globalisation increases the competition in artists' labour markets and it also raises the stakes because it enables the superstars to earn even higher incomes as markets expand, which provides the incentive to an even greater supply of artists. Another feature of globalisation is that the cultural industries can relocate or develop in 'new' countries and this can have important implications for artists' labour markets.[3]

A question that cultural policy-makers have to consider is, what are the effects of these global trends on cultural provision in their countries? What impact do they have on the quality of and access to subsidised culture and on the ability of policy-makers to influence outcomes and achieve policy objectives? The cultural industries – television, sound recording, video, Internet – have the potential to deliver arts content and information to far more people worldwide than will ever attend live performances or visit museums and art galleries, a fact recognised nearly 30 years ago by Girard (1972) (Chapter 2). Cultural policy could go much further in recognising that potential, for example by subsidising services such as the broadcast of a subsidised live performance. That necessitates a wider view of cultural policy than exists in many countries.

As for policy for the cultural industries per se, we saw in Chapter 2 that some of these industries receive revenue subsidy. Some, such as film, are assisted with capital grants. Thus they already are in the domain of the subsidised cultural sector. Most media are regulated in one way or another by censorship and decency laws, cross-media ownership rules and content quotas. This type of regulation is often viewed as part of a media policy separate from cultural policy, though; it is the responsibility of the ministry of industry rather than the ministry of culture. Some aspects of the cultural industries require a specific regulatory framework on ownership. Issues such as monopoly can and should be dealt with by anti-competition law but the cultural element makes media industries and particularly the Internet different from 'ordinary' industries covered by industrial policy. That suggests that regulation of these industries should be dealt with by a ministry of culture as cultural policy.

Culture has a public good aspect to it implying that economic policy must deal carefully with the cultural industries because of their social benefits. That is what makes policy for cultural industries particularly appropriate for study by cultural economists. Cultural economics already has a well-developed analytical framework and set of specialist concepts with which it approaches the subsidised arts. The future of cultural economics lies in its ability to turn these tools to good use in policy for the global cultural industries. A starting point for both is the recognition that markets for the traditional subsidised arts and the cultural industries are inter-related, especially labour markets for artists; creativity is central to both.

Copyright law cuts across all the creative industries and should be viewed for what it is, a *de facto* instrument of cultural policy. As we have seen, it offers incentives to cultural production and regulates the rewards. Copyright law, however, is mostly under the purview of ministries of justice concerned with jurisprudence rather than the economic outcomes in cultural markets. The lack of an empirical approach in legal studies, especially in Europe, seems especially inappropriate as the information age sweeps through the economy.

The information age offers enormous potential opportunities and threats. I do not pretend to foresee which will predominate. My contribution is concerned with one limited area, the effect of incentives and rewards on artists' supply of creative output. That is surely a key to our cultural future and I therefore argue that cultural policy should adopt an integrated approach to copyright and the regulation of the cultural industries that nurture creativity.

NOTES

1. Australia has taken this bold step by forming a Ministry of Communication and Arts.
2. The considerable number of singers and other musicians of the former USSR now working in the west is an instance of this. Equally, many Asian musicians work in Europe and the USA and many American singers work in Germany. This is and always has been a global market; recently however, there has been a significant, though unquantified, outflow from Eastern Europe.
3. The Naxos record company is an example of this. Started in Hong Kong initially, it specialised in recordings by musicians from Asia and East Europe. It has pursued a policy of paying flat fees to buy out artists' rights rather than paying them royalties, arguing with good reason that for many artists this is a preferable strategy.

Epilogue

In reviewing my work over the last ten years, I have tried to reconstruct the motives for doing it and the circumstances in which it was done. Which policy issues prompted my choice of topics? What have I learned from this work and where do I see it going in the future? After all, in its own way, academic research is a creative, on-going process of experiment, learning-by-doing, criticism and response.

Though most of my research took place in the UK and the findings are specifically about that country, it is concerned with problems common to many other countries. Cultural economics is particularly susceptible to 'national' cultural outlook as well as to country-based policy questions, even though its concerns are generally universal. My English background has undoubtedly coloured my outlook to cultural economics and this has become more obvious to me now I work in the Netherlands. Let me give a couple of examples of what I mean by different national perceptions: there has been controversy for at least the last 30 years in the UK about charging entry fees to publicly owned museums, while in the Netherlands entry is routinely charged for without comment; however, private donors and sponsors have financed significant extensions to national museums in the UK without any opposition but private sponsorship of museums is being criticised in the Netherlands. A second example is medical treatment, which in the Netherlands is privately organised, charged for and financed by regulated health insurance but in the UK is provided by a free-at-the-point-of-delivery National Health Service, financed out of taxes; the English deplore the idea of health care being paid for directly, even though there is private health insurance. Yet welfarism is far more deeply entrenched in the Netherlands than in the UK, which, by contrast, places far greater value on individualism. The point I wish to make is that we are acculturated to accept our familiar economic practices as the norm and they influence our view of what is properly private and what should be public. A similar point may be made with respect to national attitudes to the arts and the heritage; in the UK, the arts and heritage are unpopular, of interest only to top income earners and not a political issue; by contrast, in Italy, they are highly politicised and people who do not participate in the arts of heritage nevertheless have strong views about cultural policy. The point is, we all start from a different stance when we begin to discuss cultural economics and cultural policy issues.

National cultural policy-makers (ministries of culture, arts councils and suchlike) have basically two tasks: stimulating creativity and stimulating an interest in and appreciation of the arts on the part of the population – in other words, the supply of and demand for the arts. Arts policy is not usually systematic in the sense of there being stated objectives which are to be achieved by appropriate policy instruments; the arts are for some reason regarded as more sacrosanct than education or health, where policy is more explicit, even though educators and doctors are as reluctant as artists to discuss questions such as value for money and administrative efficiency. At the time I began to work in cultural economics, the Arts Council of Great Britain, the most prominent of the funding bodies, seemed to hold the belief that these tasks were two sides of the same coin: the more artists were trained quantitatively and qualitatively, the better their work would be and therefore the demand for it by an appreciative public would be bound to grow – Say's Law for the arts, that is, supply creates its own demand.

According to this view, it is impossible to spend too much money on training artists (which, however, is not under the Arts Council but the Ministry of Education) because that raises quality and spreads the arts. This was the belief at the time of all arts professionals and the 'arts elite', who produced periodic reports on crises in the arts, in arts training and so on. When I started to work on artists' labour markets, little basic data existed that could be used to address these claims and my intention was simply to collect information on the economic and social characteristics of artists (initially just on trained singers) such as earnings and employment. I was lucky to get grants for this research and to get support from a few people who insisted on taking the topic seriously because initially the Arts Council felt unable to finance expensive research on the economics of the arts (which many individual members regarded as an oxymoron). This was in part because they believed they already knew what they needed to know and also because they did not want to know that artists were typically underpaid, suffered long periods of unemployment and that more of them were being trained than could be supported by the market – to which the Say's Law answer was that training should be improved, of course by spending more on it!

The specific policy issue that was looming in the UK when I conceived my project on the economic aspects of the training and employment of singers was that the policy of free higher education and student maintenance grants, introduced in the 1960s, was under fire; now it has been abandoned and fees and loans have been introduced instead. I wanted to analyse the connection between subsidised training and the role it played in the employment of singers – pay, hiring practices, career development and so on. At the time almost none of the required data on any group of artists existed and data are still not fully adequate. Now that these changes in the finance of higher education and artist training have been made, research should be undertaken to see if the predicted fall in the number of singers and other artists entering higher education has taken place. Much bigger questions presented themselves in the course of this research, however: the role that talent – meaning natural facility – plays in this market and whether it can it be 'produced'; and the matter of how amenable artistic motivation is to economic analysis. I shall continue to think about these questions.

The introduction of student loans was a sort of 'natural experiment' that offered the possibility of before and after comparison. I had the same type of natural experiment in mind when I started work on copyright because, in the 1990s, the harmonisation programme of the European Union was causing changes to be adopted in UK law and I wanted to trace the empirical effects on payments to artists and in the creative industries where they are employed. In many ways, that was hopelessly naive; very few experiments in social science allow *ceteris paribus* assumptions to be made and technology in this area was changing so fast as to swamp the effects of legal changes. Even so, I succeeded in finding 'before' data and shall continue to look for 'after' effects. En route I have learned a great deal about the economics of copyright and its important role in almost every area of economic life. It is extraordinary to me that so few economists have woken up to this fact.

What lessons emerge from these two bodies of work? One is that government intervention by subsidy and regulation in this area has had unintended consequences, indeed even the opposite of the desired effect. Subsidy to artist training resulted in a significant expansion of the number of courses offered by universities, music, art and drama colleges which produced more and more graduates of uncertain talent and ability, who flood labour markets and produce vast over-supply of product – performances of all kinds, books, pop music, film scripts, game shows, works of art. In the Netherlands, subsidies to trained artists in the visual arts have similarly led to a flood of works on the art market, making it more and more difficult for talented artists to make their way and for consumers to discern quality. The response of consumers and of producers in the creative industries to this superabundance is to focus on superstars and on any other available means of filtering information to reduce the costs of information overload. A second area in which the unintended consequences of government intervention are to be found is in copyright, where law that is perceived as intended to assist artists (mistakenly, in my opinion) has fostered the growth of large multinational corporations which dominate the cultural industries. These firms produce goods and services that face uncertain reception on the market so they concentrate where possible on reinforcing success and this also leads to the promotion of superstars, cutting out smaller artists and narrowing artistic supply. Copyright law is being increasingly criticised from many different angles, among the critics being academics from law, economics and cultural studies. This topic will continue to be an issue as the information age encroaches further into cultural life.

I have also been inspired by Landes and Posner's (1989) view of creativity which is presented in their economic analysis of copyright law; had I understood its full implications earlier, I would certainly have wanted to include it somehow in my research on artists. Landes and Posner's insight is that copyright law draws a line between what is in the public domain and therefore available to be used freely and what is private, that is, exclusively owned by the creator, author or publisher. In common with many cultural theorists, they view creativity as a cumulative process in which the present generation of artists takes material, ideas and inspiration from the past generation of artists and creates something new to pass on to future generations. The 'line' copyright draws – a simple feature is its duration – creates winners and losers through the benefits (free use) and costs (of using protected material) that a given copyright regime determines; thus, shorter duration frees up past material but offers less incentive to its creators and a longer duration raises the cost of producing new works of art but offers a greater incentive. That is the trade-off and it hinges on both empirical economic information about the costs and benefits of copyright and on this theory of creativity. It is about what is the right balance of public and private ownership of information as well as what economic organisation creates the best incentives. But this is not only a matter of efficiency as it also impinges on distribution, on free access to created work, and so the question strikes at the heart of liberal democratic values because it has to do with freedom of expression and freedom of information. These are questions that are fundamental to cultural economics as well as to other disciplines.

An old question in the economics of copyright (and patents) is do we need statutory protection of intellectual property at all or would rewards by means of prizes, grants or honours not provide an equivalent incentive to creativity? The digital revolution is raising this problem again as there is a question of whether copyright can survive the changes in trading methods that the new technology may bring. It has often been suggested that a public reward system be introduced to encourage artists, leaving the creative industries to survive with lead time advantages of being first to market with a new product. However, little consideration has been given by those who suggest this solution to the problem of how such a system of prizes and grants would be administered in the arts. The experience of the nineteenth-century academies in the arts and sciences and the last 50 years' experience of arts councils and the like as public arbiters of taste and artistic development demonstrate some of the difficulties of such a proposal. Private markets are less arbitrary, though they also have inherent problems (as the commercialism versus culture debate has shown). This topic is an interesting one to pursue further.

At the end of the day, what much of this discussion is about is the appropriate divide between the private sector and the public sector in the context of information goods and their creation. Like innovation and entrepreneurship, creativity is something in which we all have a public interest, even though it is privately produced by individuals. Creativity comes to the fore in the information age and plays the role in the post-industrial world that innovation did for economic growth in the industrial era. Artists are the engineers of the information age in the twenty-first century.

References

Acheson, K. and Maule, C. (1994/95) 'Understanding Hollywood's Organisation and Continuing Success', *Journal of Cultural Economics*, **18** (4), 271–300.

Acheson, K. and Maule, C. (1999) *Much Ado about Culture: North American Trade Disputes*, University of Michigan Press, Ann Arbor.

Adler, M. (1985) 'Stardom and Talent', *American Economic Review*, **75**, 208–12.

Albert, S. (1998) 'Movie Stars and the Distribution of Financially Successful Films in the Motion Picture Industry', *Journal of Cultural Economics*, **22** (4), 249–70.

Albert, S. (1999) 'Movie Stars and the Distribution of Financially Successful Films in the Motion Picture Industry: A Reply', *Journal of Cultural Economics*, **23** (4), 325–9.

Alexander, P. (1994) 'New Technology and Market Structure: Evidence from the Music Recording Industry', *Journal of Cultural Economics*, **18** (2), 113–24.

Allen, D. (1990) *Report of an Enquiry into Remuneration of Welsh National Opera Musicians*, Welsh National Opera/Musicians' Union, Cardiff.

Arts Council of England (1998) *The Arts Council of England Annual Report 1998*, Arts Council of England, London.

Arts Council of Great Britain (1993a), *A Creative Future*, HMSO, London.

Arts Council of Great Britain (1993b), *National Review of Opera Singer Training: The Ritterman Review*, The Arts Council of Great Britain, London.

Bagella, M. (1995) 'The Buy-Out/Property Right Share Choice in Film Financing: Financial Rationing, Adverse Selection and the Bayesian Dilemma', *Journal of Cultural Economics*, **19** (4), 279–304.

Bagella, M. and Becchetti, L. (1999) 'The Determinants of Motion Picture Box Office Performance – Evidence from Movies Produced in Italy', *Journal of Cultural Economics*, **23** (4), 279–304.

Baker, A. (1991) 'A Model of Competition and Monopoly in the Record Industry', *Journal of Cultural Economics*, **15** (1), 29–54.

Baumol, H. and Baumol, W. (1984) 'The Mass Media and the Cost Disease', in Hendon, W., Shaw, P. and Grant, N. (1984) *The Economics of Cultural Industries*, Association for Cultural Economics, Akron, reprinted as

Chapter 16 in Towse, R. (ed.) (1997) *Baumol's Cost Disease: The Arts and other Victims*, Edward Elgar, Aldershot.

Baumol, W. and Bowen, W. (1966) *Performing Arts: The Economic Dilemma*, The Twentieth Century Fund, Hartford, Conn.

Belinfante, A. and Johnson, R. (1982) 'Competition, Pricing and Concentration in the US Recorded Music Industry', *Journal of Cultural Economics*, **6** (2), 11-24.

Bell, T. (1998) 'Fair Use vs. Fared Use: The Impact of Automated Rights Management on Copyright's Fair Use Doctrine', *North Carolina Law Review*, **76**l, 558-619.

Bender, T. and Sampliner, D. (1997) 'Poets, Pirates and the Creation of American Literature', *Journal of International Law and Politics*, **29**, 255-70.

Benhamou, F. (1999) 'The Growth of Employment in the Audiovisual and Performing Arts Activities in France and the UK Over a Period of Ten years: Two Different Models of Labour Market Adjustments', mimeo, Université de Paris I Panthéon-Sorbonne, Paris.

Bennett, O. (1991) 'British Cultural Policies 1970-1990', *Boekmancahier*, Sept., 293-301.

Besen, S. and Kirkby, S. (1989a) *Compensating Creators of Intellectual Property*, RAND Corporation.

Besen, S. and Kirkby, S. (1989b) 'Private Copying, Appropriability and Optimal Copying Royalties', *Journal of Law and Economics*, **32**, 255-80.

Besen, S., Kirkby, S. and Salop, S. (1992) 'An Economic Analysis of Copyright Collectives', *Virginia Law Review*, **78**, 383-441.

Bettig, R. (1996) *Copyrighting Culture*, Westview Press, Boulder.

Bianconi, L. and Pestelli, G. (eds) (1998) *Opera Production and Its Resources*, Vol. 4, University of Chicago Press, Chicago and London.

Booij, J. (1993) *The Economic Importance of Copyright in the Netherlands*, SEO Foundation for Economic Research, Amsterdam.

Breyer, S. (1970) 'The Uneasy Case for Copyright: A Study of Books, Photocopies and Computer Programs', *Harvard Law Review* **84**, 281-351.

Brighton, A., Pearson, N. and Parry, J. (1985) *The Economic Situation of Visual Artists*, London: Calouste Gulbenkian Foundation.

British Invisibles (1995) *Overseas Earnings of the Music Industry*, British Invisibles, London.

Brosio, G. (1994) 'The Arts Industry: Problems of Measurement', Chapter 2 in Peacock, A. and Rizzo, I. (eds) *Cultural Economics and Cultural Policies*, Kluwer, Dordrecht.

Bruce, A. and Filmer, P. (1983), *Working in Crafts*, Crafts Council, London.

Burke, A. (1994) 'The Demand for Vinyl LPs 1975-1988. Time Series Estimation of a Product Group in the Presence of Product Differentiation Innovation', *Journal of Cultural Economics*, **18** (1), 41-64.

Burke, A. (1996a) 'Dynamics of Product Differentiation in the British Record-Industry', *Journal of Cultural Economics*, **20** (2), 145-64.

Burke, A. (1996b) 'How Effective are the International Copyright Conventions in the Music Industry?', *Journal of Cultural Economics*, **20** (1), 51-66.

BVA (British Video Association) (1996) *The British Video Association Yearbook 1996*, British Video Association, London.

Cameron, S. (1986) 'The Supply and Demand for Cinema Tickets: Some UK Evidence', *Journal of Cultural Economics*, **10** (1), 38-62.

Cameron, S. (1988) 'The Impact of Video Recorders on Cinema Attendance', *Journal of Cultural Economics*, **12** (1), 73-80.

Cameron, S. (1990) 'The Demand for Cinema in the United Kingdom', *Journal of Cultural Economics*, **14** (1), 35-47.

Casey, B., Dunlop, R. and Selwood, S. (1996) *Culture as Commodity?*, Policy Studies Institute, London.

Caves, R. (2000) *Creative Industries; Contracts between Art and Commerce*, Harvard University Press, Cambridge, Mass. and London.

Chambers, T. (1998) 'Who's on First? Studying the Scholarly Community of Media Economics', *Journal of Media Economics*, **11**, 1-12.

Cheung, S. (1986) 'Property Rights and Invention', in Palmer, J. (ed.) *The Economics of Patents and Copyrights*, Research in Law and Economics Series 8, JAI Press, Greenwich, Conn. and London, pp. 5-18.

Christiansen, R. (1984) *Prima Donna: A History*, Penguin Books, London.

Coase, R. (1966) 'Economics of Broadcasting and Government Policy', *American Economic Review*, **56** (2), 440-47.

Commission on Social Justice (1994) *Social Justice*, Vintage, London.

Cotterell, L. (1993) *Performance*, 3rd edition, Sweet and Maxwell, London.

Cowen, T. (1998) *In Praise of Commercial Culture*, Harvard University Press, Cambridge, Mass. and London.

Cowen, T. (2000) *What Price Fame?*, Harvard University Press, Cambridge, Mass. and London.

Cox, R., Felton, J. and Chung, K. (1995) 'The Concentration of Commercial Success in Popular Music: An Analysis of the Distribution of Gold Records', *Journal of Cultural Economics*, **19** (4), 333-40.

Creigh-Tyte, S. (1998) 'British Policy for the Creative Industries', paper presented at the Symposium on Crafts and Design Management, Kuopio, Finland.

Dane, C., Feist, A. and Laing, D. (1996) *The Value of Music*, London, National Music Council.

Dane, Cliff (1995) *The UK Record Industry Annual Survey 1995*, Media Research Publishing Ltd, Weston-Super-Mare.

David, P. (1993) 'Intellectual Property Institutions and the Panda's Thumb: Patents, Copyrights and Trade Secrets in Economic Theory and History', in Mogee, M. and Schwen, R. (eds) *Global Dimensions of Intellectual Property Rights in Science and Technology*, National Academy Press, Washington DC, pp. 19–61.

DCMS (1998) *Creative Industries Mapping Document*, Department of Media, Culture and Sport (DCMS), London.

Domingo, P. (1983) *My First Forty Years*, Viking Penguin Inc., New York.

Dore, R. (1976), *The Diploma Disease: Education, Qualification and Development*, University of California Press, California.

Doyle, G. (2000) 'The Economics of Monomedia and Cross-media Expansion: A Study in the Case Favouring Deregulation of TV and Newspaper Ownership in the UK, *Journal of Cultural Economics*, **24** (1), 1–26.

EC Directive (1992) *Rental Right and Lending Right and on Certain Rights Related to Copyright in the Field of Intellectual Property*, 92/100/EEC, Luxembourg.

Educational Recording Agency (1999) http://www.era.org

Ehrlich, Cyril (1989) *Harmonious Alliance. A History of the Performing Right Society*, Oxford University Press, Oxford.

Equity (1993) *Equity/PACT Agreement for Cinema Films* (1 July), Equity, London.

Equity (1996a) Sample film contract, mimeo, Equity, London.

Equity (1996b) Letter from Angela Lyttle, 16 Feb.

European Commission (1998) *Culture, the Cultural Industries and Employment*, Commission Staff Working Paper, Brussels.

Fernández Blanco, V. and Baños Pino, J. (1997) 'Cinema Demand in Spain: A Co-integration Analysis', *Journal of Cultural Economics*, **21** (1), 57–75.

Filer, R. (1986) 'The Starving Artist: Myth or Reality? – Earnings of an Artist in the United States', *Journal of Political Economy*, **94** (1), 56–75.

Filer, R. (1987) 'The Price of Failure: Earnings of Former Artists', in Shaw, D., Hendon, W. and Waits, C. *Market for the Arts*, Akron University Press, Akron.

Filer, R. (1990) 'The Arts and Academe: The Effect of Education on Earnings of Artists', *Journal of Cultural Economics*, **14** (1), 15–38.

Frank, B. (1994) 'Optimal Timing of Movie Releases', *Journal of Cultural Economics*, **18** (2), 125–34.

Frank, B. (1996) 'On Art without Copyright,' *Kyklos*, **49** (1), 3–15.

Frey, B. (1997) *Not just for the Money*, Edward Elgar, Cheltenham.

Frey, B. (1999) 'State Support and Creativity in the Arts: some new considerations', *Journal of Cultural Economics*, **23** (1/2), 71–85.

Frey, B. and Pommerehne, W. (1989) *Muses and Markets*, Blackwell, Oxford.

Garvin, D. (1981) 'Blockbusters: The Economics of Mass Entertainment', *Journal of Cultural Economics*, **5** (1), 1–20.

Giardina, E. and Rizzo, I. (1994) Chapter 5 in Peacock, A. and Rizzo, I. (eds) *Cultural Economics and Cultural Policies*, Kluwer, Dordrecht, 125–42.

Gibbs, L. (1993) *Private Lives*, Goldsmith's College, London.

Ginsburgh, J. (1998) Authors and Users in Copyright, 1997 Brace Lecture, 45 J, Copyright Society 1.

Ginsburgh, V. and Menger, P.-M. (1996) *Economics of the Arts*, Elsevier, Amsterdam.

Girard, A. (1972) *Développement Culturelle*, UNESCO, Paris.

Girard, A. (1981) 'A Commentary: Policy and the Arts: The Forgotten Cultural Industries', *Journal of Cultural Economics*, **5** (1), 61–8.

Golding, P. and Murdock, G. (1997) *The Political Economy of the Media*, 2 vols, Edward Elgar, Cheltenham.

Gordon, W.J. (1982) 'Fair Use as Market Failure: A Structural and Economic Analysis of the Betamax Case and Its Predecessors', *Columbia Law Review*, **82**, 1600–1659.

Granger, B. (1986) 'The Social Situation of Performing Artists in the United Kingdom', mimeo, Polytechnic of Central London (now University of Westminster).

Greco, A. (1999), 'The Impact of Horizontal Mergers and Acquisitions on Corporate Concentration in the U.S. Book Publishing Industry: 1989–1994', *Journal of Media Economics*, **12** (3), 165–80.

Hansmann, H. and Santilli, M. (1997) 'Authors' and Artists' Moral Rights', *Journal of Legal Studies*, 95–143.

Hardy, I.T. (1988) 'An Economic Understanding of Copyright Laws Work-Made-For-Hire Doctrine', *Columbia-VLA Journal of Law and the Arts*, **12**, 181–227.

Heikkinen, M. and Koskinen, T. (eds) (1998) *Economics of Artists and Arts Policy*, Arts Council of Finland, Helsinki.

Heilbrun, J. and Gray, C. (1993) *The Economics of the Arts and Culture: An American Perspective*, Cambridge University Press, Cambridge.

Hendon, W., Richardson, J. and Hendon M-A. (1986) *Bach and the Box: The Impact of Television on the Live Arts*, Association for Cultural Economics, Akron.

Hjorth-Andersen, C. (2000) 'A Model of the Danish Book Market', *Journal of Cultural Economics*, **24** (1), 27–43.

Holzhauer, R. (1999) '"Fair Use" in Law and Economics', paper presented at European Association for Law and Economics, mimeo, Erasmus University, Rotterdam.

Hoskins, C., McFadyen, S., Finn, A. and Jackel, A. (1997) 'Evidence on the Performance of Canada/Europe Co-productions in Television and Film', *Journal of Cultural Economics*, **21** (2), 129–38.

Hughes, G. (1989) 'Measuring the Economic Value of the Arts', *Policy Studies*, **9** (3), 33–45.

Hurt, R. and Schuchman, R. (1966) 'The Economic Rationale of Copyright', *American Economic Review*, **56**, 421–32.

Hutchison, R. and Feist, A. (1991) *Amateur Arts in the U.K.*, Policy Studies Institute, London.

IJdens, T. (1999) *Schotts en Scheef*, PhD Thesis, Erasmus University, Rotterdam.

ILO (International Labour Organisation) (1992) *Conditions of Employment and Work of Performers*, International Labour Office, Geneva.

Irjala, A. (ed.) (1992) *European Symposium on the Status of the Artist*, Finnish National Commission for UNESCO, No. 64, Helsinki.

Jackson, C., Honey, S., Hillage, J. and Stock, J. (1994), *Careers and Training in Dance and Drama*, Institute of Manpower Studies, Brighton.

Jeffri, J. and Throsby, D. (1994) 'Professionalism and the Visual Arts', *European Journal of Cultural Policy*, **1** (1), 99–108.

Jeffri, J., Greenblath, R., Friedman, Z. and Greeley, M. (1991) *The Artists' Training and Career Project*, Columbia University Research Centre for Arts and Culture, New York.

Jenkins, G. (1965) *Making Musicians*, Calouste Gulbenkian Foundation, London.

Johnson, W. (1985) 'The Economics of Copying', *Journal of Political Economy*, **93**, 158–74.

King, B. (1989) *1987-88 Equity Income and Employment Survey*, Equity, London.

Klamer, A. (ed.) (1996) *The Value of Culture*, Amsterdam University Press, Amsterdam.

Knott, C.A. (1994) *An Independent Socio-Economic Study of Craftspeople in England, Scotland and Wales*, Crafts Council, London.

Kretschmer, M., Klimis, G. and Choi, C. (1999a) 'Increasing Returns and Social Contagion in Cultural Industries', *British Journal of Management*, **10**, 561–72.

Kretschmer, M., Klimis, G. and Wallis, R. (1999b) 'The Changing Location of Intellectual Property Rights in Music: A Study of Music Publishers, Collecting Societies and Media Conglomerates', *Prometheus*, **17** (2), 163–86.

Landes, W. and Posner, R. (1989) 'An Economic Analysis of Copyright Law', *Journal of Legal Studies*, **18**, 325-66.

Leibenstein, H. (1950) 'Bandwagon, Snob and Veblen Effects in the Theory of Consumers' Demand', reprinted in Breit, W. and Hochman, H. (eds) (1968) *Readings in Microeconomics*, Holt, Rinehart and Winston Inc., New York.

Liebowitz, S. (1985) 'Copying and Indirect Appropriability: Photocopying of Journals', *Journal of Political Economy*, **93** (5), 945-57.

Liebowitz, S. and Margolis, S. (1995) 'Are Network Externalities a New Source of Market Failure?', *Research in Law and Economics*, **17**, 11-22.

Litman, J. (1994) 'The Exclusive Right to Read', *Cardozo Arts and Entertainment Law Journal*, 29-54.

MacDonald, G. (1988) 'The Economics of Rising Stars', *American Economic Review*, **78**, 155-66.

MacQueen, H. and Peacock, A. (1995) 'Implementing Performing Rights', *Journal of Cultural Economics*, **19**, 157-75.

Major, N. (1987) *Joan Sutherland*, Queen Anne Press, London.

Mas-Colell, H. (1999) 'International Trade and Art', *Journal of Cultural Economics*, **23** (1/2), 87-93.

MCPS (Mechanical Copyright Protection Society) (1996) *In Brief*, March, MCPS, London.

Menell, T. (2000) 'Intellectual Property', entry in Boukaert, B. and de Geest, G. (eds) *Encyclopaedia of Law and Economics*, Edward Elgar, Cheltenham.

Menger, P.-M. (1999) 'Artistic Labor Markets and Careers', *Annual Review of Sociology*, **25**, 541-74.

Merges, R. (1995) 'The Economic Impact of Intellectual Property Rights: An Overview and Guide', *Journal of Cultural Economics*, **19**, 103-17.

Meurer, M. (1997) 'Price Discrimination, Personal Use and Piracy: Copyright Protection of Digital Works', *Buffalo Law Review*, **45**, 845-98.

Miller, R. (1988) EPR - *Exhibition Payment Right*, National Artists' Association, Sheffield.

Ministry of Education, Culture and Science (1998) *Cultural Policy in the Netherlands*, OC&W, The Hague.

Mitchell, R. and Karttunen, S. (1992), 'Why and How to Define an Artist?', Chapter 17 in Towse, R. and Khakee, A. (eds) *Cultural Economics*, Springer, Heidelberg.

MMC (Monopolies and Mergers Commission) (1988) *Collective Licensing*, Cm. 530, HMSO, London.

MMC (Monopolies and Mergers Commission) (1994) *The Supply of Recorded Music*, Cm. 2599, HMSO, London.

MMC (Monopolies and Mergers Commission) (1996) *Performing Rights*, Cm. 3147, HMSO, London.

MPA and MPCS (Music Publishers' Association Limited and Mechanical Copyright Protection Society Limited) (1994) *Report and Accounts*, MPA Ltd, London.

MU/PACT (1996) *Agreement*, Musicians' Union, London. (Effective from 11 Oct. 1993, revised 1 Feb. 1996.)

Murph, A. (1984) 'The Classical Record Industry in the United States', *Journal of Cultural Economics*, **8** (1), 81-9.

Myerscough, J. (ed.) (1984) *Funding the Arts in Europe*, Policy Studies Institute, London.

Myerscough, J. (1988) *The Economic Importance of the Arts in Britain*, Policy Studies Institute, London.

Myerscough, J. (1994) *Cultural Policy in the Netherlands*, Ministry of Education, Culture and Science, Zoetermeer.

Nissel, M. (1983) *Facts about the Arts,* Policy Studies Institute, London.

Novos, I.E. and Waldman, M. (1984) 'The Effects of Increased Copyright Protection: An Analytical Approach', *Journal of Political Economy*, **92**, 236-46.

O'Brien, J. and Feist, A. (1995) *Employment in the Arts and Cultural Industries: An analysis of the 1991 Census*, Arts Council of England, London.

O'Brien, J. and Feist, A. (1997) *Employment in the Arts and Cultural Industries: an Analysis of the Labour Force Survey and other Sources*, ACE Research Report No. 9, Arts Council of England, London.

O'Connor, J. and Wynne, D. (1992) 'The Great and the Good or High Art on Hard Times', *Boelemancahier*, March, 105-11.

Office of National Statistics (1999) *Annual Abstract of Statistics*, London.

PAMRA (1996) 'New Rights for Performers', press release, April, London: The Performing Artists Media Rights Association.

Papandrea, F. (1999) 'Willingness to Pay for Domestic Television Programming', *Journal of Cultural Economics*, **23** (3), 149-66.

Peacock, A. (1979) 'Public Policy and Copyright in Music: An Economic Analysis', *The Economic Analysis of Government*, Martin Robertson, Oxford.

Peacock, A. (1986), *Making Sense of Broadcasting Finance*, reprinted in Towse, R. (ed.) (1997) *Cultural Economics: The Arts, the Heritage and the Media Industries*, Vol. 1, Edward Elgar, Cheltenham, pp. 435-48.

Peacock, A. and Rizzo, I. (eds) (1994) *Cultural Economics and Cultural Policies*, Kluwer, Dordrecht.

Peacock, A. and Weir, R. (1975) *The Composer in the Marketplace*, Faber, London.

Peacock, A., Shoesmith, E. and Milner, G. (1982) *Inflation and the Performed*

Arts, Arts Council of Great Britain, London. Excerpts reprinted in Towse, R. (1997) *Cultural Economics*, Vol. II, Edward Elgar, Cheltenham, pp. 319–60.

Perloff, J. (1998) 'Droit de Suite', entry in *New Palgrave Dictionary of Law and Economics*, Macmillan, London, pp. 645–48.

Plant, Arnold (1934) 'The Economic Aspects of Copyright in Books', *Economica*, May, 1, 167–95.

Posner, R. (1992) *Economic Analysis of the Law*, 4th edition, Little, Brown and Company, Boston/Toronto/London.

PPL (Phonographic Performance Limited) (1994) *Annual Report and Financial Statements for the Year ended 31st May 1994*, PPL Ltd, London.

PPL (Phonographic Performance Limited) (1996*) The Rental Directive*, PPL Ltd, London.

Prag, J. and Casavant, J. (1994) 'An Empirical Study of the Determinants of Revenues and Marketing Expenditures in the Motion Picture Industry', *Journal of Cultural Economics*, **18** (3), 217–35.

Pratt, A. (1997) 'The Cultural Industries Production System: A Case Study of Employment Change in Britain, 1984–91', *Environment and Planning*, **29**, 1953–74.

PRS (Performing Rights Society Ltd) (1995) *The Performing Right Yearbook*, PRS, London.

Puffelen, F. van (1996) 'Abuses of Conventional Impact Studies in the Arts', *Cultural Policy*, **2** (2), 241–54.

Reichman (1996/7) 'From Free Riders to Fair Followers: Global Competition Under the TRIPS Agreement', *New York University Journal of International Law and Politics*, **29**, 11–93.

Reinbothe, J. and von Lewinski, S. (1993) *The EC Directive on Rental and Lending Rights and on Piracy*, Sweet and Maxwell, London.

Rosen, S. (1981) 'The Economics of Superstars', *American Economic Review*, **71**, 845–58.

Rosselli, J. (1984) *The Opera Industry in Italy from Cimarosa to Verdi*, Cambridge University Press, Cambridge.

Rottenberg, S. (1975) 'The Remunerations of Artists', reprinted in Towse, R. (ed.) (1997) *Cultural Economics: The Arts, the Heritage and the Media Industries*, vol. I, pp. 590–94.

Rushton, M. (1998) 'The Moral Rights of Artists: Droit Moral or Droit Pecunaire?', *Journal of Cultural Economics,* **22** (1), 1–13.

Rutten, P. (1996) *Music in Europe*, European Commission, Brussels.

Santagata, W. (1995) 'Institutional Anomalies in the Contemporary Art Market', *Journal of Cultural Economics*, **19** (2), 187–97.

Santos, F. (1976) 'Risk Uncertainty and the Performing Artist', in Blaug, M. (ed.) *Economics of the Arts*, Martin Robertson, London.

Schulze, G. (1999) 'International Trade and Cultural Products', *Journal of Cultural Economics*, 23 (1–2), 109–36.

SCONUL (Standing Conference of National and University Libraries) (1999) www.sconul.ac.uk.

Scottish Arts Council (1995), *A Socio-Economic Study of Artists in Scotland*, Scottish Arts Council, Edinburgh.

Seaman, B. (1987) 'Arts Impact Studies: A Fashionable Excess', reprinted as Chapter 43 in Towse (1997a).

Seaman, B. (1992) 'Considerations in Adapting Industrial Organisations Theory to International Trade in Cultural Goods', in Towse, R. and Khakee, A. (1992) *Cultural Economics*, Springer, Heidelberg.

Sedgwick, J. and Pokorny, M. (1999) 'Movie Stars and the Distribution of Financially Successful Films in the Motion Picture Industry: A Comment', *Journal of Cultural Economics*, **23** (4), 319–23.

Shapiro, C. and Varian, H. (1999) *Information Rules*, Harvard Business School Press, Boston.

Smith, Adam (1776) eds Campbell, R. and Skinner, A. (1976) *An Inquiry into the Nature and Causes of the Wealth of Nations*, Oxford, Clarendon Press.

Smith, D. (1986) 'Collective Administration of Copyright', in Palmers, J. (ed.) *Research in Law and Economics*, **8**, 137–51.

Solow, J. (1998) 'Economic Analysis of Droit de Suite', *Journal of Cultural Economics*, **22** (3), 209–26.

Stein, J. (1997) 'Some Economic Effects of Artists' Follow-up Rights', *Journal of Cultural Economics*, **1** (1), 82–4.

Strobl, E. and Tucker, C. (2000) 'The Dynamics of Chart Success in the UK Pre-recorded Popular Music Industry', *Journal of Cultural Economics*, **24** (2), 113–34.

Szenberg, M. and Lee, E. (1994) 'The Structure of the American Publishing Industry', *Journal of Cultural Economics*, **18** (4), 313–22.

Taylor, M. and Towse, R. (1998) 'The Value of Performers' Rights: An Economic Approach', *Media, Culture and Society*, **20** (4), 631–52.

Thomas, H. (1992) *Equal Opportunities in the Mechanical Media*, Equity/Goldsmiths College, London.

Throsby, D. (1994) 'A Work-Preference Model of Artist Labour Supply', Chapter 6 in Peacock, A. and Rizzo, I. (eds), *Cultural Economics and Cultural Policies*, Kluwer, Boston/Dordrecht.

Throsby, D. (1997) 'Artists as Workers', reprinted in R. Towse (ed.) *Cultural Economics*, Edward Elgar, Cheltenham, 261–8.

Throsby, D. and Mills, D. (1986) *Occupational and Employment Characteristics of Artists*, Australia Council, Sydney.

Throsby, D. and Mills, D. (1989) *When Are You Going to Get a Real Job? An Economic Study of Artists in Australia*, Australia Council, Sydney.

Towse, R. (1991a) *Feasibility of a Survey of Artists' Earnings and Employment*, mimeo, Arts Council of Great Britain, London.

Towse, R. (1991b) *The Economics and Social Characteristics of Artists in Devon*, mimeo, South West Arts, Exeter.

Towse, R. (1992a) *The Economic and Social Characteristics of Artists in Wales*, mimeo, Welsh Arts Council, Cardiff.

Towse, R. (1992b) 'The Earnings of Singers - an Economic Analysis', in Towse and Khakee (eds).

Towse, R. (1993) *Singers in the Marketplace: the Economics of the Singing Profession*, Clarendon Press, Oxford.

Towse, R. (1994) 'Achieving Public Policy Objectives for the Arts and Heritage', in Peacock, A. and Rizzo, I. (eds) *Cultural Economics and Cultural Policies*, Kluwer, Dordrecht, pp. 143-65.

Towse, R. (1996) 'Economics of Artists' Training' in Ginsburgh, V. and Menger, P.-M. (eds) *Economics of the Arts*, North Holland, Amsterdam.

Towse, R. (1997a) *Cultural Economics: The Arts, the Heritage and the Media Industries*, 2 Vols. Edward Elgar, Cheltenham.

Towse, R. (ed.) (1997b), *Baumol's Cost Disease: The Arts and other Victims*, Edward Elgar, Cheltenham.

Towse, R. (1997c) 'Book Review: Bernard Casey, Rachel Dunlop and Sara Selwood, *Culture as Commodity? The Economics of the Arts and Built Heritage in UK:* Cliff Dane, Andy Feist and Dave Laing, *The Value of Music, Journal of Cultural Economics*, **21** (4), 355-60.

Towse, R. and Khakee, A. (eds) (1992) *Cultural Economics*, Springer, Heidelberg .

UNESCO (1980) *Recommendations Concerning the Status of the Artist*, UNESCO, Paris.

Van Asselt, E., Hakfoort, J. and Minkman, M. (1997) *De Economische Betekenis Van het Auteursrecht in 1994*, SEO Report 432, Sdu Uitgevers, Den Haag. English Version, *The Economic Importance of Copyright in the Netherlands in 1994*, Stichting Auteursrechtbelangen, Amstelveen.

Vany, A. de and Walls, D. (1999) 'Predicting Movie Success', *Journal of Cultural Economics*, **23** (4), 285-318.

Waits, R. and McNertney, E. (1980) 'Uncertainty and Investment in Human Capital in the Arts', in Hendon, W., Shanahan, J. and McDonald, A. (eds) *Markets for the Arts*, ABT Associates, Cambridge, Mass.

Wallace, W., Seigerman, A. and Holbrook, M. (1993) 'The Role of Actors and Actresses in the Success of Films; How much is a Movie Star Worth?' *Journal of Cultural Economics*, **17** (1), 10-27.

Wassall, G. and Alper, N. (1985) 'Occupational Characteristics of Artists: A Statistical Analysis', *Journal of Cultural Economics*, **9**, 13-34.

Wassall, G. and Alper, N. (1992) 'Toward a Unified Theory of the Determinants of the Earnings of Artists', Chapter 18 in Towse, R. and Khakee, A. (eds).

Wijnberg, N. (1994) 'Appropriability in the Arts', *Journal of Cultural Economics*, **18** (1), 1–12.

Winkler, D. (1985), 'Screening Models and Education', entry in *International Encyclopaedia of Education*, Pergamon Press, Oxford.

Withers, G. (1983) 'The Cultural Influence of Public Television', in Shanahan, J., Hendon, W., Hilhorst, I. and van Straalen, J. (eds), *Markets for the Arts*, Association for Cultural Economics, Akron, pp. 31–46. Reprinted in Towse, R. (1997a) pp. 449–64.

Withers, G. (1985) 'Artists' Subsidy for the Arts', *Australian Economic Papers*, **25**, December, 290–95.

Woodmansee, M. (1994) *The Author, Art and the Market*, Columbia University Press, New York.

Index